The Highway Revolution, 1895–1925

The Highway Revolution, 1895–1925

How the United States Got Out of the Mud

I.B. Holley, Jr.
DUKE UNIVERSITY

CAROLINA ACADEMIC PRESS
Durham, North Carolina

Library of Congress Cataloging-in-Publication Data

Holley, I. B. (Irving Brinton), 1919–
   The Highway revolution, 1895–1925 : how the United States got out of
the mud / by I.B. Holley, Jr.
      p. cm.
   Includes bibliographical references and index.
   ISBN 978-1-59460-353-2 (alk. paper)
   1. Roads--United States--History. 2. Road machinery--United States--
History. I. Title.

HE355.H58 2007
388.10973'09041--dc22   2007021265

Carolina Academic Press
700 Kent Street
Durham, NC 27701
Telephone (919) 489-7486
Fax (919) 493-5668
www.cap-press.com

CONTENTS

PREFACE

Several years ago I wrote a family memoir in which I included a chapter on my father's business as a highway contractor. He and his partner were pioneer builders of concrete highways in Connecticut and New York state. In compiling that chapter, I was surprised at the paucity of historical writing about highway building in general and road-building equipment in particular. There are, to be sure, some excellent studies on some aspects of the road-building story. Bruce Seely's *Building the American Highway System* is an outstanding account, but it offers largely a top-down administrative view. I have endeavored to present a muddy-boots view at the tactical level, reconstituting as far as possible what was actually involved in building inter-urban highways.

Apart from a scattering of finds such as the excellent article on the early steam shovel by Samuel Stueland and the illustrated volume on steamrollers by Robert Rhode and Ray Drake, there are few scholarly studies. Stone crushers, rock drills, asphalt machinery and concrete mixers all lack comprehensive studies, although there are a few company histories, usually produced for advertising purposes. My original goal was to provide a technological history of each piece of road-building equipment, but the absence of adequate secondary literature forced me to settle for descriptive accounts in more instances than I wished. More than one lifetime will be required to compile an exhaustive history of road-building machinery. I have spun off an article on asphalt and another on steamrollers. No one has yet scratched the surface of wagon technology culminating in dropbottom wagons, which were widely in vogue just before the coming of gasoline-powered trucks. Finally, historical studies of highway contracting as a business are notably lacking.

In the chapters that follow I have made only a sparse beginning. They definitely fail to accomplish all I originally intended to achieve, but I hope I have presented a sufficiently detailed account to give a reasonably well-rounded picture of the various elements that constituted the "highway revolution." Like any good historian, I set out to tell a chronological story, but I soon found it wouldn't work. The development of asphalt and concrete spread over many years as did the evolution of the significant items of machinery used in road building. So I finally settled on a series of topical chapters set insofar as possible in chronological order.

I believe very strongly in Jacque Barzun's view that the historian's primary task is to tell a good story rather than concoct some great theory, in this case some great theory of highway construction. All I have tried to do is to paint a picture of the problems encountered and the solutions devised to leave the reader with a fuller understanding of this largely unheralded aspect of the nation's essential infrastructure.

The author wishes to acknowledge the extensive support he has received over a period of many years from the Reference staff of the Duke University Library, including the Vesic Engineering Library. Without the help of these dedicated individuals I doubt I could have completed this volume.

INTRODUCTION

The United States at the beginning of the 21st century has the greatest highway system the world has ever known. It goes far beyond the splendid network of roads the Romans built to hold their empires together. In what we call the automobile age, the highways of the nation are an essential infrastructure. Highway transportation characterizes our very culture, shaping the way we live even more than did the wonderful network of rail lines that spread throughout the 19th century.

How many of our citizens ever stop to think how relatively recent is our impressive highway system? Paved highways in the United States have been with us for barely two generations. When political authorities began to think about paving highways toward the end of the 19th century there were paved streets in urban areas, but highways were still largely lacking any sort of hard surface and were veritable mudholes in wet weather. Even as late as the first two decades of the 20th century, pictures of vehicles hub-deep in mud remind us of how long and slow was the process of paving.

The chapters that follow tell the story of how the nation learned to build highways, learned how to finance them, mastered the problem with intractable materials, developed the machinery required, and perfected the contracting organizations, the technical and managerial talent needed to pave soundly at a cost acceptable to the taxpayers.

The Highway Revolution, 1895–1925

CHAPTER 1

To Get Out of the Mud: Who Pays?

In the latter half of the 1900s highways, that is the rural roads running between towns, were in many respects worse than they had been in the early decades of the century. Then considerable effort had been devoted to improving road transportation. In 1802, Congress initiated construction of a national road from Baltimore to Vandalia, Ohio. About the same time, many state legislatures, especially in New England, began chartering turnpike corporations to build and maintain inter-urban highways. They were expected to recover their costs by charging tolls, usually at ten-mile intervals where toll-gate keepers collected a small fee from passing traffic.[1]

The federally funded National Highway was sound in conception but flawed in operation. Although the road itself was for the most part well constructed with excellent masonry bridges, maintenance was left to the states through which the highway passed. When these states proved unable or unwilling to raise the required tax funds to keep the National Highway in proper repair, it gradually disintegrated.

Although some of the turnpike corporations produced decent roads, many did not, and almost all of them soon ran into financial difficulties. Construction costs outstripped original estimates and maintenance costs exceeded expectations even more so. Moreover, revenues were disappointing as traffic detoured to side roads, "shunpikes" to evade the toll takers. Soon turnpike company shares were selling below cost. Very few recovered their original investment. In those instances where state legislators had appropriated funds to purchase turnpike shares, the political reaction to the incurred burden of debt shocked many of them into voting for statutes or sometimes amendments to state constitutions, forbidding future investment in schemes to finance highway building, a move which was to haunt efforts at state aid for highways many decades in the future.

In New England alone some 240 companies constructed 3,700 miles of toll roads. As these gradually succumbed to bankruptcy, the need for good highways mounted sharply. The Napoleonic Wars in Europe brought a lively demand for farm products of the United States. Getting to seaports meant a greater need for decent roads. This inspired another round of road building, but the economics of wagon traffic worked against sufficient tolls to pay for proper road building. In New England, which had the best roads in the nation, it cost $20 a ton to haul a load 100 miles. Only very high value loads would justify such a long haul. One of the big items in the European market was hay. Wellington's army in the Peninsula created an immense demand for fodder. But hay, selling at $.60 for 100 pounds, cost that much to go 60 miles. So only farmers near coastal ports could hope to cash in on the boom market unless better roads could reduce the costs of hauling.[2]

Beginning in the 1840s, a number of states attempted to improve highway travel by constructing plank roads. Wood was plentiful, and heavy planks made an excellent surface for wagon traffic. Moreover, a wooden surface was not hard on a horse's hooves. Unfortunately, in the absence of chemical preservatives, the planks rotted and the plank road experiment was abandoned.[3]

Oddly, the coming of railroads with steam engines, beginning in 1830, had an adverse impact on highway construction. By 1836 there were over 1,000 miles of railways in eleven states; 9,000 miles by 1850; over 36,000 by 1860; and over 60,000 miles of track by 1870. Freight by horse and wagon at $.33 a ton mile in 1800 cost only $.02 a ton mile by rail in 1860. As the rail net expanded, town dwellers increasingly lost interest in paying state taxes for highways. The farm population continued to suffer from poor roads, but these were no longer for the long haul, only the distance from farm to the nearest railway station. As one observer remarked, after the decline of the toll roads, the nation entered a "dark age" as far as highways were concerned.[4]

Three hundred years after the first settlers arrived, the nation's highways were still atrocious, unimproved earth roads, ill drained if drained at all, poorly graded, rutted in good weather and almost impassable in wet weather. Wagons and carriages often became hopelessly mired. Even travelers on horseback found it heavy going. One humorist of the period liked to tell about seeing a hat sitting on the mud as he rode up to a particularly bad section of highway. He leaned down from his saddle to pluck up the hat and was surprised to discover it was on the head of a man neck deep in the mud. That unfortunate individual looked up and said, "It's all right, friend; I think my horse finally has his feet on solid bottom."[5]

Very few highways had been consciously constructed; most were simply trails cleared of vegetation periodically subjected to minor improvements by local residents working out their taxes by "a day on the roads." An Ohio farmer in the 1880s recalled sallying out once a year with his neighbors and their sons to work on the roads under the eye of a county supervisor. The men were armed with garden rakes, hoes, shovels and mattocks.

> The boys worked hard catching butterflies, killing snakes, and toting water. The men were discussing politics, instructing the supervisor how to do the work, and part of the time playing with the boys.

Forty men and boys in this way did about as much work as one fourth that number could have accomplished under a competent foreman. Few road supervisors had any special skills in road construction. In some states they were elected officials. As one cynical observer noted:

> The office of supervisor is one few wish to hold, and it is often the case that a few drinks of whiskey buy votes enough to elect a man with no interest in the road and but little sense of judgment.

About the only control the road supervisor had over his crew was his signature on a certificate indicating that the property owner had indeed turned out to work on the roads. This certificate the local tax collector accepted in lieu of cash. It was a system virtually guaranteeing that rural roads would largely remain mud holes.[6]

As the 1880s wore on, more and more voices were raised to urge remedial measures. The editors of *Engineering News*, consistently in favor of greater professionalism among engineers, editorialized that better roads were impossible as long as working on the roads in lieu of cash taxes continued and as long as there were no professionally competent civil engineers supervising road work. In an effort to pique the pride of local citizenry, the editors pointed out that in many cases highways in the 1880s were even worse than when traveled by "the stage coaches and conestoga wagon of our grandsires' day."[7]

Returning to the cause in an editorial two years later the editors saw that the most persuasive argument was the economic one. Because the first cost of building a highway was, in most states, charged to the abutters, there was great resistance to such costs in the farming community. Even when the farmers agreed to pay for some improvement they most often opted for the cheapest solution which promptly fell into disrepair, leaving the farmer as badly off as he had been before shelling out for an improved road.[8]

As the editors of *Engineering News* saw the problem, a farmer ten miles from a railroad had to spend a day hauling produce from farm to station. On an unimproved road the load two horses could responsibly pull was 1,400 pounds. Given a rolled crush stone road the same team could be expected to haul more than 2,000 pounds and make the round trip in less time with less wear and tear. Using average figures, the editors concluded that the savings on transportation costs alone would net over two million dollars for the nation's farmers, savings that could pay for 30,000 miles of improved roads. It is doubtful that many, if any, farmers were reading *Engineering News*, and even if they had, some would certainly be skeptical about the use of "average" figures or that any such promised savings would accrue to them. Nevertheless, agitation year after year for better roads gradually awakened a wider, public interest.[9]

Signs of that mounting interest appeared in Ohio, for example, when the legislature of that state considered passing a law addressing the highway issue in one county. While pleased at the evidence of rising concern for highway reform, the editors of *Engineering News* wisely rejected the idea of a county by county approach. The need was for highway law for the whole states; leaving responsibility in local county hands seemed only to perpetuate the prevailing malpractice.[10]

If the advocates of road reform were disturbed by their slow progress in building up support, help was on the way from an entirely unexpected quarter, young city dwellers. In 1880 a group of cyclists in Newport, Rhode Island, formed an organization, the League of American Wheelmen, or LAW. These cyclists were riding highwheel models of what the British called "penny farthing" vehicles in light of the disproportion between the main wheel and the trailing wheel. As soon as these joy riders ventured beyond the paved streets of Newport they encountered wretched highways that discouraged jaunts into the countryside. Frequent tumbles from the highwheelers caused by rutted roads awakened a serious interest in efforts at encouraging the movement for better highways. Although LAW established chapters or clubs in other towns, the movement spread only slowly until the coming of the so-called safety bike with two wheels of equal diameter and a chain and sprocket drive. This British development gave an enormous impetus to bicycle riding and to LAW.[11]

The manufacturers of safety bikes soon brought out designs suited for female riders. And once women began acquiring bicycles, the character of LAW changed markedly as groups of young couples undertook expeditions into the countryside for weekend rambles. The safety bike was not only safer but easier to ride, even on rutted rural roads. The appearance of pneumatic tires in 1889 made such jaunts more popular than ever. By 1890 there were 312 firms in the United States attempting to satisfy what had become literally a bicycle craze.

By 1896 LAW had some 38,000 members in clubs scattered about the nation with a national organization coordinating the efforts of divisions in the several states to push for better highways. In 1891 the national president of

LAW began editing a *Good Roads Magazine*, which depicted the horrible state of the nation's highways with pictures to goad local officials into action. LAW club members became active in local politics in an effort to elect officials sympathetic to highway reform.

One of the most active protagonists for better highways was Colonel Augustus A. Pope, who rode the coat tails of the LAW Good Roads movement. The colonel was a Hartford, Connecticut, manufacturer of bicycles. He obviously had a vested interest in promoting good roads, but his efforts went well beyond encouraging the sale of bicycles. Not only did he publish a stream of pamphlets fostering good roads, he also provided the funds to establish a course at the Massachusetts Institute of Technology for highway engineers.[12]

Inevitably, the bicycle craze faded and LAW membership fell off from its peak membership of 100,000 to some 80,000 in 1898. Two-thirds of the bicycle manufacturers had withdrawn from the business by 1906. The momentum for road reform initiated by LAW was, however, not entirely lost as the enthusiasm of the cyclists waned. Another organization, the National League for Good Roads, founded in 1892, picked up where LAW left off. While the cyclists in LAW were primarily interested in better roads for their own pleasure, they had little interest in the plight of the farmer who suffered from the economic disadvantages of miserable highways. The National League, in sharp contrast, aimed directly at the farmers. General Roy Stone, the League president, wisely sought to recruit state governors as vice presidents. And with no less political acumen he looked for support from the Farmers' Grange, the popular name for the rural lobbying organization's formal title, The Order of the Patrons of Husbandry.[13]

Rallying political support from various groups with widely different interests is never easy. As one example, in New Hampshire the cyclists were taken aback when the state Grange proposed a tax on bicycles to pay for highway improvements. And in Ohio the bicycle manufacturers favored a bond issue that would fall most heavily on the farmers. Clearly, the great game in politics is to secure the benefits one seeks while passing the tax burden on to someone else.[14]

Traditionally in most states abutters were expected to pay the initial cost of better roads. Farmers with large acreage facing on highways and low cash income were reluctant to shoulder the cost of improved highways. When Colonel Pope proposed the creation of a federal Road Department at the cabinet level, the National League prudently shied away, fearing that such a move would rouse active opposition in Congress, which was still confronted with the burden of Civil War debts. Instead, the National League concentrated on state governments. By 1893 the League had already held no fewer than fifteen state conventions to tout highway reform. However, the Good Roads movement had by this time generated a momentum that ran well beyond state borders.[15]

When local newspapers began taking up the good roads cause, state legislators and governors, ever sensitive to "back home" concerns, began to take notice. Encouraged by such signs, Colonel Pope redoubled his efforts and urged the formation of state highway commissions to coordinate efforts, set standards, and disseminate information as to what constituted sound construction practices. Above all, he expounded the economic benefits of good roads.

In an article in *The Forum* Colonel Pope laid out his grand scheme for better roads. State highway commissions would provide trained engineers to ensure quality construction. No longer should the abutters be expected to bear the whole burden of construction costs, but should be shared by the state, the county, and the town. Good roads benefit everybody, so all should share in the costs. Even the railroads should be willing to share in the tax burden. Better feeder roads from remoter rural districts would bring them increased business.[16]

Although Colonel Pope urged setting the tax rate very low by spreading it widely across the population, not everybody bought his argument. Farmers caught in the agricultural depression of the 1890s were reluctant to take on any more debt. Many of them resented Colonel Pope's urging an end to the practice of working out one's taxes on the roads. And many town dwellers were skeptical, fearing that taxes to pay for highways would encroach upon the funding of in-town streets.

Despite the fears of the naysayers, the obvious economic elements of good roads increasingly won converts. Facts and figures appealed persuasively. The editors of *Scientific American*, for example, offered the evidence of a vegetable grower in Florida who cultivated ten acres eight miles from a railway station. He buys two tons of fertilizer for $70, but to get it home he has to make eight trips, each of six hours, with his one horse wagon over the miserable sand road he must travel to the station. He figures his time and that of his horse at a modest $.60 per load. With this fertilizer his ten acres produce 500 crates of vegetables requiring 71 trips to the railroad at a cost of $42.00. If he had a hard surfaced road, he could expect to haul his fertilizer home in four loads of four hours each. When the crop ripened, on hard surfaced roads he could haul his 500 crates to market in 35 trips of four hours each at a cost of $14.00. But these savings are only part of the story. On sandy roads, a six-hour trip for a single horse is a day's work. Seventy-one day trips extend beyond the growing season. To get his whole crop to market the farmer has to keep two horses. To avoid the expense of a second horse he doesn't need much of the year, he can rent a second horse from a neighbor, but in the growing season such rents come high. Seventy-one day-long trips to market consume so much of the farmer's time, he must take on a hired hand. So the farmer calculates that bad roads add up to a heavy tax on every one of his ten acres.[17]

As the crusade for better roads gathered increasing momentum, several state legislatures voted to establish highway commissions. Massachusetts led the way, then New Jersey, Pennsylvania, and Connecticut followed suit. These moves reflected growing public interest, but apart from Massachusetts, few of these states appropriated significant funds for highway construction. Members of Congress no less than the state legislators were conscious of the increasing public clamor for better roads. But they too understood that responding to constituent desires had to be tempered by the voters' unwillingness to pay more taxes. By way of compromise the congressmen established an Office of Road Inquiry in the Department of Agriculture with an appropriation of $10,000. By placing the organization in the Department of Agriculture, the move could be interpreted as an effort to get the farmers out of the mud, while the appropriation was so modest, no one could complain about the expense. Clearly the ORI was to be a source of investigation and information, no more; a $10,000 appropriation would build no roads.[18]

The Secretary of Agriculture in a shrewd political move appointed General Roy Stone as Director of the Office of Road Inquiry. Stone was not only a competent engineer but also the president of the National League of Good Roads. The Secretary laid out these objectives for ORI. Stone was to inquire into the best methods of road management and to solicit the assistance of land grant universities in disseminating his findings, including a survey of existing state laws on the subject. To placate the fears of those who worried that ORI was but an opening wedge in a scheme to secure federal funds for highways, the Secretary took great care to stress that ORI's role was inquiry only and all construction costs would remain with the states. In this the Secretary was whistling against the wind. History was against him; the natural tendency of the federal bureaucracy is to expand.[19]

Sure enough, in three years General Stone was asking for a 50% increase in the ORI appropriation. He didn't get it, but this didn't stop his experimentation. With the cooperation of the steel-making industry, he explored the possibility of laying steel planks or plates 10 or 12 inches wide as tracks for wagon wheels, leaving an earth or crushed stone path between the plates to provide a good foothold for horses' hooves. If two teams met head-on, one or the other would have to pull off on the turf berm as only one set of plates was contemplated.[20] Despite General Stone's enthusiastic backing for steel road surfacing, the project attracted little support; he was far more successful in proposing demonstration roads, short sections of crushed stone roads to show interested state highway officials and others what constituted sound construction. For want of funds, he couldn't build such demonstration roads, but the idea was sound and elicited considerable interest from land grant schools and state governments.

General Stone realized that as long as most states required the abutters to pay all or much of the cost of highway construction, he would meet serious opposition from that set of taxpayers. The only way to overcome this resistance was to show them that good roads were a sound investment, which would more than pay for the costs incurred. To this end, he circulated questionnaires eliciting statistics, which the Office of Road Inquiry published:

	Average Haul	Average cost per ton for the whole haul
Eastern States	5.9 miles	$1.80
Cotton States	12.6 miles	$3.05
Pacific Coast & Mountain States	23.3 miles	$5.12
Average for U.S.	12.3 miles	$3.02

Using the replies received by ORI, General Stone estimated that U.S. farmers hauled produce on rural roads amounting to more than 313 million ton miles at a cost of $986 million. He concluded that as much as 60% of such transportation costs could be saved by good roads, counting reduced wear and tear on the horses, shorter turnaround time spent hauling, and the reduction in the number of horses a farmer would have to maintain. He ignored another factor too difficult to estimate, the loss on perishables that a farmer failed to get to market in time for the best prices. All in all, he concluded that the incurred savings would offset the cost of improved roads.[21]

While many farmers remained skeptical about General Stone's promised savings, not all the opposition to his arguments came from them. The editors of the journal, *Engineering Record*, were particularly scathing in their criticism.

> When the careful historian of engineering of a century hence writes his history of the present progress in road construction, he will have ample material for an astonishing tale.

While admitting that the Office of Road Inquiry had done some good work, the editors deplored its practice of "scattering broadcast an avalanche of miscellaneous misinformation," especially its dubious statistics. They singled out such "trashy figures" as ORI's claim that the cost of hauling farm products to market accounted for 27% of the product's value.[22]

If the farmers couldn't be persuaded that it was to their advantage to pay for highways, it began to look as if another approach might be necessary. When both the Republican and Democratic parties wrote good road planks into their platforms, the good roads advocates had reason to believe that some form of federal aid might be forthcoming. Congressional reluctance to increase the ORI appropriation gradually weakened as the public clamor for better roads continued. A change in leadership may have helped. When Martin Dodge took over as Director, there was a decided shift in tactics. Appeals to individual congressmen were couched in terms of a demonstration road "in your district." This seems to have been effective. In 1899 Congress changed the name of the organization to Office of Public Road Inquiry, and the following year OPRI hired a graduate of Harvard University's road construction course to establish a laboratory to test samples of materials submitted by the states to determine scientifically their suitability for road construction. By 1904 the OPRI appropriation had grown from $10,000 a year to $35,000.[23]

Increased appropriations made it possible to fund or share in funding demonstration roads, usually short sections to illustrate the best way to construct a crushed stone road. The obvious contrast between the ease of hauling a heavy load of produce over such roads and the exhausting struggle teams had in pulling wagons through rutted and muddy roads seems to have won converts, for after 1900, legislators, both federal and state, introduced numerous bills calling for direct governmental appropriations for highway construction. While few of these bills secured passage, they nonetheless reflected a significant growth in popular interest.[24]

The states that led the way in providing state funding were for the most part in the east. New Jersey was first, starting in 1891. By 1900, Vermont, New York, Massachusetts, Maryland, and Connecticut were all appropriating money for highways, as did California, the sole Western state to do so. This was real progress, but many remained skeptical about the hopes for better highways throughout the nation. A.B. Hurlbert, the author of a volume in the series, *Historic Highways of America*, conceived as propaganda for better roads, complained that the United States had what were possibly "the poorest roads of any civilized nation." He blamed the railroads for the decline in public will to maintain highways, which left the farmers isolated. He lamented that in all probability they would still be without good roads a century hence.[25]

Hurlbert's pessimistic assessment was largely discounted by the evidence he himself spelled out. The railroads were anxious to support better roads in order to increase the distance farmers could afford to haul crops to the railway. A single horse could pull as much on a gravel road as four on a dirt road. In economic terms, he observed, to reach urban markets cost farmers $.25 a mile on poor roads but only $.10 a mile on improved roads in 1905. And there were other social forces favoring better roads. The notable advantages of consolidated schools over the inefficiencies of one-room rural school houses brought an additional constituency to the push for state aid to highways.[26]

Bicycle riders, Rural Free Delivery Postal Service, the parents of rural school children, railroad executives anxious to tap an ever larger watershed of growers to contribute freight, all these and many others helped swell the growing support for better highways, but it was the automobile drivers who finally brought the necessary impetus to both state and federal funding. In the early 1890s even the nomenclature was uncertain. Journalists mentioned "self-propelled road carriages" and "power vehicles." *Scientific American* reported the appearance of the first "horseless hack" in Paris, noting with satisfaction that it was only 10 feet long. Since horse-drawn hacks were 15 feet long, this promised to ease congestion. The editors presciently added, "We are witnessing the beginning of an evolution whose importance cannot be forseen."[27]

After the turn of the century, automobile registrations enjoyed an astounding growth. In 1903 there were 78,000 autos licensed in the United States. Admittedly most of these might be dismissed as rich men's toys, mere novelties. And many of them bore little resemblance to the automobiles of a hundred years later. To put the autos of the early 1900s in perspective, it is well to recall that one of the most popular models of the period was a "one lunger" Cadillac, as that single-cylinder vehicle was called. A wide variety of designs—electric cars, steamers, and gasoline-powered versions—were in fruitful competition. Some had chain-and-sprocket drives, others differential gearing as dozens of firms struggled to produce vehicles that would satisfy the performance demanded by the public.[28]

As auto registrations rose, the organizational infrastructure grew apace. Auto enthusiasts formed the American Automobile Association, AAA, in 1902 and promptly began lobbying for road appropriations. New York state started assessing fees for auto registrations and by 1913 was collecting a million-and-a-quarter dollars a year in this way, money which could be applied to road building. Massachusetts followed suit and soon was collecting well over half a million dollars in fees. By 1913 the states with auto registration requirements were collectively bringing in more than twelve million dollars in auto fees and fines.[29]

By 1916, the momentum built up by autoists had reached the point where direct Federal subsidies for highway construction were virtually inescapable. With auto registrations at more than two million, there were a lot of articulate voters demanding action from Congress. The log jam on road bills finally broke clear, and President Wilson signed a Federal road aid measure. This measure unleashed the flow of federal money, which brought the highway revolution to fruition in what one scholar has called "the golden age" of highway construction.[30]

The title of the federal road act reflects something of the adroit political manipulation required to get it passed. "An act to provide that the United States shall aid the states in the construction of rural post roads and for other purposes." Post roads! Who can be opposed to delivering the mails? And that terminal phrase left the door open for much else. This was to be no loose give away greasing the hinges of the door to the U.S. Treasury. The Secretary of Agriculture was to "cooperate" with state highway commissions in deciding which highways were to be improved and what methods of construction were to be used. States had to accept this degree of federal control or forfeit the federal funding, which was awarded by a formula based on the number of roads in a given state and the size of its population. To secure funding a state had to put up half of the actual cost of construction. In no case would the federal contribution be in excess of $10,000 per mile. Appropriations were authorized, starting at $5,000,000 the first year and rising to $25,000,000 over five years.[31]

Despite the misgivings of some eastern politicians who feared that their states would pay out more in taxes than they were to receive in highway funds, the federal road act proved remarkably successful. By 1916 all but eight of the states already had Highway Commissions, and the act induced the hold-outs to fall in line. The concept of matching funds proved to be irresistible. By the terms of the act the federal government was to specify the method of construction. But what did this mean? What kind of construction was desirable? As the sponsors of the measure admitted in the debate leading up to its passage, "Engineers have not yet figured out how to build a road that will stand up to modern traffic."[32] The problem, of course, was automobile traffic. The chapter that follows considers the early development of road building in the United States, the various methods of construction and the implements developed to assist in this effort, and some of the individuals who led the way.[33]

CHAPTER 2

WHAT KIND OF ROAD?
THE MACADAM ERA, 1816–1916

The previous chapter mentioned crushed stone roads, a term with a long history. As early as 1585 an Italian engineer, Guido Toglietta, wrote a treatise on the use of crushed stone as a cheaper substitute for the massive Roman roads, built largely with army labor. But the modern era of road building really begins with a French engineer, Pierre Marie Jérôme Tresaquet, whose succcesess as a road builder led to his appointment as head of the École des Ponts and Chaussées in the middle of the eighteenth century. Graduates of the École built or rebuilt some 25,000 miles of improved hard surface roads, giving France the best road system in the world.

Tresaquet abandoned the extremely expensive but wonderfully durable methods employed by the Romans. His method or design involved digging a trench ten feet wide down to a foundation of solid subsoil, leaving a slight crown. At either flank he placed bigger flat stones with their largest dimension against the sides of the excavated road bed. These stones served as the anchors for the arch of flat stones with their longer dimension of approximately eight inches, laid vertically following the crown of the subsoil. These were hammered in to fit tightly against the side anchor stone. Smaller stones were pounded in to fill the voids. On this substantial base, he added a layer of walnut-sized gravel. Above this, he placed a one-inch layer of crushed stone, carefully screened to include nothing but sharp-edged fragments ranging in dimension from three-quarters to one inch. When rolled, the top layer bonded firmly, making an excellent roadway for horse and wagon in all weathers. The success of Tresaquet's roads in France promptly led to emulation in Germany, Sweden and Great Britain.[1]

In Britain, Tresaquet's methods were picked up by the eminent Scottish engineer, Thomas Telford, famous for his construction of canals, bridges and roads. He argued that the heavy crowned stone base was essential to give a highway uniformity. As it advanced across country it was bound to encounter different qualities and conditions of subsoil, some wet, some dry, so the large stone base would guarantee uniformity. Telford's roads were a success, partly because he was at pains to lay them out in a way to avoid steep grades and partly because they were impressively durable. They suffered from one serious drawback, however; they were expensive, because preparing the heavy stone base was exceedingly labor intensive.[2]

Faced with the resistance of county and parish taxpayers to pay for Telford's high quality roads, one of his younger contemporaries, John Loudon McAdam, a county surveyor or supervisor of roads, conducted a series of experiments in search of a cheaper alternative. His solution was to do away with the massive foundation of large stones. His experiments were constructed by laying ten inches of broken stone directly on the earth sub-base so that it projected a few inches above the surrounding area, allowing the crushed stone to drain off any water falling on the surface.

McAdam explained his methods in a book published in England in 1816 titled *Remarks on the Present System of Road Making*. A descriptive subtitle revealed the theme of the work: "the introduction of improvements in the Method of Making, Repairing and Preserving Roads." The author stated his thesis in the first few pages: "poor roads stem from the use of rounded stones lacking the angular points of contact by which the broken stone unites and forms a solid body." The great secret revealed in these few words has a profundity that helps explain why the eponymous term *macadam* continues in use to the present.

McAdam certainly didn't originate the idea of using broken stone, a notion he adopted from Tresaquet and Telford, but he articulated the idea more effectively than his predecessors. His book ran through several editions. It was successful in part because he had a knack for clear exposition, but there can be little doubt that his ideas were widely accepted because they could be applied far more cheaply than Telford's.

McAdam specified that "any stone which exceeds an inch in any of its dimensions is mischievous." To insure compliance, he proposed arming inspectors with wire rings, one inch in diameter, as "go-no go" gauges to measure the broken stone produced by seated women, children, and "men past labor" armed with light hammers. A bed of broken stone, which rose three or four inches above its surroundings, would be self-draining, he contended. For this reason it would avoid the destruction that results when water-soaked roads freeze and then thaw. McAdam was adamant that under no circumstances should one add clay or loam "or any other matter which will imbibe water," which could be affected by frost.[3]

McAdam did not advocate rolling the broken stone surface; he left that to the horses' hooves and the wagon wheels. Letting traffic do the job took about six months and was brutally hard on the horses. Until the sharp-edged stones began to bond, they not only hurt the horses' hooves but also made pulling the load exceedingly difficult. There seems little doubt that McAdam knew rolling would be advantageous, but he also knew that rolling would add to the expense, and that would make his methods less attractive to local officials.

Over time, roads built to McAdam's design came to be called "waterbound macadam." The broken stone, properly sized, was spread on the road bed and then filled with the "fines," the dust particles produced when the stones were broken. The road surface was then sprinkled repeatedly with a water wagon to insure that all the voids were filled. The final product, whether compacted by traffic or by rolling, produced a hard, smooth surface. Surprisingly, the moist fines produced a certain amount of cementation, giving the larger stone shards a considerable stability. It was many years before the process of cementation was appreciated or fully understood.

In the United States, the first major highway construction project was the National Pike, initiated by Congress in 1806, too early to benefit from McAdam's published ideas. As originally conceived, it was to run from Baltimore to Jefferson City, Missouri, but by 1818 it had progressed no further than Wheeling, West Virginia, and it never did get much beyond Springfield, Ohio. On the whole it was well built, especially its masonry bridges. However, finding sufficient funds was a continual problem. The sale of western lands opened up by the road never produced the flow of cash anticipated, so Congress finally abandoned the whole project in 1856. By then the coming of railroads offered a substitute for highways serving long-distance traffic. McAdam's works may have influenced the later stages of construction on the National Pike, but it was left to a different undertaking to mark the effective introduction of McAdam in the United States.[4]

In 1821 various commercial interests in Baltimore recognized that their port city on the Chesapeake, especially in competition with its rival, Philadelphia, would be significantly enhanced if they improved the major feeder highway bringing produce from the interior. One stretch in particular, the highway from Boonsboro to Hagerstown, remained unimproved. This was a key link because it connected with the National Pike. The Maryland legislature passed an act incorporating a road company and bullied several Baltimore banks by threatening not to renew their charters unless they put up the money to construct the desired highway.[5]

Fortunately, the contractors hired to build the road had access to McAdam's treatise, for a Baltimore publisher brought out an edition of his famous work in 1821, just in time to be of use on the new highway. The contractors leveled the existing road with drags and scrapers and then put down a foundation of six inches of stone, all of which was broken by men with hammers "as pre-

Figure 2.1   Artist's rendering of construction of the Boonsboro Pike to McAdam's specifications. Note particularly the inspector with the ring gage for testing the sizing of the stone, the seated stone crushers with hammers, and in the background, a template or leveling device to maintain the proper curvature of the crown. Source: 31 *American Highways* (January 1952) 36–37.

scribed by John McAdam." This they rolled with an iron cylinder surmounted by a box filled with stone to give it appropriate weight. On this foundation they spread a second layer of broken stone three or four inches thick. After rolling this layer, they added a thinner surface layer, which was duly rolled. In one respect the Boonsboro Pike went well beyond what McAdam prescribed, for it was crowned with 15 inches of crushed stone at the center, tapering to 12 inches at the edges of the 20-foot wide road; McAdam had called for no more than a uniform 10 inches of stone across the whole width.

Despite the enhanced crown, the Boonsboro Pike was the first authentic McAdam construction in the United States. As such, it served as a fine demonstration or role model of what a good highway should be. It established macadam construction as an ideal to emulate. And that is precisely what happened. The Secretary of War, impressed by the quality of the Boonsboro Pike, decreed that all future extensions westward of the National Pike should be built to McAdam's standards.[6]

While the macadam link did indeed help develop Baltimore as a major port, the coming of the railroad era, beginning with the Baltimore and Ohio in 1830, effectively ended enthusiasm for highway building for many years to come. This did not mean, however, that McAdam's construction methods were no longer used. As interest in highway building declined, emphasis shifted to the construction of city streets.[7]

Even in the larger cities, most of the streets were no more than dirt roads. Some few principal streets in the early 19th Century were paved with cobble-stone, or more rarely, with granite blocks. These escaped from the mud but offered precarious footing for horses. The best alternative was macadam, which provided a sure footing for horses and a firm surface with good traction for wheeled vehicles. But macadam construction suffered from a serious limitation. Even in cities with a sound tax base in the abutting property holders, the cost of breaking stone by hand imposed a serious obstacle. Since it took about two man-days to crush a cubic yard of stone, macadam streets with layers of broken stone ten or more inches deep required a great many man-days of effort.

As late as 1870, New Haven, Connecticut, with some 90 miles of streets, had less than four miles paved with granite block or macadamized. Sometime prior to 1852 Eli Whitney Blake, a nephew of the inventor of the cotton gin who had supervised his uncle's gun factory for ten years, was appointed to a committee to oversee the macadamizing of a mile-and-a-half of Whalley Avenue, a street named for one of the regicide judges of the English civil war who fled to the colonies at the Restoration. Appalled at the labor cost involved in breaking the required rock by hand, Blake set about inventing a steam-powered stone crusher. In 1852 he secured a patent. His simple design, which incorporated a heavy cast iron frame with two converging jaws and a massive flywheel, was so successful that it has continued in use with slight modifications down to the present. At 200 rpm, the jaws exerted a pressure of 27,000 pounds per square inch. This could fracture stones nine inches by twelve inches and produce as many as seven cubic yards of crushed stone in an hour.[8]

The advent of Blake's stone crusher gave an enormous boost to macadam construction because it markedly reduced the cost of crushed stone. As orders for crushers poured in, Blake and his competitors had a powerful incentive to improve on the original model. The cast iron frame gave way to steel, and the jaws were made adjustable to produce different sizes of crushed stone. A stronger frame meant reduced breakage with less down time, which cut construction costs still further. By the 1870s, contractors were reporting costs of

Figure 2.2   Although the crusher is situated to permit gravity feed from the crusher to the waiting cart, in this illustration no provision is made to do the same for the stone emerging from the screening cylinder. Nor is there gravity feed into the crusher. Source: 34 *Scientific American* (29 April 1876) 275.

$.18 to $.41 a cubic yard. When the crusher was located at a quarry, a significant part of the cost of stone for macadam roads came from the charge for hauling from quarry to the road site. This led to the design of a portable, wheel-mounted crusher for use at the construction site. This in turn required a portable steam boiler and engine.[9]

Engineering News, greatly impressed with the Blake invention, declared "Probably no town that pretends to keep thirty or forty miles of road in good repair ought to be without one of these labor-saving machines." And *Scientific American* was sufficiently impressed to run a steel engraving illustrating not just the stone crusher but a whole system, including the quarry, steam plant, crusher, gravity feed to a waiting cart, and a most significant addition, a cylindrical steel screening device to grade the crushed stone into appropriate sizes. The accompanying text indicated that it was then probably a relatively new device.[10]

While many were convinced that macadam highways were what the nation needed, there were some who saw the problem from a larger perspective. A spokesman from the California Department of Highways, writing in *Overland Monthly* in 1896, reminded his readers that road construction had to suit a wide variety of climates and terrains in the United States. To suit the future need of the "rapidly growing empire," he warned, financial resources, legislative sagacity, and great engineering skills would be required. California, he observed, is 800 miles long and 300 miles wide; it is three-quarters as large as the whole of France. Manifestly, a type of road well suited to one section of such a great state might be utterly impossible in another section. In a similar spirit, an engineer, addressing a meeting of the American Society of Mechanical Engineers, observed that "the practice of road building is so unchrystalized that it is impossible to give hard and fast rules for road construction for any given locality." He clinched this observation by noting that so-called experts will tell you that drainage is the sine qua non of road construction while quite overlooking the fact that one-third of the nation is arid. Other experts insist that Telford or McAdam offers the best solution yet ignore the fact that in some areas, no proper source of appropriate stone can be found within 500 miles.[11]

While it was certainly true that macadamizing highways was the best available solution for much of the nation, macadam was certainly not without its problems. It was indeed well suited to horse traffic, but carriage and wagon wheels eventually rutted even the best-constructed macadam surface. Some state legislatures addressed this problem by voting to require wider wagon tires. Florida, for example, specified four-inch-wide tires for all two-horse wagons and six-inch tires for four-horse wagons. Trying to enforce such a statute was virtually impossible unless all vehicles were required to change over to the wider tires at a given date, manifestly a requirement the voters would never accept. One suggested remedy was to impose a tax on narrow-tired wheels, which rutted macadam surfaces, but waive the tax if one converted to the specified wider tires. Part of the resistance wide tire legislation provoked was the obvious fact that while wider treads worked better on poorly drained roads, narrow tires made for better traction and higher speeds on good, dry roads.

Some localities tried to limit the weight of wagons allowed on macadam surfaces, imposing fines for violations. Here again, consistent enforcement was difficult, if not impossible. It was easy enough to fine a wagoner who deeply rutted a crushed stone surface when he hauled a 35-ton ship's anchor, but in the absence of industrial scales at convenient locations, how would a farmer hauling a large load of hay know if he was violating the law?[12]

Those who advocated macadam construction as the answer for the nation's highways were sometimes greatly distressed when sections of macadam built to the very best specifications under the watchful eye of experienced contractors disintegrated rapidly under wagon traffic and in a very short time were no better than the old dirt road the macadam replaced. The obvious answer was lack of maintenance. The success of crushed stone roads in France rested upon well-organized and continuous maintenance. The workmen assigned to upkeep for designated sections of highway promptly filled potholes and ruts as soon as they appeared. Relying upon local taxpayers working out their taxes to undertake routine maintenance was the worst possible way of effecting repairs. Hiring contractors to do the job was scarcely better. In both cases, the critical defect was lack of adequate supervision and the tendency to use whatever materials were readily at hand, whether they were suitable or not. Experience showed that it was cheaper in the long run to haul in the proper kind of stone to insure enduring results.[13]

One potential response to the problem of macadam raveling and rutting under wagon traffic was proffered at a Good Roads convention by a delegate from California. He reported that oily sand from leaking oil wells had proved useful in patching rutted roads. John D. Rockefeller, impressed by this potential market, donated a tank of oil for further experiments. Using a water-sprinkling cart as an improvised oiler, a 200-foot section of road was treated with some success, as the oiled section did not rut after a rain as did an untreated section. If oiling didn't entirely resolve the problem of rutting, it did hold considerable promise in reducing dust clouds, "so disagreeable to people in the vicinity" as the journal *Engineering Record* complained.[14]

Although crushed stone macadam construction dominated the discussion as to what kind of highways should be constructed, in areas where stone was not readily available a number of alternatives attracted attention. In some states with ample sources of clay, the use of this material in vitrified form provided a substitute for stone. When crushed to form sharp angled shards, it would bond in much the same way as conventional crushed stone. On the other hand, it suffered from the expense of baking. In Southern and Western states with excessively sandy soil, sand-clay construction offered an alternative to conventional macadam.[15]

In an area of heavy clay, sometimes it was possible to plow the dry roadbed to loosen it up and then dump sand on it dry, followed by harrowing to mix the two ingredients. The hard sand particles had no adhesive properties but resisted abrasion, thus making a durable wearing surface. The clay provided the necessary binder for the sand. When thoroughly mixed, the road was sprinkled, dragged to shape a crown, then rolled. Sand-clay could produce a reasonably durable road, but it was difficult to secure just the right proportions. Too much sand makes a less durable road and too much clay tends to disintegrate when wet.[16]

Out of the 2,200,000 miles of roads in the United States prior to World War I, about two million miles were dirt roads. To make these viable in all weathers, they would have to be drained, better aligned, their grades reduced, and, ultimately, provided with some form of durable surfacing. Therein lay the problem. Accomplishing these objectives required widespread knowledge and experience. The chapter that follows tells the story of how ever greater numbers of individuals received instruction on the mysteries of sound highway construction even as the kinds of construction evolved as innovations in materials and machinery advanced year by year.[17]

CHAPTER 3

EDUCATING THE RURAL HIGHWAY BUILDERS: GETTING OUT THE WORD ON CONSTRUCTION METHODS

Chapter I of this study was primarily concerned with the effort to sell the public on the need for good roads and the importance of finding ways to pay for them. In this chapter, the focus is on educating a somewhat different audience, the state and local officials who would direct the process, and the engineers and contractors who would actually do the constructing. There were upward of 2,000 counties and similar political entities to be informed about the intricacies of road building within widely differing environments and geological contexts. The term intricacies is peculiarly appropriate, as it is derived from the Latin meaning, "to entangle." Defining what needed to be done and how to do it was a task calling for the most careful investigation. This chapter looks at some of the individuals and organizations who led the way, as well as the solutions they advocated.

The bicycle manufacturer mentioned in the first chapter, Alfred Augustus Pope, was on the right track when he helped introduce courses in road building at both Harvard and MIT. He never built a road himself, but he understood that doing so presented a complex problem requiring sound knowledge as well as practical experience. As an officer of the Union Army during the Civil War, he learned the importance of good roads, and his business as a bicycle builder gave him an economic incentive to work toward a solution. One of his most useful contributions was his agitation for the creation of a state highway commission in Massachusetts, the first in the nation.[1]

The push to induce the Massachusetts state legislature to establish a highway commission extended over several years, beginning about 1887. By 1892 the movement had enough momentum to secure the creation of an investigating committee, whose findings led to the establishment of a permanent three-man commission to advise the state on highway construction and maintenance. One of those selected to serve on the commission was Harvard geologist Nathaniel Shaler, who had been among those most active in urging highway reform. In an article in the *Atlantic Monthly*, he argued that with respect to highways, the U.S. ranked at the bottom of the civilized world. Remedying this situation, he observed, would involve educating the public and would cost a great deal of money. He accentuated this marked realism with the further warning that the call for better highways would succeed, "providing we guard the existing movement from ignorant enthusiasm."[2]

Shaler recognized that public enthusiasm was needed to get legislators to act, but without knowledge of the many difficulties, obstacles, and frustrations, the demand for immediate results could become counter-productive. He saw "the great petition," which colonel Pope had spearheaded to gather 150,000 signatures to present to Congress, as useful propaganda but liable to result in "much blundering" if the public failed to see that highways required a great deal of engineering skill. Such skills were scarce. As he put it, "the learning of the craft is limited." Engineering schools in the United States had scarcely begun to teach highway engineering. There were indeed treatises on the subject, textbooks, but these were for the most part used by supervisors in city street departments. They were all but unknown to village and small-town political officials of rural districts who grappled with highway problems on a part-time basis.[3]

General Roy Stone, writing from his post in the newly created Office of Road Inquiry in the Department of Agriculture, echoed Nathaniel Shaler's views: the best roads for farming districts, he declared, "must not be too costly." The ideal highway, he said, would be a dirt track, easy on the horse, noiseless, and less destructive of the vehicle. Dirt tracks had the further advantage of holding snow better for sleighing than did gravel roads. But dirt roads simply would not do in the wet season. By way of compromise, Stone proposed a single wagon-width, crushed stone macadam road with dirt tracks for passing on either side. This would minimize the cost but still allow the farmer to haul loads to the city in seasons when his fields were too wet to cultivate.[4] In this context of horse and buggy thinking, the Massachusetts Highway Commission set to work.

George A. Perkins, the Massachusetts Commission chairman, reported in 1894 on the work in progress. There were 20,000 miles of roads in Massachusetts, not counting city streets. About 20% of these roads were main-line routes, highways handling through traffic. With but $300,000 appropriated for construction and 14 counties to satisfy, the commission decided to stress

Figure 3.1   Original caption: "THE FARMER'S SLOUGH. The main road between Cleveland and Warrenville, Ohio, about two miles from Cleveland city limits, April 7, 1891." Source: Nathaniel Shaler, *Amerian Highways* (New York, 1896) 21.

one-mile demonstration sections to show off the virtues of crushed stone macadam roads to as many people as possible. Few counties owned stone crushers, so they had to buy their stone from commercial quarries equipped with crushers. Given the cost of hauling wagon loads, some 30 or 35 tons per mile of macadam highway, to remote highway sites, towns and counties had a powerful incentive to acquire steam-powered crushers along with their related equipment, bucket elevators, sorting cylinders or sizing drums, and gravity feed storage bins.[5]

Two years later, Nathaniel Shaler published a book titled *American Highways: A Popular Account of Their Condition and the Means by Which They Can be Bettered*. This reflected his experience as a member of the commission and offered practical advice to highway builders. To make the case for better roads, there was the usual picture of horses struggling to pull a heavily loaded wagon deeply mired in a muddy roadbed. Shaler deplored the wastefulness of allowing citizens to pay their taxes by working on the roads, a practice he compared to the forced labor or corvée of the *ancien* regime in France. But most of the book was devoted to giving sound advice on highway construction practices with the various kinds of machinery available.

At the most primitive level, there was the drag, a locally fabricated frame of heavy beams bolted together and faced with a steel strip to provide a cutting edge. Drawn by two horses, a drag could smooth out the ruts in a dirt road suitably softened by a heavy rain. At best, however, the drag did little more than fill in the ruts with loose material. Wagon traffic soon made new ruts, so the effort was scarcely worth the cost. Road machines or bladed scrapers were somewhat better. The adjustable pitch blade could be used to cut and clear ditches on either side of a road to provide adequate drainage. This was useful, but Shaler was quick to deplore the common practice of letting the spoil turned up from the ditch pile up in the center of the road, where it could be rolled into a crown. While this might be the theory, in practice the soft soil mounded to a crown was soon rutted again by passing wagons. This practiced Shaler dismissed as "irrational and mischievous," as subsequent rains only served to return the soil as mud to the ditches.[6]

Shaler's whole conception of the highway problem was definitely centered on the notion of horse-drawn vehicles. Perhaps the best evidence of this is the symbolic illustration that graces the cover of his book; it depicts a horse-drawn road roller with its characteristic box, loaded with stone to add weight. But to his credit, he also looked to the future. When discussing horse-drawn road graders, he went on to comment, "It is likely that in time steam power will be used for this service." Sometimes, however, his anticipation of the future was somewhat flawed. This was evident when he suggested that the costly damage done to road surfaces by the iron-shod hooves of horses would be obviated if "power carriages" displace animal-powered vehicles.[7]

Shaler's open-mindedness is evident in his description of the steam-powered stone crusher as "the most important piece of road machinery now in use." But even the smallest crusher cost some $1,600. With an eye to impoverished rural communities, he backed away somewhat apologetically from suggesting that crushers were obligatory. Even though a crusher drastically cut the cost of macadamizing a highway, he went on to say, "it does not follow that hand-broken stone should everywhere be abandoned."[8]

By way of practical advice, Shaler urged local officials to buy crushers with adjustable jaw sizes to accept large stones since sledging to break fragments down to suitable size added expense. While there was an advantage in having a portable crusher which could be moved to the construction site, limiting the expense of hauling, lighter models of crushers tended to break down more frequently. Although Shaler was not himself an experienced contractor, it is evident that he was a careful observer as he traveled from one Massachusetts county to another, picking the brains of those he met.[9]

Many communities, when building macadam crushed stone roads, sought to avoid the expense of compacting by leaving the job to the traffic moving over the road. Shaler deplored this practice as excessively hard on the horses. The sharp edges of newly crushed stone hurt their hooves and the rough surface of the uncompacted stone made loads more difficult to haul. He favored using horse-drawn rollers, which were commonly available. These could be hauled empty to the construction site, where stones could be loaded into the box and water to the roller cylinder to add weight. Horse rollers, he had to admit, suffered from certain drawbacks. Even with the added weight, they were seldom heavy enough to compact the crushed stone as thoroughly as desirable. Moreover, the horses' hooves tended to disturb the crushed stone road surface, especially on upgrades where they had to dig in to pull the loaded roller.[10]

Steam rollers, which were increasingly being used on city streets, gave promise of doing what was necessary for rural highway construction faster and better than horse-drawn rollers. Shaler's progressive outlook and enthusiasm for the newest technology is evident in his assertion that "In its existing form the steam-roller appears to have attained very nearly to its possible development." There were, however, he admitted, substantial drawbacks, especially the roller's initial high cost. Furthermore, machines heavy enough to compact the crushed stone roadway risked breaking down the light bridges and culverts so frequently found on rural highways.[11] Strangely, for all his enthusiastic endorsement of the steam roller and the steam-powered stone crusher, Shaler's book never mentions the steam engine and its accompanying boiler needed to power the crusher. This may have been because portable wheel-mounted boilers and steam engines were by the 1890s commonly seen at sawmills and large farms with threshing machines where power was conveniently transmitted by leather belting.

Clearly, men like Roy Stone, Nathaniel Shaler, and George Perkins, who had been reared in the horse and buggy era, were striving to understand and exploit effectively in highway construction the machinery appearing with increasing frequency in urban areas. There the tax base was sufficient to justify the development of specialized machinery for contractors to use in street paving. The problem for the state highway commissioners was to persuade local officials and contractors that it was to their advantage to acquire these labor-saving machines despite their high cost and to accept commissioners' specifications and quality standards. This meant agreeing to supervision and inspection by state engineers if one accepted state financial assistance in road building. On this point, Shaler was adamant. The big problem, in his view, was the prevailing misconception that effective road building could be accomplished "by any dabster." On the contrary, the task called for a high degree of engineering skill, a career field crying for development.[12]

Shaler's most persuasive argument was the economic one. County officials with little or no understanding of highway construction were wasting large sums annually dragging and scraping their dirt highways. This merely shuffled the dirt to and fro, giving no permanent solution. As one state study revealed, annual maintenance expenditures on dirt highways ranged from $50 a mile to as much as $90 for the worst sections. A good crushed stone macadam road constructed under competent supervision would, Shaler contended, cost more initially to build but could be maintained for as little as $10 a mile annually.[13]

The good beginning made by the Massachusetts Highway Commission was gradually followed by other states such as Connecticut, New Jersey, and New York as the popular drive for Good Roads gathered momentum. But progress was slow. By 1905, some 14 states had established highway commissions. However, it took more than two decades for the rest of the nation to follow the eastern leaders. As late as 1901, some states and counties were still letting citizens work out their taxes on the roads despite the notorious inefficiency of this approach. And even some of the more progressive states were slow to acquire the specialized equipment needed for building good macadam roads.[14]

Awakening literally thousands of state and local officials to the need for expert knowledge of highway building was a slow process. Counties that bought stone crushers sometimes may have thought they were building macadam roads when they spread the broken stone. But if they lacked the appropriate screening to insure the proportioning of sizes, they were inviting failure. Without the necessary "fines," the dust particles for filling the voids, there would be little compaction, let alone cementation. Such a road would soon rut and unravel.[15]

While individuals like Nathaniel Shaler worked conscientiously to educate key state and local officials about the technical problems of highway building, there was actually a far more comprehensive source available, a textbook by an engineer with considerable experience. Austin T. Byrne, a graduate of Trinity college, Dublin, published in 1892, *A Treatise on Highway Construction*, which proved to be so popular that it went through eleven editions by 1913. Although most of Byrne's construction experience was on urban streets, his book did include several chapters dealing with the construction and maintenance of "country roads." A final chapter on the tools of the trade provided illustrations of the whole range, from handtools such as picks and shovels to massive steam rollers.[16]

Where individuals like the members of the Massachusetts Highway Commission seemed to address primarily the political officials who would be concerned with highways, Byrne's textbook was manifestly written for these actually involved in the construction, whether professionally educated engineers or those whose qualifications were based on practical experience as supervisors working for town or county officials. That few contractors in the 1890s actually read Byrne's text is scarcely to be doubted. Many, if not most, road contractors then were small-scale operators who conducted their business "out of their hats" as the saying was. Many were Irish or Italian immigrants with but slender capital, who employed their fellow countrymen for what was largely pick-and-shovel work. As for equipment, few of such contractors had more equipment than a cart or two with teams to haul them. Such firms seldom left archival sources about their existence.

Nowhere in his text does Byrne define his intended readership. However, implicit in his content is the engineer or supervisor hired by local political officials to specify the work to be done and to oversee its accomplishment. For such individuals, the textbook was a gold mine of practical advice on obtaining the most economical performance by a contractor. For example, in addressing the problem of making cuts to reduce the gradient of a highway, the author gives explicit advice on the alternatives. Shovelers can throw dirt twelve feet horizontally and six feet vertically. For greater distances up to 200 feet, wheelbarrows running on planks should be used. Hauls from 200 to 500 feet can use one-horse, two-wheeled dump-carts economically. For any distance over 500 feet, a two-horse, four-wheel dump-cart, which the author describes as "a recent invention," is preferable.[17]

Further evidence that Byrne's book was primarily intended for engineers and others involved in directing state and county highway projects is evident in a chapter on "specifications and contracts." These pages also offered highly practical advice. When specifying tests, Byrne suggested, care must be taken not to be too demanding, for in such cases contractors will feel they are unreasonable and will do everything they can be evade compliance. Bear in mind, he cautioned, "the more stringent the demand, the greater the difficulty in enforcing it." This kind of comment bespeaks the experience of an engineer who has actually worked with contractors on the job. Again, when discussing clearing land for a highway, he recommended that care be taken to save all useful timber, which should be stacked in a way suitable for marketing. Clearly Byrne had had a wide range of experience as an engineer and understood how many considerations well beyond the details of construction which should be taken into account when drawing up highway contracts.[18]

One stipulation for contracting prescribed by Byrne is curious in that it strongly suggests he did not fully understand the macadamizing process. The specification for crushed stone should, he said, call for square-faced cubes with sharp edges ranging in size down from two inches to quarter-inch chips, "but the proportion of stones below one and one-half inches shall not exceed 20 percent of the whole quantity." This would seem to indicate that he may not have understood the cementing role played by "the fines." This inference is further suggested by his additional stipulation that "The broken stone shall not be screened but will be delivered as they come from the breaker."[19] Despite this apparent aberration, Byrne's book was a remarkably useful compilation. That it went through eleven editions and remained in print for more than twenty years is sufficient evidence of this.

As more and more states took up the Good Roads movement, a competitor for Byrne's textbook appeared in 1905. By then the demand for works on highway engineering had obviously become acute, for John Wiley and Sons, the New York publisher who had brought out Byrne's text, published a rival text, *A Treatise on Roads and Pavements*, by Ira O. Baker, a civil engineer and a professor at the University of Illinois, in spite of the fact that Byrne's volume was still selling briskly. Baker's study also was a publishing success. Between 1903 and 1920, it appeared in three editions, a dozen printings, and sold tens of thousands of copies.[20]

Baker left no doubt as to his intended readership. He wrote for the engineer constructing city pavements and country roads, devoting four of his twenty chapters to the latter. Baker's treatment of macadam construction was far more advanced than Byrne's because in the ten years between the appearance of Byrne's book and Baker's, much had been learned about the character of crushed stone roads. Baker was sensitive to the importance of screening. He specified screens with a 100 mesh, that is 100 to the square inch, because he understood the role of "the fines," the rock dust particles which helped bind a crushed stone road together.[21]

A 100 mesh screen would select out the fine rock particles needed to insure cementation, a phenomenon identified by experiments undertaken by the Massachusetts Highway Commissioners and published in their annual report for 1900. Baker admitted that this cementation was not well understood, but it appeared to be a chemical reaction of the powdered particles when wetted and subjected to pressure by rolling. The extent of cementation depended upon the type of stone employed. Traprock offered excellent cementing properties, granite somewhat less.[22]

One of the good features of Baker's text was the author's readiness to mention negative views. For example, he recognized that not everyone was willing to accept the glowing statistics issued by the Office of Road Inquiry on the great savings good roads allegedly accrued to the farmer. While the added cost of an all-weather macadam road would certainly benefit farmers who produced perishable fruits and vegetables which must get to market when ripe, farmers producing non-perishable crops such as hay and grain could afford to wait out the weather, so costly good roads were of less interest to them. Furthermore, not every farmer was enamored with macadam highways, many claiming that the stone surfaces "stiffened up a horse."[23]

Another feature of Baker's text was his care in defining terms. He pointed out that raveling of a macadam road was not the same thing as rutting. Raveling was the phenomenon of stones working up and floating about on the surface. Similarly he was at pains to distinguish between gravel and crushed stone. Gravel applied to stones rounded by water action in contrast to the sharp-edged broken stone produced by a rock crusher. While gravel dumped on the surface of an earth road had some advantage in wet weather, it was by no means as effective as a crushed stone macadam road in the rainy seasons. On the other hand, a gravel road could be made cheaply at little more than the cost of hauling gravel from the borrow pit, since there was no need for crushers and rollers. But such roads required an infusion of clay to act as a binder. When the clay dried, it contracted and ceased to act as a binder. To prevent this, gravel roads required periodic sprinkling in dry weather, and this added to the cost.[24]

Wiley and Sons in 1913 brought out yet another volume, *Textbook on Highway Engineering* by Arthur H. Blanchard and Henry B. Drowne, faculty members at Columbia University. This book went through three editions but never enjoyed the success of the Byrne and Baker texts, in part, no doubt, because it continued to be horse-oriented, just as the automobile was beginning to have a major impact on highway construction.[25]

The many thousands of copies of these textbooks sold in the twenty-odd years after Byrne's work first appeared in 1892 offers a rough measure of the extent to which increasing numbers of state, county and local township officials were employing informed talent to supervise road construction. By no means all of these individuals were graduate engineers, but the availability of texts for experienced practitioners had a decided impact on the character and quality of highways produced. By 1900 there were 20,000 civil engineers of all kinds in the United States, not just highway engineers. By 1910 that number had doubled. But there were over two million miles of rural roads in the nation in 1900 and only about 150,000 of them were macadamized. So it is evident that in relation to the total miles of rural highways needing skilled attention, the available pool of talent was small but growing.[26]

Even where highway work was being done by contractors who could be held to a certain level of quality by the withholding of payments to insure compliance, competent supervision was essential. How much more so was this true where road work was accomplished by citizens working out their taxes by labor on the roads. And as late as 1902, when Baker's textbook was first published, in all but five states it was still possible to work out one's taxes on the roads.[27]

Also important in educating highway supervisors were the engineering journals, notably *Engineering News* and *Engineering Record*, which eventually merged. Although it is doubtful that many township- and county-level highway supervisors who were not graduate engineers were reading these journals at the turn of the century, their pages often contained valuable advice. A common shortcoming was the lack of a uniform system of accounting for highway costs. While statistics for total costs and total number of miles constructed or repaired were often available, such information was insufficient to make useful comparisons between jobs. For cost figures to be meaningful, they needed to show the outlays for labor, materials, supervision, equipment, and interest, divided by miles of road. But even such computations were not enough. True costs also involved consideration of the volume of traffic, cost per mile divided by the number of vehicles using the road, as well as the cost of maintenance for a given period of time. The journals regularly urged the pressing need for trained engineers to avoid the all-too-common waste of tax money resulting from poorly supervised construction and repair by men unskilled in cost analysis as well as construction methods. To offset the shortage of trained men, one journal suggested that some currently enrolled students should be diverted from railroad engineering to highway engineering.[28]

The journals, appearing monthly, played an important role in updating the information provided by the textbooks, which were only infrequently revised. Baker's important treatment of the cementation process in macadam construction identified by the Massachusetts Highway Commission was amplified by journal articles publicizing the more recent laboratory reports of the Department of Agriculture Office of Road Inquiry. These lab reports showed that limestone had a cementation value of 20, whereas granite dust had a value of but 6. However, when the two were combined, the value rose to 82. This could be critically important information to an engineer supervising the construction of a macadam highway. In fact, the editors of *Engineering Record* chided Austin T. Byrne when he brought out the fifth edition of his text. They pointed out that it contained much old and obsolete material, saying he should have rewritten the book entirely, given the rapid progress in highway engineering. Since Byrne's text with but modest revisions continued to sell for more than a dozen years after this criticism strongly suggests that there was an enormous need for elementary instruction in road building, and many lagged far behind the cutting edge of this rapidly developing technology.[29]

Yet another participant in the education of highway supervisors was the Office of Road Inquiry, ORI, in the Department of Agriculture, beginning in 1893, and its successor agency, the Office of Public Roads, OPR. These organizations turned out a steady stream of bulletins and advisories on a wide variety of subjects. These ranged from simple advice on the use of the split-log drag for scraping dirt roads to a rather sophisticated report on the cementing power of road materials, giving the adhesive properties of different materials found in different localities. Other bulletins discussed the construction of culverts, short span bridges, advice on the selection of appropriate stone, and testing procedures. The OPR laboratory would test samples for road builders and provided detailed instructions on how to submit specimens for analysis. Other bulletins and circulars dealt with the construction of sand clay roads where stone was unavailable for conventional macadam.[30]

Most of these governmental publications were brief compilations which could be had for as little as ten or fifteen cents, making them readily available for local road makers once they learned about the role of ORI and OPR and managed to overcome the vagueries of the Government Printing Office monthly catalog. Sometimes the compilers of the catalog injected their own opinions as to the significance of their publications. In 1910, for example, they announced that "The two great problems of road construction at the present time are preservation of the road bed and dust prevention." If dust prevention was widely perceived as one of the major problems confronting road builders, it suggests why understanding more about cementation in macadam highways was of such interest; for the long reign of macadam surfaces as the ideal for highways was beginning to be seriously questioned.[31]

One of the most effective vehicles for getting out information on sound highway construction methods was the Good Roads Train. In 1901 the President of the National Good Roads Association dreamed up the idea and persuaded the Illinois Central Railroad to contribute an eleven-car train to transport a road show from community to community. The train transported items of equipment contributed by manufacturers of road machinery along with experienced operators to demonstrate the use of the equipment. The Office of Road Inquiry assigned a representative to accompany the train with its nine flatcars of machinery and two sleeping cars. Between April and August, the train visited fifteen towns in five states, stopping to build demonstration roads of half a mile or more. Not all were crushed stone macadam; some were clay, some were gravel, depending on local conditions. Frequently, more than a thousand people attended these demonstrations.

The incentive for cooperation in highway building by the railroads was articulated by a Southern Railroad official who explained that where poor roads prevailed, the railroads could attract farm products from two to five miles on either side of their tracks. With improved roads, this range could be extended to 20 or 30 miles. Some rail firms even went so far as to build short sections of good roads out from their stations to the nearest muddy highway to play up the contrast. Actual demonstrations of how good roads could be constructed seemed to be more effective than endless written instruction. "Seeing is believing."[32]

The Good Roads Train idea proved to be so effective that it was soon copied as numerous other railroads volunteered trains to carry demonstration teams across the country. Sometimes these consisted of no more than a "museum on wheels" with small-scale models of road machinery to go along with a magic lantern lecture by an ORI or OPR representative. However, the actual demonstration of road construction using the equipment provided by manufacturers with materials provided by the local community had the greatest impact. Advance party teams drummed up interest in towns along the route by putting up circus-style lithograph posters. In 1911 alone, Good Road Trains gave 52 demonstrations. Between 1910 and 1917, two-and-a-half million people in hundreds of towns attended the displays. Even if no more than a small fraction of this total was directly involved in highway construction, there can be little doubt that the demonstrations were beneficial.[33]

Over the years between the early days of the agitation for better highways and the period immediately prior to World War I, those who addressed the problems of highway construction were aiming at a moving target. From the hesitant steps of such early spokesmen as General Roy Stone, who was almost afraid to go all-out for macadam construction because it might be too expensive for the farmers, down to the Good Roads Train demonstrations and the 1916 Federal funding enactments, those who spoke for highway reform had to struggle to stay abreast of the times. It was an age of transition from the horse to the automobile. As sources of funding became increasingly available, so too did the technological advances in road machinery, the subject of the next two chapters.

CHAPTER 4

HORSE-DRAWN ROAD MACHINERY

For readers in the early part of the 21st century accustomed to seeing a single operator mounted on a powerful bulldozer move hundreds of tons of earth in a single working day, it may be difficult to recall that in the early years of the 20th century, a contractor working on the same sort of task would often employ as many as a hundred workers, most of them pick-and-shovel men. In cutting down a grade where it was only a short distance to the fill site, they would load a succession of wheelbarrows. For longer hauls, they would have to expend more effort, tossing each shovelful into the higher body of a two-wheel cart drawn by a single horse.

The two-wheel cart was not designed for very long hauls, as there was no seat for the driver. He walked and led the horse by a hand on the bridle. Such carts were especially suitable for construction work in cramped areas; they could be brought about in a relatively small turning circle. Early versions of these carts had to be shoveled out to empty. Improved models hinged over the axel could be dumped, but only if the driver was able to tilt the load. A still later version was equipped with rollers so the loaded body could be pushed to the point where its bulk would be far enough behind the hinge point to tilt of its own weight. Such improvements may seem modest, but in an era of muscle power, these modifications helped a contractor reduce his labor costs and increase his efficiency. When horsepower could be substituted for human effort, the savings in cost mounted still further.[1]

One of the first pieces of road machinery other than the cart was the horse-drawn slip, or drag scraper, shaped like a metal-bodied wheelbarrow with two handles for the operator to adjust the depth of the cutting edge as a single horse pulled. Although the slip held only three or four cubic feet of earth, about the same as a wheelbarrow, it was self-loading and faster. Moreover, it was inexpensive; one could be procured for less than $10 at the turn of the century.

Figure 4.1   One horse drag scraper. Source: A.T. Byrne, *A Treatise on Highway Construction* (1892) 571.

The normal procedure in using a slip to cut down a highway grade was to have a conventional farm plow soften the earth ahead of the scoop to a depth of three or four inches. Protracted use tended to wear out the sheet iron body, so manufacturers took to welding iron straps to the bottom to absorb the wear and reduce friction in use. Larger slips, sometimes called fresnos, drawn by two horses, substantially increased the amount of soil moved, but were more difficult for the driver to dump at the end of the run. If the distance to the dumping site was great, sometimes it was advantageous to use a wheeled drag scraper, but these were more expensive. When the ground was excessively hard, sometimes contractors used a snatch team, a pair of horses hitched in front of the team dragging the scraper.[2]

Not surprisingly, the simplicity and self-evident advantage of the slip as an efficient means of moving earth relatively short distances without excessive labor costs led to its appearance early in the 19th century. Oliver Evans, the famous designer of an automated gristmill, credited the invention in 1805 to one Gershom Johnson, who secured a U.S. Patent on the device. With it, he claimed, three horses could do the work of twenty men. Versions of this device were used in constructing the Erie Canal and early railway roadbeds.[3]

Probably antedating the slip and even simpler and less expensive as a horse-drawn road machine was the road drag. This primitive device consisted of beams or split logs bolted to form a frame to be drawn behind a horse to scrape a road surface and fill in ruts. An iron strip bolted along the face of the leading edge provided a durable cutting blade. The driver would stand on the frame while steering the horse, his weight insuring a suitable bite to the iron strip. Because it was simple and thus cheap, the drag was the commonest road device used on rural highways. Many communities encouraged farmers to make such drags to maintain the roads fronting their property.

The effort to develop a better way to level the surface of dirt roads has a long history. During the 1870s various designs of graders appeared with metal blades mounted under the box of a conventional farm wagon. In 1877 one Samuel Pennock of Ithaca, New York, secured a patent for a "road machine" to scrape and level dirt roads by means of a blade fixed at a 45-degree angle under a frame mounted on two wheels. Levers fixed to each end of the blade controlled the depth of the cut. A scarifier or set of teeth mounted in front of the blade could be raised or lowered with a lever. The whole rig was designed to be hauled behind a farm wagon. A later four-wheeled version, also with a wooden frame, proved more satisfactory. Sam Pennock and sons manufactured this grader for some years before becoming the Good Roads Machinery Company of Kennett Square, Pennsylvania. In 1877, two other individuals developed road machines: H.C. Moore designed a wheeled scraper and C.H. Smith and Company, a railroad constructor, perfected a grader. These two designs became the prototypes of the road machinery manufactured by the Western Wheeled Scraper Company of Aurora, Illinois.

In 1886, George W. Taft of Abington, Connecticut, patented a significant improvement on the Pennock design by substituting hand wheels in place of levers to adjust the blade. This greatly erased the burden on the operator, who could set both the depth and horizontal tilt of the blade. Taft also introduced the reversible blade. Where earlier designs had a rigidly fixed blade angle, Taft's design could swivel the blade so that it faced in the opposite direction, allowing the operator to level either side of the road without turning his team around. Taft joined E.L. Lathrop in manufacturing wooden frame reversible graders for some years in Kennett Square, Pennsylvania, and the enterprise eventually became the American Road Machine Company.

The 1880s seem to have been an especially fruitful period for the development of road machinery. Improved graders were so much more efficient than a simple log drag that manufacturers found a ready market for them. In 1887 Goulds and Austin, a mill supply firm in Chicago, developed an all-steel road grader, which they had fabricated by a subcontractor, Kilbourne and Jacobs in Columbus, Ohio. The heavier, all-steel model proved so successful the company built its own plants in Chicago and eventually became one of the major road machine builders in the United States, the Austin Manufacturing Company. Still later it merged with the Western Wheeled Scraper Company of

Mount Pleasant, Pennsylvania, which had in 1888 developed an all-steel scraper.

The heavier and sturdier all-steel graders, soon demonstrated that they not only shaped a road surface inexpensively but could also be used to cut a suitable ditch at the roadside to carry off surface water. When making such cuts with the right-hand rear wheels leaning into the sloping cut, there was a tendency for that wheel to bind on the axel. So J.D. Adams of Illinois in 1885 invented wheels that would tilt to alleviate this strain. Similarly, when Taft and Lathrop observed that the rear wheel of their grader had a tendency to slue to the right when ditching or cutting a bank, they developed an adjustable axle, which allowed the operator to extend the right rear wheel so it would track beyond the blade edge. This allowed the operator to place the wheel against the unplowed edge of the roadside to keep the machine from twisting under the load of earth piling up in front of the blade.[4]

One of the most efficient road machines was the elevating grader, invented in 1883 by W.J. Edwards, who assigned his patent to the Austin Manufacturing Company. In this machine, a coulter or harrow-like cutting disc sliced the earth ahead of a moldboard plow, which turned the dirt on to a rubber belt geared to the rear axel. This continuous belt elevated the dirt at right angles to the machine's line of motion and eight or more feet above the ground, giving sufficient clearance for a wagon to draw alongside the grader as it moved ahead, taking on the dirt being brought up by the elevating belt. With two or more wagons to haul away the dirt, the grader could remain in almost continuous operation. Depending on how hard the roadbed happened to be, four, six, or even more horses might be required.[5]

While the elevating grader was an impressive improvement over its predecessors, it was not without its problems. The horsepower required to break hard earth coupled with that needed to operate the rubber belt meant that more horses and mules were needed than the team ordinarily used to pull a conventional grader. Few if any of today's readers will have had experiences driving six, eight or more animals. Eight horses were difficult to manage, but eight mules were even worse. The problem was to get all of them to start up in unison. And while the elevating belt was efficient in discharging dirt into a waiting wagon, it also generated clouds of dust, which soon covered wagoners and grader operators alike.

The creative inventiveness that introduced so many improvements in graders and other road machines in the years leading up to the turn of the century did not stem from designers associated with large manufacturing establishments. Virtually all the significant, innovative ideas appear to have

Figure 4.2 The Austin elevating grader, shown here with its accompanying teams, was said to be capable of excavating over a thousand cubic yards of earth in a 10-hour day, loading into a wagon moving alongside or piling it upon an embankment. In difficult soil, an additional team could be harnessed to a shaft attached to the rear of the machine to assist the horses pulling up ahead. Source: 22 *Engineering News* (30 Nov. 1889) 521.

come from individuals actually working on highway maintenance, most of them individuals of modest means working for townships or county officials. A few developed their own manufacturing establishments, but most assigned their patents to existing firms with manufacturing capabilities. J.D. Adams, who came up with the idea for tilt wheels, offers a typical example. A man of limited means, he had to have his machine fabricated by someone else while he went out to demonstrate the utility of his invention to community officials as potential buyers. Eventually, like Pennock, he acquired his own factory and developed a highly successful business.[6]

While wagons may not seem particularly complex technologically, they do in fact have a history of mechanical development. For road work especially, the principal problem was to simplify the task of unloading the wagon box. The labor cost of shoveling out a load of dirt or gravel was not inconsiderable, so much thought was devoted to designing a suitable method of dumping. The long survival of the two-wheel cart as a contractor's vehicle was based on the fact that a man could with some difficulty tilt the body and discharge the contents of about 20 cubic feet. But a four-wheel wagon with the load in the body box over both sets of wheels could not be readily manhandled in this way. To meet this difficulty, wagon builders designed a box fitted over rollers, so the load could be pushed back until its center of gravity was beyond the rear axel to dump of its own weight. This was an improvement over shoveling out the load, but it still involved a great deal of muscle power when the wagon was filled to capacity, which was about 40 cubic feet, or twice what a two-wheeled cart handled.

Various alternative methods for dumping were tried. The least desirable was a scheme by which individual boards running the length of the wagon box could be pulled out one by one to dump the load. This required a great deal of strength to accomplish. Moreover, it was slow and took time to reinsert the floor boards after the load was discharged. Time was critical if a contractor was to get the most efficient use of the wagon, driver and team, not to mention the shovelers who would be standing idle while the wagoner replaced the floorboards.[7]

Early in the 1890s the Austin Manufacturing Company came out with a dump wagon designed to reduce the manhandling required. It achieved this by mounting the wagon box on rollers so the driver could push the box aft of the center of gravity, over the rear axel. The displaced wagon box was held in position by a catch or lock. When the driver tripped a lever, the box pivots down and dumps its load. While this was a significant improvement, it suffered from the fact that it placed more weight on the rear wheels and stressed the wagon unevenly.[8]

A few years later, the American Road Machinery Company of Kennett Square, Pennsylvania, brought out its "Champion" dump wagon on the same lines as the Austin, but with improved details. To ease the burden of dumping, it had a crank which operated a pinion gear and rack. This allowed the driver to set any desired angle when dumping. The tailgate was also adjustable to limit the amount of sand or gravel eased out on the highway as the wagon moved along. A further refinement allowed the driver to set the horizontal angle of the gate so that more gravel could be dropped in the center of the road than at the edge to establish a crown more readily. Moreover, the tailgate was divided into two panels so that the load could be dumped to half the

Figure 4.3   An Austin dump wagon. This is a later model than the wagon described at note 8. In this version, the wagon box is tapered to be larger in the rear so that the center of gravity is aft of the horizontal member, which sustains it midway between the front and rear wheels. Source: 28 *Engineering News* (1 Sept. 1892) 212.

width of the wagon. This was for use in building side strips on either flank of the highway to accommodate wagons passing one another. Despite these useful modifications, the "Champion" still suffered from placing too much of the weight on the rear wheels, making the wagon harder for the horses to pull.[9]

To overcome this drawback, the Shadbolt Manufacturing Company of Brooklyn, New York, in 1902 came up with a novel design. The company was engaged in excavating for the Manhattan subway system and was experiencing all the difficulties of hauling off tons of rock. The Shadbolt design had the enlarged portion of the body box toward the rear, but seated the box on a set of leafs prings placed in front of the rear axel. This shifted the center of gravity one foot ahead of the rear axel. A chain to the tailgate latch allowed the driver to open it for dumping the load without leaving his seat.[10]

Three years after the appearance of the Shadbolt dump wagon, the Moore Manufacturing Company of Syracuse, New York, came up with a vastly superior solution. Instead of dumping by tilting the entire body box, this wagon design simply dropped its load by opening two doors in the floor, one behind the other. To close the doors, the driver spun a wheel at the side of his seat to turn a windlass, which drew up chains attached to the doors. To open the

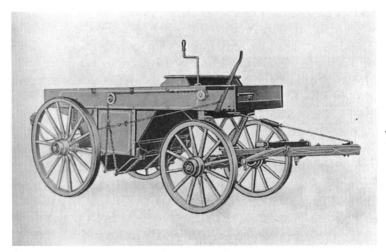

Figure 4.4 Good Roads Machinery drop-bottom wagon. Source: A.H. Blanchard and H.B. Drowne *Textbook on Highway Engineering* (1913) 163.

doors under the load, the driver kicked a foot pedal, which released the ratchet holding the windlass. To control the rate of dumping, the driver could check the extent to which the doors opened by holding the wheel. By this means a driver could even drop a load of bricks without breaking them.[11]

Other wagon makers followed suit with similar designs with doors hinged crosswise. The Good Roads Machinery Company of Kennett Square, Pennsylvania, brought out a drop-bottom wagon with a V-shaped hopper body. Two doors, hinged crosswise and facing one another, discharged the load quickly, entirely by gravity. An upright crank controlled the chains that checked the doors. The Moore and Good Roads company drop-bottom designs were a significant improvement over their several tilt-body predecessors, but the most popular drop-bottom wagon, one produced by the thousands, had a somewhat different door arrangement.[12]

The drop-bottom wagon, which became the virtual standard of the type, hinged its doors along the sides of the wagon fore and aft so that it dumped along its centerline, leaving the wheels free to pull beyond the load. The Watson Wagon Company of Canastota, New York, is advertised as the originator of this particular design. The firm certainly was one of its major manufacturers. Although its wagons were more expensive than several of its competitors, Watson wagons enjoyed a high volume of sales based on the superior quality of its product.[13]

Figure 4.5   Western drop-bottom wagon. Source: J.L. Allhands *Tools of the Earthmover* (1951) 100. The crank visible to the left of the driver's seat winds the chains on the transverse bar seen below the driver's seat.

There were plenty of competitors, for soon almost all the firms building heavy wagons for contractors brought out versions of the drop-bottom with longitudinal doors. Among them were the Studebaker Corporation of South Bend, Indiana; the Austin-Western Co. of Chicago, Illinois; and the Bain Wagon Company of Kenosha, Wisconsin, to name only a few of the more prominent firms. Studebaker produced over 100,000 wagons of various sorts annually. The company boasted of its 80-acre lumber yard. To appreciate the significance of this, one has to recognize the importance of thoroughly dried lumber in making quality products. That this was an advantageous advertising claim is suggested by the boast by the Bain Wagon Company of its 60 years of experience and its adequate capital "to buy and hold lumber until properly cured."[14]

Numerous other firms turned out drop-bottom wagons, confirming its status as the favored vehicle for heavy-duty hauling of broken stone and the like. Among these firms were the Tiffin Wagon Company of Tiffin, Ohio; the Eagle Wagon Works of Troy, New York; the Troy Wagon Works of Troy, Ohio; and the Moore Manufacturing Company of Syracuse, New York. Each introduced some variant in the levers, cranks, and winches to secure the bottom doors in the search for competitive advantage. One simple modification was to add a rolled form iron strip to the edge of one of the doors to provide an overlapping lip so sand and other particles of the load wouldn't drip out where the doors met.[15]

Innovations in wagon design offer a contrast to innovation in road machines such as graders. In the latter, many if not most of the creative designs came from individuals working on the roads, practical men, who "invented," but having little capital and no manufacturing plant of their own, assigned their patents to some metal-working firm because there was no established road machinery industry. On the contrary, in the latter years of the 19th century and the first decade of the 20th century, there was a well-established and prospering industry of wagon builders. In 1909 somewhat more than 5,000 wagon and carriage builders in the United States manufactured 587,685 wagons. Of these, 154,631 were for non-farm use; not all of these, of course, were for road construction purposes. Innovative designs for wagons came from within this established industry. And because the industry had a long tradition of working in wood, wagon designs continued to employ wood construction much longer than the other types of road machinery, such as graders, where there was no well-established industry.[16]

The wagon makers were not averse to involving metal-workers' innovations. As early as 1899, some began experimenting with ball bearings for heavy-duty wagons. When the spokes of a stoneboat's wheels collapsed under loads approaching fifty tons, a resourceful firm developed steel spokes. Several firms turned to sheet-metal doors in drop-bottom wagons to resist the abrasion of sharp, crushed stone particles. But the skills of the labor force and the machinery of the traditional wagon builders were wood oriented, so it was probably inevitable that they would continue to seek wooden solutions. This is evident in the design of sprinkling wagons so essential to the construction of waterbound macadam highways.[17]

Firms producing sprinkling carts that had skilled coopers among their employees and the necessary woodworking machinery continued to fabricate wooden tanks long after it became evident that metal tanks would be less leak-prone, cheaper, and probably lighter. However, competition and the requirements of highway construction eventually forced the wagon builders to move increasingly into metal working. So long as sprinkling carts had been used almost exclusively in urban areas, they could be refilled from hydrants, but highway construction out in the country meant filling up from a brook or pond, and filling a thousand-gallon tank using a handpump was manifestly impractical. So Studebaker came out with a sprinkler that had a steel tank and a pump driven by a small gasoline engine, which could be used to pressurize the tank as well as to refill from a convenient wayside source.[18]

Studebaker retained its leading position in the field by continual innovation. One example of this was the nozzle it developed to send out a fan-shaped spray arcing some distance to either side of the wagon, allowing it to cover a wide road surface. A competitor, still using the traditional horizontal bar perforated with holes, attempted to justify its older design by advertising that pointing the spray downward avoided wetting pedestrians! For waterbound macadam too vigorous a spray was undesirable because it led to gushing streams which washed away the fines so essential to proper cementation. For this reason, the gentle drip from a perforated horizontal piper was entirely appropriate. Studebaker met this consideration by equipping its sprinkler with a valve by which the driver could adjust the spray to any desired intensity.[19]

One persistent problem confronting the wagon builders was to determine the proper width of the steel tires on the heavy-duty vehicles they produced. On this subject they received conflicting advice. In 1897 the Office of Road Inquiry conducted a series of dynamometer tests to determine the tractive power required to pull loads on different road surfaces. They found accuracy difficult to obtain, as the jerky motion of the horse's exertion made as much as a 50-pound difference in the readings. The rougher the road, the greater the jerking motion that increased the fatigue experienced by the horse. The ORI experimenters speculated on the potential reduction in fatigue if some sort of elastic link could be added to the harness. This study didn't address tire width, but it was an early effort to give scientific precision to the problem of maximizing horsepower.[20]

A year later, engineers at the University of Missouri conducted experiments with different tire widths on various types of road surfaces. They concluded that broad tires consumed less energy than narrow tires, except when the surface was sticky clay or deep sand, where narrow tires performed better. They defined broad as six inches and narrow as one-and-a-half. A few years later, University of Washington engineers conducted tests that led to somewhat similar results: narrow tires were best for smooth surfaces; broad tires were best for compressible dirt surfaces; narrow tires were best for soft mud. From a contractor's point of view, these "scientific" experiments may have seemed of little use, for a team pulling a heavy drop-bottom wagon or a thousand-gallon sprinkler on a waterbound macadam construction job might easily encounter all three types of surface in a single hauling job.[21]

There were in fact other considerations than tractive power to be evaluated in deciding upon optimum tire width. The broader the tire, the harder the vehicle is to turn. Further, when a broad-tired vehicle drives down the center of a crowned macadam highway, the slope of the surface on either side tends to rest the whole load on the edge of the tire rather than its broad surface. This resulted in excessive wear on the tire and a tearing motion, dislodging the broken stone surface of macadam. Oddly, both Byrne and Blancher, two of the leading textbook writers on highway engineering, suggested using tires up to eight inches wide on sprinkling wagons. So the wagon manufacturers would have found the advice of the academic community somewhat ambiguous when it came to tire widths.[22]

There were, however, some areas where the increasingly frequent research projects of the engineering schools offered useful and valuable advice to manufacturers of road equipment. Because drop-bottom wagons used by highway contractors normally operated on rough ground and were subjected to far greater stresses than vehicles confined to use on graded roads, it was important to determine just how strong to build them. Purdue University subjected a 4.5-ton drop-bottom wagon manufactured by the Troy Wagon Company of Troy, Ohio, to a load of 36.5 tons before it collapsed. Wheels deeply mired in ruts are vulnerable to severe sidewise stress when a team making a sharp turn jerks abruptly to start the load. To simulate this condition, the Purdue engineers supported a wooden wheel horizontally at the hub and applied pressure at the rim of the felloe until it broke. This didn't happen until almost twice the design strength of the wooden wheel.[23]

Of all the horse-drawn road machinery, the horse roller was probably the least effective. It suffered from several drawbacks. Most notable was the damage the horses inflicted on the crushed stone roadway they were rolling. Their hooves dug into the rolled surface as they strained to pull the heavy roller. And their manure droppings, unless promptly removed, formed a slippery layer after a rain and in time worked down below the surface, where they collected water and, when frozen in winter, disrupted the macadam. Another drawback of the horse roller was the damage it inflicted when, at the end of a run, a team attempted to turn around, the heavy roller churned up the crushed stone it had just rolled. To overcome this defect, one manufacturer came out with a reversible roller. The massive iron roller stayed in place, but the towing frame and shaft were pivoted, allowing the horses to swing about to roll in the opposite direction.[24]

Road machinery makers showed considerable ingenuity in making horse-drawn rollers more effective. To lessen the load imposed on the horses during what was sometimes a long trip from the contractor's base to the highway construction site, they designed a box above the roller, which could be filled with stones to add weight only after arriving at the job site. Another design relied on a water- or sand-filled roller cylinder to add weight. But sometimes design ingenuity over-reached itself. This seems to have been the case of the hand-powered roller, which required three men working at cranks to maneuver the roller to and fro. In advertising this contraption, the manufacturer pointed out that there was no need to get up steam before setting out in the morning, no need to worry about supplying coal or water. And what is more, this roller wouldn't "frighten horses" the way noisy steam machines did. Needless to say, this roller design found few buyers. Workmen willing to engage in the kind of toil involved in propelling it throughout a ten-hour day were hard to find.[25]

By 1915, the journal *Engineering and Contracting* was declaring that horse-drawn road machinery was "out of date" and various forms of power-driven equipment would replace animal power. This was certainly true, but horses continued to be widely used by highway contractors. As late as 1925, the editors of *Public Roads* were still touting the merits of elevating graders, which were said to load as much as 5,000 cubic yards into wagons drawn alongside during a ten-hour day. For maximum efficiency, they pointed out that the two-yard wagon was better than a 1.5-yard wagon. The heavier load required an additional horse, but for a 14% increase in cost, one could get a 33% increase in the yardage of a road graded and there would be fewer exchanges of empty wagons for loaded ones in the course of a day. Clearly, the economics of horsepower continued to command attention. Replacing animals by steam and gasoline power was a slow process. Many contractors and communities had a considerable investment in animals, barns, harness, wagons, and other horse-drawn equipment, a sunk cost not to be squandered.[26]

Of course, the days of animal-powered highway construction were numbered, but not everyone was willing to concede the fact. The members of the Carriage Builders Association complacently assumed that prudent consumers would continue to favor wagons. For some, the gasoline-powered vehicle was a fad that would fade away just as rapidly as the bicycle craze. When the United States entered World War I, the Army flooded the industry with orders for wagons because the gasoline-powered truck was yet too unreliable to replace wagons entirely and the auto industry too small to meet the demand. So the demise of the wagon industry was briefly delayed by one last gratifying gasp of production. In this, it repeated the pattern of the clipper ship industry. Wooden shipbuilding was well on its way out when the forty-niner gold rush created a temporary boom for the clipper ship builders.[27]

CHAPTER 5

STEAM-POWERED MACHINERY FOR HIGHWAY BUILDING

A previous chapter mentioned the importance of Eli Whitney Blake's 1852 invention of the steam-powered stone crusher, which revolutionized the construction of macadam highways by drastically lowering the cost of broken stone. Blake got the idea for a jaw-type crusher upon observing an attempt to employ a trip hammer to break stone against an old furnace grate. This approach sent shards of stone flying about dangerously. It took Blake several years to perfect his scheme for a steam-powered set of jaws in a cast gray iron frame with a large flywheel to the point where he could secure a patent in 1858.[1]

Until the patent expired, the Blake Crusher Company of New Haven, Connecticut, enjoyed a brisk sale not only in the United States but also in the export market. Thereafter, a number of competitors appeared, most of them offering minor variants of the essential Blake design. Competition led to improvements: replaceable face plates in the jaws, which wore down rapidly, a capacity to adjust the size of the crushed stone product without stopping the machine, and steel rather than gray iron construction. The most important modification appeared when several manufacturers brought out portable crushers, which could be hauled to the construction site. This obviated the former considerable expense of transporting wagon loads of crushed stone to remote construction jobs.[2]

As is often the case in the early days of a new industry, there was some confusion over terminology. What should one call the new machine? The editors of the *Index to Engineering Periodicals* suggested "stone breaker," "disintegrator," then "pulverator" or "pulverizer," although the latter two were usually applied to a large gyratory model designed to crush ore rather than stone for highways. In the end, of course, common usage decided the question and rock or stone crusher became the standard terminology.[3]

By the 1890s, manufacturing stone crushers had become big business. No community of any size could be without one if it aspired to have good macadam roads. The road machines firm, F.C. Austin of Chicago, produced

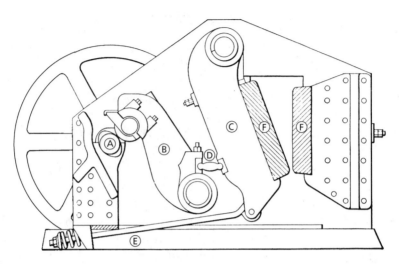

Figure 5.1   The Blake stone crusher imparted reciprocating motion by means of an elliptical cam, A, on the driveshaft at the opposite end from the flywheel. The revolving cam imparts a backward and forward motion to the rocker arm, B. The rocker arm imparts motion to the moveable side of the jaws, C, by means of a small breaker arm, D. The breaker arm is the weakest part of the crusher, protecting the rest of the machine from breaking in case unexpectedly hard material such as iron is ingested in the jaws. The size of the discharge opening at the bottom of the jaws can be adjusted by the threaded rod, E, or by inserting shims behind the jaw face plates, F, which can be replaced when worn. Source: Wm. H. Walker, Warren H. Lewis, and Wm. H. McAdams. *Principles of Chemical Engineering* (New York, 1927) 277.

a number of models ranging up to one capable of turning out 14 tons an hour. The Farrel Foundry and Machine Company of Ansonia, Connecticut, offered buyers ten different sizes, while the Totton and Hogy Foundry Company of Pittsburgh, Pennsylvania, boasted of having sold some 1,500 crushers. At the 1892 Colombian Exposition in Chicago, seven different firms displayed crushers. Clearly, this simple piece of machinery had caught the industry's fancy.[4]

As contractors acquired more experience with crushers, they came to realize how differences in design affected their operations. A crusher with its flywheel extending parallel to the jaws inhibited the ability of a cart to dump stone directly into the jaws, thus raising labor costs. They discovered that manganese steel jaw liners lasted three times as long as regular steel liners. They also found that stone dust tended to work its way into bearings and cause them to bind. Repair parts for crushers were not inordinately expensive, but down-time means idle labor and horse expense, emphasizing the importance of investing more initially for the highest quality machine. Also, contractors soon learned that a larger jaw opening was of importance since it cut the amount of sledging required to reduce the quarry product to fit into the jaws. All jaw-type crushers suffered from excessive vibration, but it wasn't until many years had passed that it was found this could be substantially reduced by balancing the flywheel, which apparently the manufacturers had failed to do.[5]

As long as crushers were located at a quarry or at a municipal site where uncrushed stone was hauled in from a distant quarry, they could be powered by a fixed steam engine. But when portable crushers became available for use on rural highways, obviously some portable source of steam power became essential. Oddly enough, the engineering journals and texts dealing with highway construction largely ignore the question of steam power. They seemed to assume it was readily available. And indeed it was, but unlike other pieces of specialized road construction machinery, it was available because it had been developed to a highly practical state for a completely different purpose.

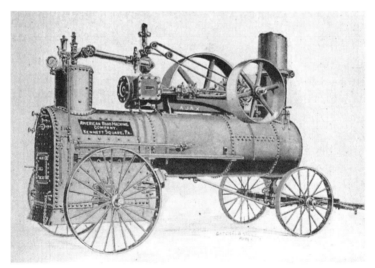

Figure 5.2 Portable steam engine manufactured by the Good Roads Machinery Company of Kennet Square, Pennsylvania, illustrated in Blanchard, Arthur H. and Drowne, Henry B., *Textbook on Highway Engineering*. Such engines were commonly available up to 50 hp capacity.

Back in 1849, when agriculture was the major industry of the nation, one A.L. Archambault designed a steam engine fitted to a boiler and firebox mounted on wheels for use in threshing grain. Steam was to replace the previously used horse sweep or capstan, which powered threshing machines. The continuous circular motion of the horses on the sweep tended to gall their necks because of the sidewise tug on the horse collar. Horses, worn out from a summer's cultivation, would often collapse while powering the thresher. So a steam substitute was greatly desired. Unfortunately, a 30-hp portable steam rig cost about $3,300 at mid-century, a sum very few farmers could afford. The solution of course was the itinerant "for hire" thresher, who moved from farm to farm with his thresher and portable steam rig, taking his charge in grain which the farmer could pay in lieu of cash. In winter, portable steam engines were extensively used in lumbering. By 1860, some 22 firms were producing portable steam engines with forced draft, governors, and safety valves. Safety was an important consideration, for conservative farmers were often fearful of this strange new source of power. Manufacturers sensitive to this concern wisely put the flywheel at the far end of the engine, away from the door to the firebox and controls, where the operator would be standing. This sheltered him from the tendency of the broad leather driving belt to fly off its pulleys on occasion, a common cause of injury. So by the time a portable steam engine was required to operate crushers out on highway construction jobs, there was a substantial industry ready to satisfy the need.[6]

For many years after Blake introduced his crusher, contractors used the stone as it came from the jaws with a random assortment of sizes up to the maximum opening at the bottom of the jaws. Normally this would be not more than two inches, or slightly more than John Loudon McAdam specified when he said no stone should be larger than one could put in one's mouth! This random mix of sizes was not ideal for macadamizing, as it wasted much of the fines on the lower courses rather than the finishing course where they were most needed. Somewhat prior to 1890, manufacturers began to offer cylindrical screens, which sorted the crushed stone according to size. An advertisement of the Farrel Foundry and Machine Company of Ansonia, Connecticut, in Blanchard's 1893 textbook provides an excellent illustration of this primitive screening mechanism.[7]

As the illustration clearly shows, the cylindrical screen was powered by a belt running off the hub of the crusher flywheel. The crusher, mounted on steel wheels, is shown carefully chocked with wooden blocks for operation on site. This screening process was manifestly inefficient, since the several sized products had to be shoveled into a wagon. This represented no improvement over

Figure 5.3   This illustration, showing a Farrel portable stone crusher, an early version of a screening cylinder, is from Austin T. Byrne's 1893 *Treatise on Highway Construction*, advertising section, p. 4.

the 1876 *Scientific American* picture (Figure 2 in Chapter II), illustrating Blake's original New Haven operation. Fortunately, a markedly more efficient solution for handling the screened and sorted crushed stone was readily available.

By using an endless chain of buckets, the product of the crusher could be elevated and poured into the screening cylinder mounted on top of a storage bin equipped with separate sections for each size of stone. Sloped bottoms in the bins delivered the sized stone to chutes in the side of the storage structure. These chutes could be opened or closed to load by gravity wagons positioned below. The highway builders didn't have to invent this solution, for it already existed in another industry.

The concept of an endless chain of buckets goes back a long way. In 1582, Jacques Besson published *Theatrum Industrumentorum et Machinarum*, a volume illustrating various mechanical devices, including one depicting an endless chain of baskets used to hoist soil 25 feet or more by the efforts of a man cranking a worm gear. The device may well be fanciful, for it is doubtful that such an arrangement would overcome the friction inherent in the design, let along the weight of the load. However, it did illustrate the principle of the endless chain elevator. A more practical application had to await the development of power sources.[8]

Figure 5.4   Stone-crushing plant, consisting of crusher (portable steam engine as source of power, not shown, would be connected to the crushers by wide belting), continuous belt bucket elevator (chain and sprocket transmits power from crusher to elevator) screening cylinder (with power take-off by gearing from head of elevator) and storage bins with delivery chutes. From I.O. Baker, *A Treatise on Roads and Pavements* p. 216.

Around 1848, ice harvesters in New England were using steam power to operate endless belt devices to lift cakes of ice for storage in ice houses. The coming of railways soon adapted the principle for the efficient transfer of wheat and coal to storage bins. This developed a large market for endless chain elevators. A major manufacturing concern, the Link Belt Engineering Company, with factories in Philadelphia and Chicago, was already producing a wide range of lifting devices when the highway builders first sensed the need.[9]

There were many problems to solve. Once the screening cylinder was lifted to the top of the heavy timbered elevated bin, means had to be devised to transmit power from the steam engine to the shaft on which the cylinder rotated. Experiments with screening cylinders revealed that a slope of one inch to the foot gave the best results. A ten-foot-long cylinder divided into three or four sections with holes of different sizes, typically ranging from ¼ to 2 ½ inches in diameter, became the more-or-less standard configuration. The first section at the highest point would sift out everything from the finest rock dust up to ¼-inch particles. Any stone larger than 2½ inches would fall out the end of the cylinder as tailings to be recirculated to the crusher. Operators learned that over-charging the screening cylinder in an effort to increase production only resulted in the loss of much of "the fines," the pulverized rock dust so valuable for cementing the surface course in macadam, because it tended to pass beyond the initial screen. To maximize the recovery of rock dust in the first section, some operators added dust shields around that portion of the cylinder to insure that most of the valuable fines were deposited in the first bin section.[10]

Although most contractors who did any considerable volume of highway work had their own crushing plants, some of the larger commercial firms selling crushed stone formed an association of producers, and in 1917 they agreed upon standard sizes and terminology. This was important because many states had begun to specify the sizes of stone to be used in highway construction. Without standardization there was bound to be confusion and waste, as well as needless expense when a contractor had to replace his screening cylinder to comply with a state specification.[11]

By the 1890s those who advocated the use of steam-powered crushers and their accompanying screening plants could argue that they reduced the cost of crushed stone for macadam roads by some 200% over hand hammering. What is more, using machines increased output from the 1-cubic-yard per day by hand hammering to 50 for the crusher. Despite this, one prize-winning essayist as late as 1890 still claimed that hand-hammering produced a better product, which bonded more effectively.[12]

Crusher plants were not cheap to operate, although contractors could count on a normal life expectancy of ten years for the crusher unit itself. Despite its heavy construction, repairs were frequent. By the very nature of its operation, crunching chunks of stone, the machine was subjected to continual vibration and abrasive wear and tear. The elevator buckets, made of relatively thin metal, wore thin from the continuous grating of sharp stone particles. And the exposed metal surfaces were vulnerable to rust. Crusher plant repairs could run as much as 60% of initial cost in a year's operation. This could be reduced somewhat by systematic preventive maintenance, especially daily lubrication, but this involved significant labor costs. The life of the wooden storage bin could be extended by installing sheet iron on the sloped flooring facing the delivery chutes. But even with this modification, bins often had to be replaced in four or five years, especially when they had to be knocked down and set up anew at successive highway sites.[13]

When the stone crusher was first developed, it was logical to locate the crusher at the quarry site adjacent to its source of stone.[14] Workmen using hand drills and hammers could drill up to ten inches in an hour. They inserted a black powder blasting charge developed in 1859 by DuPont, and broke off chunks of stone from the quarry face. Most of these fragments were too large for the crusher, so they had to be sledged into smaller sizes. All this labor intensive effort ran up the cost. But here too, steam came to the rescue. In 1849 J.J. Couch developed a steam-operated flywheel and crank-driven rock drill, which he patented. It was exceedingly heavy, clumsy to use and inefficient. However, an associate of Couch, J.W. Fowle, came up with a major modification. He did away with the crank and fly-wheel by attaching the drill bit directly to the piston. Like so many inventors, Fowle lacked the capital to perfect his drill, so he sold his patent to Charles Burleigh. In October 1866, Burleigh's improved model was employed in the Hoosac Tunnel, which was planned to provide a direct rail connection between Boston and Albany.

Although the Burleigh tool was a great improvement over the hand drilling which had been used when the Hoosac project began in 1858, it was still a heavy and complicated instrument. And part of the faster tunneling achieved after switching to machine drilling was attributable to the use of newly available nitroglycerin. Critics also complained about the drill's expense. As one put it, "Only a corporation backed by a state's Treasury could afford to use it." Perhaps the most important contribution of the Burleigh drill and its use in the Hoosac tunnel was the competition it inspired. In the following decade, several inventors brought out alternative designs. Among these were Simon Ingersoll, who devised a tripod stand, and the brothers E. Addison and J.R. Rand, who built drills for mining. Henry C. Sergeant at one point was called upon to repair an Ingersoll drill and decided it could be developed further. So he formed the Sergeant Drill Company, but the Ingersoll patents were significant, so he persuaded a wealthy investor to buy up the Ingersoll patents in order to organize an Ingersoll Rock Drill Company, which he merged with the Sergeant Drill Company in 1885. This firm in 1905 merged with the Rand firm, creating the corporation which continues to the present.[15]

Although the mergers, which consolidated the rock-drill manufacturers, had the advantage of pooling all the important patents to produce an all-around better tool, until the 1890s, rock drills continued to be heavy and unwieldy. In 1896 J. George Leyner introduced a major improvement in the form of a free-floating drill bit. Hitherto all the various models had the drill attached to the driving piston. Leyner's innovation had the piston hit the drill bit like a hammer. This modification greatly reduced the shock and made possible a much lighter tool. Leyner also introduced the hollow drill bit, allowing water or compressed air to cool the cutting tip and flush out the cuttings. Leyner also perfected a pneumatic bit sharpener. Ingersoll-Rand promptly brought up Leyner's patents.[16]

When air compressors replaced steam engines, ease of operation was greatly facilitated, but hose lines were still a problem. In an effort to obviate this difficulty, Samuel Lessen of Denver, Colorado, as early as 1894 developed an electric drill in which two alternately actuated solenoids kept the bit flying back and forth. Electric cable was more convenient in use than high-pressure hoses, but the merits of pneumatic drills allowed them to survive this alternative design.[17]

Powered rock drills remained largely quarry tools for many years, along with their use in mining and tunneling. Until significant State and Federal funding became available, powered rock drills played only an indirect role in highway construction. They helped supply the quarry stone, which fed the contractor's crushers. Prior to 1916, highway construction was largely a matter of providing a sound macadam surface. Cutting down grades, cut and fill work, was sharply limited by the problem of cost. With Federal funding, it became feasible to undertake far more extensive efforts at reducing grades. And where such efforts encountered ledge rock, contractors began to acquire rock drills, which they could operate with their portable steam plants.

Next to the crusher, no powered road machine of the 19th century was more important than the steam roller. The first steam-powered roller appeared in France, designed in 1859 by a man named Lemane. It was not a success, but the idea once launched was sure to be emulated. In 1862 another Frenchman, M. Ballaison, came up with an improved design, which the manufacturing firm, E. Gellerat and Company of Paris, began to produce in considerable numbers. The British were intrigued and promptly sent various representatives to France to learn what they could about the Gellerat machine. A nation which claimed pride of place in manufacturing steam engines was sure it could do better than the French, and soon local firms were busy developing various types of steam-powered road rollers.[18]

Aveling and Porter, a firm in Rochester, Kent, which manufactured steam traction engines for agricultural use, had little difficulty in modifying its existing design into a steam road roller. Subsequent improvements helped Aveling and Porter to capture most of the British domestic market, and a substantial export trade as well. As early as 1869, the Park Commissioners of Brooklyn, New York, purchased an A&P roller. They praised its "great savings of expense." A day of operation with the steam roller cost $10 but did as much as eight horses in two days at $20 per day. The high U.S. tariff on the imported machine made it cost half again what it sold for in Britain, but even so sales in the United States were brisk.[19]

The original Aveling and Porter machine was a giant 30-ton roller, but the company's designers decided that a less unwieldy 15-ton model was sufficient. A 15-ton version, they observed, was well beyond the weight feasible for any horse-drawn roller. As the weight of a roller increased, horses had to dig their hooves into the rolled surface to pull the load, disturbing the very surface they were supposed to be compacting. The revised 15-ton model created the design so widely copied in the United States that for many years it was the standard configuration for steam rollers. Two large driving wheels in the rear also served as rollers. By placing the driving wheels in the rear, the machine achieved greater traction when climbing a grade. The space between the driving wheels was compacted by the smaller front rollers, which ran freely on unpowered axels on either side of a supporting column that allowed the front rollers to pivot in order to steer the machine.[20]

Even the most carefully constructed waterbound macadam surface eventually unravels under heavy traffic. When this occurs and the road has lost its smooth surface, the conventional practice was for maintenance crews to break up the surface with picks to begin the sprinkling and rolling process all over again. To cut the cost of this process, A&P introduced a novel feature in their 15-ton model. They drilled holes at intervals in the treads of the driving wheels and inserted spikes into the wheels, which then could be used to tear up the old road surface, loosening the stone for reworking. When the machine was not being used in this way, the spikes could be removed and the big rear driving wheels reverted to their compacting function.[21]

By 1879 there were several different types with locally manufactured designs competing with Aveling and Porter for sales in the United States. One, by a designer named Lindeloff, was manufactured by the Pioneer Iron Works of Brooklyn, New York. Lindeloff produced light three- and five-ton rollers with front and rear rollers covering the same space. His machines were used primarily for rolling asphalt pavings.

The second type of roller was patented by a man named Ross. This 22-ton machine combined a roller with a tamping or ramming capability. This was accomplished by five steam-operated tampers positioned across the rear of the machine. An unusual feature was a steam line from the boiler to heat the main roller when working with asphalt.

The third model available in the United States was the imported French machine manufactured by the Gellerat company of Paris. The unique feature

Figure 5.5   Steam Roller Spiking a Road. Source: Ira O. Baker, *Roads and Pavements* (Wiley and Sons 1905) 255. Sometimes spikes were called porcupines.

of this machine was its ability to cant both rollers to assist in turning. This can readily be seen in the illustration on page 64.

The fourth type of steam roller available in the United States was the latest Aveling and Porter design imported from England. The illustration on page 65 shows the essential features: the worm-gear steering mechanism, the simple, readily accessible single piston engine atop the boiler, and the split-front roller to assist turning by allowing the outer roller to turn faster on a curve than the inner roller. Despite the local competition, A&P machines, offered in 8-, 10-, 15-, and 20-ton versions, continued for some years as the most widely used rollers in the United States. The success enjoyed by this firm stemmed largely from maintaining high quality and from a policy of continually introducing improved designs by adding such features as a compound

Figure 5.6   The Lindeloff Steam Roller. As this illustration clearly reveals, the design offered little room for the operator standing at the steering wheel, and his all-around view was somewhat obstructed by the vertical boiler. The twin pistons actuate the power train through a bevel gear driving the main roller. This gearing was vulnerable to fouling by mud and dirt picked up by the roller.

   In an 1895 advertisement the manufacturer of the Lindeloff machine suggested it was also good for rolling lawns, thought it is doubtful many estate owners accepted this suggestion. Source: 8 *Transactions of the American Society of Civil Engineers* (May 1879) 136 ff.

engine to save fuel and reduce the noise of the exhaust. A power takeoff to use the steam power of the roller to operate a stone crusher made A&P rollers especially attractive to smaller communities with minimal road maintenance equipment.[22]

   Despite the heavy transatlantic shipping charges and the tariff, A&P continued for some years to enjoy a near monopoly on steam roller sales. Eventually, of course, local U.S. manufacturers overcame the teething problems of their early designs and began to take an increasing share of the domestic market. Among these were the O.S. Kelly Company of Springfield, Ohio, offering

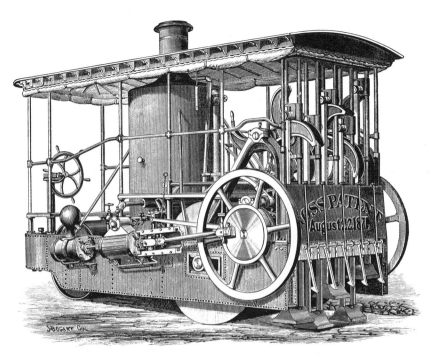

Figure 5.7   The Ross Patent Roller and Rammer. The novel tamping mechanism of this roller is evident. The complexity of this roller made it difficult to maintain. Source: 8 *Transactions of the American Society of Civil Engineers* (18 May 1879) 136 ff.

5- and 10-ton models; the Harrisburg Foundry and Machine Company of Harrisburg, Pennsylvania, with a 10-ton version; the Pioneer Iron Works of Brooklyn, New York; and Russel and Company of Massilon, Ohio, with a 12½-ton version.[23]

From the perspective of a hundred or more years later, it is easy to forget that in the latter years of the 19th century, a steam engine was "high tech." There were many details for a roller operator to check. Assuming that a night watchman had fired up the boiler before the crew arrived to begin the working day so there would be no delay in getting underway, the driver would begin by checking all the oiling points and grease cups. He would then fill the water reservoir and replenish the coal box. In winter, the boiler and reservoir had to be drained completely overnight to prevent freezing. With steam up he would blow the condensers to clean them, then run up the boiler pressure to

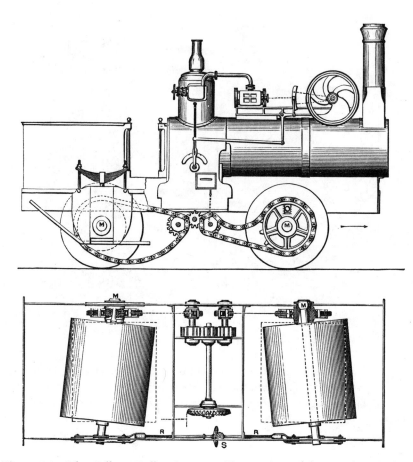

Figure 5.8   The Gellerat Roller. Source: 8 *Transactions of the American Society of Civil Engineers* (May 1879) p. 136 ff.

make the safety valves pop off to be sure they were not stuck. During the day's operation, the driver would have to clean out the ash pan several times. Forgetting to do so could burn out the furnace grates. The list of chores, things to do and not to do, went on and on.[24]

Not least among the cares involved in running a steam roller were the spikes or picks fitted into the driving wheels. They gave endless trouble. If they hit a solid rock in the roadway, they were prone to break or bend. When thus distorted they were often difficult to remove. Once removed, the spike holes had to be filled with wooden plugs. If these weren't driven in absolutely flush with

Figure 5.9   The Aveling and Porter Roller. This engraving shows the modified A&P roller exported to the United States by the 1870s. This model included a friction brake, but since it was operated at 2 mph there was little occasion for braking. The mud scrapers on the driving wheels were designed to function when the machine was moving forward or backwards. Source: 8 *Transactions of the American Society of Civil Engineers* (May 1879) 136 ff.

the wheel surface, they would catch on the scraper blade, which cleared mud or asphalt from the wheel surface. Roller operators continually complained about the difficulties raised by the spikes, although some of them found spikes useful in getting a roller freed from a slick, muddy stretch, where the driver wheels spun with no traction. Inserting a few spikes solved this difficulty, but it was obvious that the disadvantages of spikes outweighed the advantages.[25]

By 1912, an alternative to wheel spikes widely used in England was beginning to appear in the United States. This was a scarifier mounted on a steam roller. Previously, scarifiers other than wheel spikes used in the United States had consisted of teeth set in a cast iron block on wheels which could be towed either by horses or a traction engine. Several different versions of the British

Figure 5.10   Scarifier produced by the Huber Manufacturing Company of Marion, Ohio. The spikes are lowered and raised by steam power. Source: 37 *Engineering and Contracting* (10 Jan. 1912) 36.

steam roller scarifier appeared in the United States, but all were variants of the same principle, a set of teeth fitted in a frame behind the driving wheels. Lowered into the road surface, these teeth could tear up a dirt, crushed stone, or asphalt surface for reworking far more efficiently than the wheel spikes or "porcupines." One such design produced by the Huber Manufacturing Company of Marion, Ohio, had nine teeth slightly curved forward to penetrate more effectively as the roller advanced. The teeth were controlled to a set depth by a steam piston. If they hit ledge rock or some other obstruction they moved up against the steam pressure and rode over the obstruction.[26]

Other improvements were soon introduced. The Kelly Springfield Road Roller Company of Springfield, Ohio, offered a scarifier with pneumatic controls. Certainly one of the most useful modifications was one of the simplest.

It consisted of replaceable teeth made of tool steel held into their frame by massive set screws.[27]

Although the introduction of scarifiers vastly increased the general utility of the steam roller, horse-drawn equipment continued in use well beyond the turn of the century. As late as 1914, the state of California was still using teams of 12 to 20 horses to scarify a macadam highway for rebuilding. A steam roller could do the job at half the cost of such an unwieldy large team, which must have been incredibly difficult to turn around.[28]

Just as steam power gradually replaced horse power, the days of the steam roller were numbered. Around the turn of the century, a French firm, Coutant-Dujour, began experimenting with a roller powered by a four-cycle single cylinder kerosene engine. One of their engineers came to the United States and joined the Austin Manufacturing Company of Chicago, but the first internal combustion roller manufactured in the United States appears to have been produced by the Kelly-Springfield Road Roller Company.

Gasoline-powered rollers caught on slowly, but by the 1920s some 2,000 were in use in the United States. The greater ease of operation and maintenance of gasoline and diesel engines made inevitable the eventual displacement of their steam predecessors, which continued in operation for many years, some as late as the 1950s. Steam rollers are now to be found in a few scattered museums of farm implements and heavy construction machinery and in the possession of enthusiastic collectors.[29]

A remarkable feature of the steam roller was its stability of design. Once the Aveling and Porter engineers put their original 30-ton behemoth behind them, the functional design they came up with was so sound that it became the standard which most of their imitators in the United States copied. County officials and contractors well into the 20th century seemed to feel that they could not build roads successfully without stone crushers and powered rollers, even if these were the only steam-driven machines they employed.

In sharp contrast to the steam roller was the steam shovel, which evolved along a very different path. The first steam-powered excavating machine appeared in 1796, when a man named Grimshaw of Sunderland, England, hired the famous engine firm, Boulton and Watt, to install a 4-hp steam engine in a scow to power a dredge. In the United States, Oliver Evans, the famed millwright, built a similar dredging device in 1805.[30]

The first true dry-land steam shovel in the United States was the work of William Smith Otis, the 19-year-old son of a railroad contractor, who secured a patent in 1839 on a novel design in which a cast iron kingpost, conceptually reminiscent of contemporary derricks, supported the dipper boom. The ma-

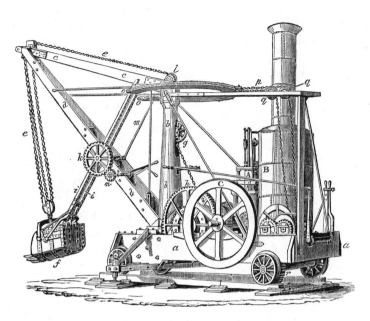

Figure 5.11   The Otis steam shovel, which he termed the "Yankee Geologist." One of the outriggers to stabilize the machine is clearly visible just behind the left front wheel. The gearing at K permitted the dipper to be moved under power to a position parallel to the horizontal plane on which the shovel stood, giving it an ability to make horizontal cuts later described as "crowding." The horseshoe-like collar embracing the cast iron kingpost, b, power operated through chains p, swiveled the shovel left and right for dumping. Source: 5 *Journal of the Franklin Institute* (1843) 3rd Series, p. 324.

chine rode on a temporary track as the roadbed under construction advanced. The wooden-framed machine had detachable outrigger arms projecting from either side to stabilize the shovel in action. An inefficient vertical boiler served a 16-hp engine in the largest Otis model. A chain from the engine to the swinging boom pulled the dipper into the bank it was excavating. The boom had sufficient side-to-side rotation to dump the loaded dipper into waiting wagons. Crude as it was, the Otis shovel allegedly did the work of 60 to 100 men with its 1½ cubic yard dipper. As long as its patent lasted, the Otis firm built a few shovels for the market but was primarily interested in cutting the firm's labor costs to stay ahead of the competition. When the extended patent expired in 1860, the company authorized John Strother, an experienced locomotive builder in Boston, to manufacture the Otis design for commercial sale.[31]

The economic advantages of the Otis machine were impressive. For an investment of around $6,500 including interest at 6% on the cost, the powered shovel could excavate 1,000 cubic yards in a 12-hour day at about $.03 a yard. A pick-and-shovel laborer at $1.00 a day could move about 12½ yards. Even taking account of wages for three or four operators and the cord of wood the boiler consumed each day, the shovel was not only a money saver but a time saver.[32]

By 1880 there were four firms producing steam shovels. These included Starbuck Brothers Iron Works of Troy, New York; the Vulcan Iron Works of Chicago, Illinois; and John King and Company of Oswego, New York. The fourth firm was organized by a Toledo, Ohio, contractor, H.T. Stook, who had purchased two Otis machines for use on a construction project. He made several modifications to improve the shovel, especially fitting it to ride on a standard guage railroad track, and began to construct shovels for sale. All four of these firms were job shops for whom making steam shovels was an occasional undertaking. However, in 1880 a wealthy bank president and railroad investor founded a company in Bucyrus, Ohio, to specialize in building steam shovels, which it began turning out in ever larger numbers.[33]

As contractors purchased increasing numbers of steam shovels, ingenious designers came up with various improvements. For example, the Industrial Works of Bay City, Michigan, brought out a model with a steam piston operating the dipper arm directly. In 1883 H.M. Barnhart and Edward Huber of Marion, Ohio, came up with a radical new chain drive thruster, which led them to found the Marion Steam Shovel Company. Another notable improvement appeared when the Bucyrus company introduced powered broad steel-tired wheels, giving the shovel mobility apart from railway track.[34]

One of the more interesting developments came in 1895, when a retired Great Lakes ore boat captain, Richard P. Thew, tried to improve the efficiency in wharf-side loading operations. He had the Variety Iron Works of Cleveland, Ohio, manufacture a shovel to his design. Like the Bucyrus, it had broad tread wheels to travel under its own power on the wharf. One of its novel features was full-circle swiveling, so the shovel could turn about on its own axis. Even more importantly, it was so designed that the dipper could be thrust parallel to the wharf flooring, so its teeth in collecting a load didn't tear up the wharf planking. Which is to say, the hinged end of the dipper handle could move along a five-foot track so the dipper could, in the terminology of the trade, "crowd" parallel to the surface of the wharf. This was a development of considerable future importance to highway construction, for it allowed the shovel operator to dig the subgrade to the level specified by the layout engineer's grade stakes.

Thew formed the Thew Automatic Shovel Company of Lorain, Ohio, in 1899 and eventually became a major supplier of shovels for highway contractors. The all-around rotation of Thew shovels had several advantages. It allowed greater flexibility in spotting wagons to receive the load dumped from the dipper, and it avoided the twisted hoist chain, which commonly happened in earlier models. And all-around swiveling meant the shovel could use its powered wheels to roll off the massive plank platform often used to provide a stable base, use its dipper teeth to snag the chain or hawser loop attached to the platform, and swivel the platform around until it was out in front, and then crawl up on it again to go back to excavating once more mounted on a stable support.[35]

Although the Thew shovel was optimized for highway use, that does not mean that highway builders began to use it when Thew first produced shovels. Not many contracts that specified significant reductions in grades were signed for the construction of rural roads until State and Federal funds became generally available. Austin T. Byrne's famous text, *A Treatise on Highway Construction*, first published in 1896, makes no mention whatever of steam shovels, although he offers illustrations of most of the other road machines. Ira O. Baker's 1905 *Treatise on Roads and Pavements* mentions steam shovels dismissively:

> The steam shovel and dump cars afford the most economical method
> of handling earth when the amount to be moved justifies the outlay
> for the plant, but as that would seldom be the case in highway work,
> this method will not be considered.[36]

Even more surprising is the absence of any mention of steam shovels in Arthur H. Blanchard and Henry B. Drowne's 1913 *Textbook on Highway Engineering* at a time when highway contractors were already beginning to use steam shovels extensively. One reason for the delay in using such shovels on highway jobs, apart from funding, was the difficulty of moving such a heavy piece of equipment, which traveled only about 3 mph under its own power on the highway. A 1913 report of moving a shovel on a house-moving trailer pulled by two traction engines traveled 24 miles a day at a cost of $48 per mile. And the two steam traction engines needed a five-ton auto truck "to help out with the starts." Five years later, with more powerful trucks available, moving an 18-ton shovel seemed less daunting. Mounted on a heavy stoneboat trailer, one was moved along at 8 mph and was able to climb a 3½% grade "with no trouble."[37]

A highway construction contract had to involve extensive excavation before it became economically feasible to employ a steam shovel. In 1908 a widely used engineer's handbook suggested that a shovel costing $15,000 including interest on investment would cost $164 per 10-hour day to operate. But given the short fair-weather construction season, a shovel was an impressive time saver. Two dipper loads would fill a waiting two-cubic-yard wagon.[38]

As with any expensive piece of equipment, a contractor had to keep his steam shovel continuously busy if he hoped to recoup his capital investment. This led manufacturers to introduce modifications, giving shovels an increased capability. For example, the Ball Engine Company of Erie, Pennsylvania, brought out a model in 1915 with a gear and pinion on the dipper arm, driven by a separate engine, which provided a "crowding" capability of eight feet on the horizontal. In the hands of a skilled operator, this shovel could even cut a properly crowned subgrade. Many other modifications followed. The Ball company also introduced a shovel mounted on crawlers. That idea was not new, but previous cleated track arrangements had shown a tendency to become clogged with mud, leading to breakdowns and costly delays. The Ball version added a system of lubrication to overcome this difficulty.[39]

For highway contractors, probably the most important innovation was the introduction of the gasoline engine in place of steam-powered shovels. There were many good reasons to switch to gasoline engines. Shovels using a ton of coal a day meant hauling fuel to a distant highway job site. Water was often difficult to find on highway jobs, so there was more hauling. And some localities demanded licensed firemen and operators for steam equipment. Although several firms introduced gas engines around 1915, the Marion Shovel Company of Marion, Ohio, was the leader in this move, adding such features as a flywheel to relieve the stresses encountered under sudden changes of torque. Wisely, the designers retained the same set of control levers used on steam versions to make the transition easier for operators. Despite the manifest advantages of gas engine shovels, contractors were slow to switch. The early gasoline engines were often unreliable, and relatively few operators were skilled at maintaining them.[40]

If delayed, the replacement of steam by gasoline engines was inexorable. So too was the pace of innovation. By the 1920s, there were diesel shovels, power steering, rubber tires for road transit, ball bearings, and manganese steel for parts subjected to heavy wear. Previously, wearing out two sets of dipper teeth in a season was not unknown.[41]

To hold down costs, a contractor must synchronize each aspect of his operation to insure that there is but a minimum of lost time and unproductive labor when men working on one operation have to stand idle until other men arrive to perform another sequential operation. Steam shovels were faster than laborers with shovels loading wagons to haul off earth. To keep up with the speed of the steam shovels, more wagons were required. The greater the distance the wagons had to travel to dump in a fill, the more wagons would be needed if the economies of the steam shovel were not to be lost. But more wagons, drivers, and teams would run up costs, offsetting the savings produced by the power shovel. The pace of a team of horses set the practical limit on the time it took to make a round trip between cut and fill. Steam power offered a potential solution for this problem.

Steam-powered traction engines pulling a train of wagons provided one alternative. Another was to employ a narrow gage railroad using portable track. By the time contractors began building rural highways at a rapidly expanding pace after the turn of the century, both of these alternatives were readily available. Traction engines for agricultural use were being manufactured by several firms. And portable narrow gage railway systems already existed in connection with mining operations. These were generally known as "industrial railroads."

Both systems could haul greater loads and faster than horse teams. Moreover, neither had to be fed during the off-season. Traction engines pulling a long train of wagons were difficult to turn around, but this drawback was overcome when manufacturers began to produce steel-bodied, double-ended wagons; the traction engine could unhitch and go to the end of the line of wagons to haul in the opposite direction. However, traction engines had difficulty hauling on rainy days. The industrial railroad, on the other hand, could move in both directions without repositioning the engine. Laying sections of track was labor intensive, but once laid, track permitted a lower-powered engine to pull greater loads than the traction engine working on rough surfaces. Moreover, the industrial railroad offered a variety of cars suited to contractor needs: flats to haul rail, equipment such as pumps, lumber, forms and the like, as well as material such as bags of cement. Side-dump cars served to move sand and gravel. Even without the use of a steam engine, one man pushing a car on rails can push five to eight times more than he would with a wheel barrow. Using track, a horse can haul far heavier loads than possible with a wagon.

Although portable railroads were widely used in Germany and elsewhere in Europe, they were not extensively used in the United States until after State and Federal funding made the construction of multi-mile highway construction commonplace. A German firm, Orenstein-Arthur, with a plant in Koppel, Pennsylvania, was the dominant supplier in the United States. The company claimed that even using horses to haul their cars on track, the cost per cubic yard of material would run about $.05, which is to say $20 per day on

Figure 5.12   A narrow gage, portable track Koppel industrial railway showing a Koppel 20-hp engine hauling a string of two-way V-dump 36-cubic feet cars being loaded by a Marion steam shovel, about 1914. Source: Orenstein-Arthur Koppel catalog 910, courtesy of Smithsonian Institution.

rails as opposed to $90 per day using 18 wagon teams to do the same amount of work.[42]

A 7½ ton Koppel steam engine rated at 20 hp along with a mile of track and 18 two-way V-dump cars of 1½ cubic yards' capacity could be purchased for about $6,000, including an allowance for track laying and freight delivery charges. The company claimed such an outfit could operate for $17.50 per day, including 6% interest on investment. The track came in 15-foot sections, which two men could easily carry and lay. With 18 cars, an engine could spot nine under a steam shovel for loading while hauling the other nine to the job site, alternating the full and empties for maximum efficiency. With such a rig, the company claimed material could be delivered at $.02 a cubic yard. A friction brake on one car in each nine could control the descent of cars on down grades.[43]

The Koppel company offered contractors several options: one could rent a compelete outfit or any item; one could buy outright, or, alternatively use a combination rent-purchase scheme. A contractor with a stable of horses could rent track and cars without an engine, and if the experiment proved effective subsequently add an engine. Unless a job required at least three or four miles of hauling, procuring an engine probably wouldn't be economical. Contractors contemplating investing in an industrial rail system had to do some close calculations on the estimated cost. The Koppel catalogs didn't mention all the expenses involved. On many sites a certain amount of grading had to be done before the track could be laid. To this expense the cost of hauling the track, cars, and engines to the job site also needed to be added. Moreover, a considerable amount of time had to be spent daily in watering and coaling, time which could upset one's cost estimates if neglected.[44]

Moving the engine of an industrial railway was no small undertaking in the years before World War I. One contractor in 1914 reported moving an engine by mounting it upon a massive stoneboat-type wagon with wide tires. This he hauled using a Locomobile truck with five tons of stone on board to give traction. Using a gasoline-powered truck proved to be 40% cheaper than using teams of horses to transport the steam engine.[45]

For a few years at least, portable railroads were widely used by contractors. With sand, for example, some 90% of the cost lay in transporting it to the job site. So the economics of using a multicar train appealed to contractors. As demand rose, Koppel encountered competitors. The Lima Locomotive Company of Lima, Ohio, to mention but one, put a narrow gage engine on the market. A few years later, the Fate-Root-Heath firm of Plymouth, Ohio, came out with a gasoline locomotive with a high cab so the driver could see over the cars he was pushing or hauling. The appearance of gasoline-powered locomotives only presaged the end of the industrial railway era of highway construction as automotive power began to replace narrow-gage railways, but that is a story for a later chapter.[46]

The foregoing chapters in this narrative of the highway revolution have dealt primarily with crushed stone macadam as the principal form of "improved" road surfacing. But even before the appearance of automobiles in significant numbers after the turn of the 20th century, the subject of paving materials for roads and streets was well-advanced in towns and cities. There the tax base was sufficient to finance various kinds of paving that were far too expensive to be considered for use on rural routes. However, the experience towns and cities acquired in building paved streets provided a valuable resource when the coming of state and federal funding made it possible to consider paving highways. A later chapter, which recounts the nation's urban experience in paving streets, most particularly with asphalt, deals with the nation's early experience with this versatile material.

CHAPTER 6

THE CONTRACTOR

With funds increasingly available and state highway commissions empowered to call for bids, along with the availability of a wide variety of road building machinery, the final factor needed to pull all these elements together was the contractor, whether an individual, a partnership, or a corporation. Who were the contractors? What did they know and where did they learn it? What experience did they have? Where did they get their capital and their skilled labor? When the surge in rural highway building came, did they have the requisite managerial skills to cope with multi-mile contracts to build surfaced roads out in the open countryside?

Because many, if not most, of the contractors who undertook to build state highways, especially in the early years, were relatively small-scale operators, detailed records as to their existence, their business practices, and their managerial skills are exceedingly hard to come by. Most contractors who ventured into highway building in the late 19th and early 20th centuries had small beginnings, taking on contracts to build short sections of urban streets. Some learned the business on an even smaller scale, building sidewalks before bidding on street contracts.

As one observer put it, looking back over 50 years from the mid-1920s, contractors then had their "offices under their hats." The boss directly supervised a gang of men armed mostly with hand tools and perhaps a wagon or two and a couple of slips, horse-drawn scrapers. With newly arrived immigrant manpower willing to labor with pick and shovel for 10 or 12 hours a day, an enterprising contractor who plowed his profits back into plant could gradually take on bigger contracts, which enabled him to buy a stone crusher or a steam roller. By establishing a reputation for competence on small jobs, he gradually qualified as a responsible bidder. Competence reflected more than obvious success in achieving quality results. A successful urban street builder had to persuade bankers and bonding agencies that he was a good risk.[1]

A contractor building several miles of highway had to borrow money to meet his weekly payroll and the cost of materials. Even if the state agreed to make progress payments, there would always be a need for capital up front, notably if the job involved renting specialized equipment. The highway building season is about 150 days of good summer weather, give or take a few weeks on either end. To keep a whole stable full of horses eating their fill all winter when jobs were few was uneconomical, so a contractor often rented additional teams and wagons, if he could get them, for in summer farmers with teams and wagons were in the midst of their busy season.

The essential skill for a successful contractor lies in the ability to make sound estimates of his costs, *all* his costs, when preparing a bid. Experience is essential, but so too is record keeping. And many small-scale contractors building short sections of urban streets relied upon judgment based on past experience rather than upon written records. Moving to multi-mile highway contracts involved a host of novel factors. Longer hauls, the absence of readily accessible sources of water, and the problem of getting labor and materials to relatively distant sites all conspired to complicate the matter of estimating. The more progressive contractors introduced rudimentary cost accounting in the 1890s, but there were many who did not, continuing to "guestimate" when bidding.

Contracting to build city streets meant doing business directly under the eye of the banker and civil authorities; contracting with the highway commission in the state capitol, remote from the construction site, was a very different proposition. Larger scale meant greater risks and state contracts as a consequence became more complex. Without extensive cost accounting records it was difficult to persuade bankers that one's estimates were sound enough to ensure completion of the contract and payment in full by the state.[2]

Older engineers, fully competent in design work, gradually came to recognize their deficiency in cost accounting and began to register complaints against the engineering schools for failing to offer instruction in this form of accounting. They wanted to know how to find the most efficient solution to a construction problem, one which identified the optimum cost among alternatives. The difficulties are evident in a typical instance. A contractor building a waterbound macadam highway found that teams hauling gravel an average of 1 ¼ miles cost $.33 per ton-mile. Further, he had learned from experience that because of delays in loading and unloading, it cost him $.40 a cubic yard for the first mile but only $.20 for each additional mile. In contrast to this, he reported that a traction steam engine hauling four 7-yard wagons an average distance of three miles cost $.15 a ton-mile. But he admitted that these figures included neither interest on the money invested or depreciation.[3]

How was a contractor to make sense of such figures? To begin with, omitting interest on money invested, the opportunity cost, and ignoring depreciation robbed the given figures of real significance. And comparing a 1 ¼ mile haul employing teams of horses with a three-mile haul by a traction engine offers no true basis for evaluation. If time to completion is critical, then the faster speed and longer haul of the traction engine might be more advantageous, but against this must be set the capital cost of the traction engine compared with the teams.

Given the short construction season for highways, time spent performing is almost always critical. Equipment, which contractors term "plant," is a substitute for labor. It is worth substituting for labor if it can do the job at lower cost and in less time. But given the capital costs of equipment, a contractor must calculate closely on just how far to invest in plant, which commonly ran between 20 and 30 percent of total cost. For the small-scale local street contractors venturing to become highway contractors, a common practice was to estimate their first big highway job at no profit except for the cost of the added machinery. Then on subsequent contracts they might add no charge for the previously acquired machinery in order to keep their bid low. Failure to include some increment for depreciation would eventually show the folly of this practice when the equipment had to be replaced. Sale of old equipment seldom brought as much as 25% of its initial cost.[4]

A common cause of disaster, faulty estimating leading to bankruptcy, was a failure to calculate accurately the cost of excavating the subgrade of a highway. There are many variables to trap the inexperienced or unwary contractor. These included the distance between cut and fill, the relative difference in cost between wagon teams and various mechanical alternatives. Not least of the difficulties was the unexpected encounter with hardpan or ledge rock, which greatly increased a contractor's costs. Prudence would suggest the advisability of conducting test borings on suspected sites, but such tests ran up costs even before one submitted a bid. This hazard cast a cloud over bidding, at least until state highway commissions began including rock clauses in their contracts to protect bidders against such unforeseen burdens.[5]

Many state highway commissions specified lump-sum contracts. They were easy to administer, but suffered from rigidity if the state wished to add certain work after the contract was signed. To overcome this difficulty some states introduced the so-called "unit cost contract." This form of contract set a price on each square-yard of paving laid or each cubic yard of soil excavated. For the contractor, lump-sum contracts were at high risk. No matter how carefully one estimates cost and tries to take into consideration every reasonable eventuality, it is still impossible to foresee every contingency, especially weather. Even if a contract omits penalties for delays caused by weather, interest on borrowed funds goes on relentlessly during such periods when no work is accomplished.[6]

One way to reduce the risks assumed by a contractor entering a contract for a multi-mile highway was to subcontract parts of the overall task. By so doing, the prime contractor got the benefit of closer supervision through the efforts of his subcontractors, who could be given incentives to optimize their contributions. And for the prime contractor, he benefited additionally by employing their capital as well as his own.[7]

In the 1890s, the cost plus fixed fee contract was sometimes employed to reduce the risks a contractor had to accept. By the early 1900s, it was more commonly employed. Under this form of agreement, the state highway commission engineer estimates the probable cost of the job. Then the state authorizes a certain percentage of this estimate, say 10 percent, as the contractor's fee if he performs within the specified time. The state pays all his expenses as reported and certified by the state's supervising engineer. If the contractor finishes the job ahead of schedule, his fee might be enlarged by a specified percentage. If he is delayed in finishing, his 10 percent fee would be reduced by the same formula. This gave the contractor an incentive to push hard to complete the contract in less than the specified number of days. While this form of contract saved a highway builder from catastrophic loss if his costs escalated unexpectedly by market fluctuations in labor and materials, it did suffer from one serious flaw. Its effectiveness hinged largely upon the state engineer's initial estimate of the probable total cost of the job. State highway contracts often specified that the execution of certain details should be "satisfactory to the engineer" supervising the job for the state. This, of course, readily led to ample opportunities for discord between the contractor and the engineer, since it left the former almost entirely vulnerable to the whim of the latter. The high risk character of highway contracting is evident in the report that surety firms lost more than 30 million dollars on defaulting contracts in five states during 1924.[8]

No matter what type of contract was employed, the burden of risk remained largely upon the contractor. A contractor cannot sue a state unless that state's legislature has explicitly prescribed an appeals process. The inability to sue, to resort to the courts for remedy of unresolved differences, suggests that signing any sort of agreement with the state is never really a true contract. By definition, a contract is "an enforceable agreement." If the ground were really level, then the contractor should be able to compel compliance by the state as well as vice versa. Any road builder who signs a contract with a state should recognize as a given that the ground is not level and the best he can hope for is that the state highway commissioners are men of integrity and fair play. To insure completion of a contract if the contractor simply walked off without finishing the job, most states required contractors to furnish bonds or sureties. Bonding agencies charged fees ranging upward from 10% of the contract depending upon their appraisal of a contractor's reliability.

While it may be reasonable to assume that most highway commissions were honest, occasionally one would be encountered which jiggered the specifications offered to bidders to force them to use products available only through a politically favored supplier. One such case was reported by the media in 1913. In this instance, the specifications required the use of a reinforcing steel patented by the politically favored supplier, even though the required material was significantly more expensive than that sold by competitors. When unable to sue the state in such cases, probably a contractor's best recourse was to hope for exposure by investigative journalists. Contractors bidding on state highways obviously should understand the rudiments of state politics. The editors of one engineering journal chided practicing engineers for writing extensively about the technical aspects of their work but almost never about the political problems they encountered. Politicians are here to stay, the editors concluded, so engineers better learn how to cope with them. This was undoubtedly good advice, but was it addressed to the right audience? Only the larger highway building firms employed formally educated professional engineers. The vast majority of smaller contractors were educated in the school of practical experience.[9]

Although highway building went into high gear in the 1920s as states and the federal government poured millions into multi-mile paving contracts, reasonable profits seemed to elude most road builders. One survey of 11,000 contractors in 1923 revealed that they averaged only 1¾% on their highway contracts after state and federal taxes. "What is the matter with contracting?" the editors of one engineering journal asked. The answer, of course, lay largely in poor estimating. In preparing bids in response to a state's invitation, a contractor is under great pressure to beat the competition by coming in with the lowest possible cost figure. To do so, he must estimate every one of his costs as closely as possible. By miscalculating or to omitting significant items of expense, he may end up losing money on the contract or even bankrupting his company if his bid is markedly below his expenditures in performing on the contract.[10]

So estimating is at the heart of successful contracting. There is no single formula or check list for sound estimating. Every situation is different. Great care must be exercised to include all the factors. And for each element, labor, materials, plant or machinery, the estimate must be based on the quantities derived from the plans and specifications submitted by the state, coupled with records of prior experience. How many cubic yards must be removed to achieve the specified grade on a segment of highway? How many shovelers will be required to fill a two-yard wagon in how much time? How far must the wagon travel to the fill where it dumps its load? Was the excavation loose soil or hardpan?

A contractor who had previously kept good records on cost accounting discovered that his costs on different jobs for shovelers loading wagons ranged between $.07 and $.25 a cubic yard. The low figure, he found on inquiry, resulted because the wagon drivers jumped down from their wagons and pitched in with the shovelers. The high figure, he discovered, was the result of "frost and firewater." In short, all estimating requires judgment based on experience. Cost accounting data derived from numerous cases, whether shovelers or steam shovels loading motor trucks, will give average costs, but the estimator must inject his judgment based on his knowledge of the particular situation.[11]

Some states, sincerely interested in helping contractors remain solvent, explored various alternative solutions. One was to employ a cost plus fixed fee, CPFF, contract mentioned above. The statutes in some states mandated the use of fixed-price contracts. When precluded from using CPFF contracts, these states sometimes sought to ease the risks to contractors by including a contingency fund to cover "add-ons" or additional work beyond that specified in the original contract.

The worst form of contract is the cost plus percentage of cost, CPPC, form. This was used and abused during World War I when there were more jobs than experienced contractors willing to bid, and the state needed to induce firms reluctant to bid during a period of escalating inflation. With the CPPC form, a contractor had no incentive to strive for efficiency. The greater his costs, the greater his profit. The only justification for using the CPPC form was the state's dire need to attract inexperienced firms to undertake jobs that established firms were too busy to bid on. In effect, the state was paying a premium to educate an inexperienced contractor. As one perceptive observer of the contracting scene put it, as soon as it becomes known that the contract is cost plus, "even the mules on the job learn to loaf."[12]

Sometimes state engineers preparing specifications inadvertently made their demands too rigid. Even when there was no intention of political favoritism, an engineer might use the specification of a certain product simply because it was at hand. A supplier wanting to bid on the item would find that his product of comparable quality but differing in some slight detail, would be technically disqualified from bidding. One way around this was to submit two bids. In one he would show that, given time, he could modify his product to comply with the specification in the state's request for bids, but indicate that would increase the price. In the other, he would submit his product, as is, at a substantially lower price, possibly lower than the bids of other firms. In short, just as a state highway commission had to educate and help cultivate inexperienced contractors, so too contractors had to educate state engineers on the larger implications of writing specifications.[13]

As more contractors lost money or went bankrupt, especially during the inflationary period of World War I, there appeared frequent complaints that bidders simply did not understand estimating. The editors of the journal *Engineering and Contracting* charged, with some asperity, that contractors simply failed to read Halbert Powers Gillette's *Economics of Road Construction*, which, first published in 1901, was filled with good advice on the art of estimating. Somebody must have been reading the book, for it went through several editions, but its readers were probably more often supervising state and county engineers than self-educated contractors. Gillette published several other titles, all of them filled with suggestions on sound estimating practices.[14]

The comment that contractors too often failed to read Gillette's useful studies was undoubtedly true. A survey conducted by the federal Office of Public Roads in the 1920s revealed that contractors seldom compiled adequate cost records on their own operations. And without carefully assembled and detailed records, estimating becomes guesstimating. Cost accounting is not the same thing as bookkeeping, which is concerned with debit and credit, profit and loss. Cost accounting is concerned with the number of units of labor or materials used in a given time. Cost accounting for the highway contractor is far more difficult than for the factory manager. Highways are built in rural areas under variables in weather and terrain. The highway contractor's plant, his machinery, is continually subjected to the roughest kind of travel. His workmen, those capable of the heaviest kind of labor, often work over long distances far from close supervision. Under such conditions, it is obviously exceedingly difficult to accumulate accurate and detailed records of itemized costs.

While it is undoubtedly difficult to record costs under field conditions, it is essential if a contractor is to prepare sound estimates when bidding. There are many advantages to cost accounting besides the aid it renders to estimating. Cost figures, if carefully recorded, help to identify inefficient workmen, padded payrolls, time lost by breakdowns of machines, the lack of available spares, and the excessive or wasteful use of materials. Diligent cost keeping helps a contractor economize on labor and materials.[15]

A contractor must decide what form of measurement is most effective. When buying gravel from a supplier at a sand and gravel bank, a common measure is the truck or wagon load. But what constitutes a "load"? The cubage of a load of washed gravel at the purchase point may be somewhat less at the distant construction site as the jolting journey shuckles down and compresses the cubage. Weighing is a more exact measure, but it is often not convenient to make platform scales available in the field.[16]

There are so many factors to take into consideration that it is easy, even for an experienced contractor, to omit some from his calculations. Back in the days before automobile ownership was common, workmen often lived on the job in bunkhouses or shanties provided by the contractor, who sometimes also had to provide meals and a commissary for his laborers. These items, while not construction costs as such, were nonetheless significant factors in estimating on a highway contract. Transporting the workers to and from the remote construction site was an easily overlooked cost. Probably the most common source of error in estimating costs was in excavating, where there were so many variables. Another source of difficulty arose from a failure to plan for the most efficient use of machines, proper sequencing of the movement of heavy equipment to have each item where it is needed when it is needed and not sooner, to avoid unavoidable unproductive idleness. Every day a steam shovel stands idle, its overhead charges mount inexorably.[17]

A common problem for all contractors was in deciding how to handle depreciation. They had the usual options not unique to roadbuilding equipment. They could use the straight-line method, charging off the replacement cost each year with an equal increment down to the point where the item was discarded. Or, alternatively, they could front-end load the depreciation, writing off ever-decreasing sums over the life of the equipment, an approach that assumed that the machine was increasingly less efficient as it aged. In either case, the determination hinged on the anticipated life of any given item. What was the probable useful life of a drop bottom dump wagon? Or a stone crusher? An inexperienced contractor could be woefully wrong if he heeded the overly optimistic predictions of the manufacturer's representative who sold him the item.

To inject greater realism into the computation of depreciation, an organization known as Associated General Contractors, AGC, surveyed large numbers of contractors to compile tables showing the average life of each of the typical items of plant used by road builders, from pneumatic jack hammers to steamshovels. In addition, they assembled data showing the annual percentages of cost devoted to shop repairs, field repairs, and number of months in a year that the equipment could be used. The reports went further, expounding how successful contractors actually interpreted the concept of depreciation. Their findings indicated that sound practice was to consider the life of any item of plant, whether a concrete mixer or a bunkhouse, to end when it had been depreciated to 25% of its original cost, including delivery charges. For the inexperienced contractor, this sort of guidance could spell the difference between profit or loss. Unfortunately many, probably most, of the contractors engaged in road building were not reading the professional journals, nor were many of the smaller firms members of the AGC. However, the guidance on how to handle depreciation provided by the AGC was typical of the benefits that Secretary of Commerce Herbert Hoover sought to foster by encouraging the formation of such business combinations and trade associations.[18]

While exchanges of information such as that provided by the AGC helped road builders enterprising enough to secure it, the anti-monopoly statutes ran distinctly contrary to the kind of cooperation Secretary of Commerce Hoover encouraged. Bidding on state highway contracts was still highly competitive. Preparing a proper bid was a demanding task, and a road builder who came within a few hundred dollars over the winning bid had nothing to show for his effort except some gain in experience in compiling a bid. Because competition was often intense, a bidder was under great pressure to minimize every item of expense. However, experience taught that it was folly not to include a generous allowance for the inevitable contingencies. But since the scale of anticipated contingencies could never be ascertained in advance, it was tempting for a bidder to understate this item in his bid in the hopes of winning the contract. In at least one state, the highway commission proposed an effective solution: have all the bidders agree to a 15% figure for contingencies, thus removing the contingency factor from competition. Enlightened state highway commissions recognized that it was in their best interest to help contractors remain solvent in order to insure a healthy competition when they issued invitations to bid.[19]

Who were the contractors who confronted the formidable challenge of preparing bids on highway contracts? Some had evolved in the 19th century, digging canals and building railway lines. Far more evolved from small-time operators who learned the trade building town and city streets. Many, though by no means all, of the early road builders were Irish immigrants who had nothing but their labor and a willingness to put in long hours, often ten or twelve in a day. The ablest of these immigrants became contractors. An amusing anecdote attributed to the brother of William Otis, who designed the first successful steam shovel, offers some insight on the evolving Irish labor force. When an Irish pick and shovel man found himself ousted from his job by the newly developed steam shovel, he shouted at the machine, "Ye can dig, but be jabbers, ye can't vote!"[20]

Later waves of immigrants, especially the Italians settling in the Northeast, entered the road building business in considerable numbers. Coming from a region of scarce lumber and extensive reliance upon masonry construction, many of them were familiar with stonework and concrete, skills which readily led them into the construction industry. Contractors' records were usually sketchy at best.[21]

In the preface to this volume, the author explained the circumstances of the family connection which led him to write this book. That family connection made available a modest collection of records which provide some insights on how a relatively small local contractor with a limited inventory of machinery grew into one of the leading highway builders of the region. The story is most readily told as a personal narrative.

The author's father was a student at the Hotchkiss School in Sharon, Connecticut, preparing for Yale, when he contracted tuberculosis. After rusticating in the Adirondacks to cure, he cast about for employment that would offer him healthy outdoor work. A chance encounter in his home town, Torrington, Connecticut, with a local street contractor induced him to form a partnership with Mr. Joseph Mascetti, a professional stonecutter from northern Italy. After some years cutting granite curbstones, in 1901 Mr. Mascetti established a road-grading firm. With horse and wagon, along with a slip, he soon acquired contracts to grade streets and set curbs in suburban developments.[22]

By the time Father entered into the partnership agreement in 1910, Mr. Mascetti had already built up a substantial business grading roads, not only in his hometown but also in several surrounding towns. The partnership agreement signed before a justice of the peace with its inventory of the firm's equipment gives a fair picture of the character and scope of the business: there were thirteen horses, eight dump carts, one wheel boat (a wheeled stoneboat for excessively heavy loads), three lumber wagons, three tram cars and an unspecified number of feet of narrow gage track on which to push the cars, two steam drills, two steam pumps, one hand pump, one sprinkling cart, one road grader, two buggies, one surry, one business wagon, one stone crusher and storage bin, one steam boiler and engine, two hoisting engines for derricks used in quarrying, along with one heavy motor truck and one steamroller. Also included were all hammers, drills, implements, and unitemized supplies used in quarrying and road building. Along with these items of equipment were three shanties with wheels and one without, structures which served as bunk houses and offices.[23]

For a half interest in this equipment and all the future profits and losses of the partnership, father put up $5,000 from an inheritance he had received.

The partnership came at a most opportune time; the state in 1895 had created the Connecticut Highway Department, and under the exceptionally able leadership of Commissioner James H. MacDonald, was developing sound procedures for dealing with contractors. By 1910 state legislatures were voting ever larger appropriations for highway construction. Most of the early Mascetti and Holley contracts were for waterbound macadam highways. For labor, Mr. Mascetti drew upon the Italian community, many of them relatives. Newly arrived immigrants found the arrangement congenial. Until they learned English, they often lived with relatives. Mr. Mascetti encouraged his employees to start businesses of their own. He helped his master mechanic, Andrew Oneglia and his friend, Romeo Gervasini, to buy trucks which they could rent out to build capital. That was the foundation of what years later became the giant construction company, O & G, a Fortune 500 firm.

Mascetti and Holley prospered by emphasizing quality work and completing contracts on time. They pursued a policy of plowing most of their profits back into the company, buying more and better machinery so as to be able to take on larger contracts. Each success induced their bankers to extend larger loans to meet up-front costs and weekly payrolls long before the state finally paid them for a finished stretch of highway. On only one contract did the firm lose money seriously. This was a New York State contract for an 18-mile concrete highway from Carthage just south of Fort Drum to Crogan to Lowville (the "Cheese Capital" of the state). Mr. Mascetti signed that $250,000 contract in June of 1914 just before war broke out in Europe. With the war, labor costs soared upwards. Where day labor usually earned $1.70 an hour, M & H paid $1.90 to attract quality workmen. But Carthage was 300 miles from their home base in Torrington, an expensive trip for workmen wishing to return home for weekends. And as wartime inflation escalated, the partners' workforce began drifting off to other jobs nearer home, although their hourly wage had been raised to $4.50. As these experienced men gradually departed, the partners had to hire whatever they could find, in Father's words, "hillbillies, foresters and villagers," who knew nothing about road building, so labor costs grew beyond all expectation.

With inflation threatening to bankrupt construction companies, many contractors sought relief by petitioning the state to rewrite their agreement to take account of the escalating labor charges. But Father and Mr. Mascetti reasoned that a contract was binding and they would fulfill it, even if it meant acquiring what was for them a fearful load of debt. They valued their reputation for square dealing. As a consequence, they staggered off that contract $50,000 in debt, an appalling burden in relation to their total capital. As it turned out, however, their decision to abide by the contract was a sound one. The Connecticut State Highway Commissioner was so impressed with the firm's integrity it granted them several subsequent contracts on highly favorable terms.[24]

Father greatly enjoyed the contracting business and its challenges. Firms that achieve efficiency soonest will profit the most, he said. "The old businessman carried the figures in his hat, but the new way is scientific management." Years later, after his death when the author was closing out his father's estate, he found in his study several books on scientific management dating from the 1920s. In 1920 the partners called in a firm of professional consultants and accountants in an effort to get better control over their expenses.

The consultants found the partners already had a sound system of accounting but suggested various ways to allocate overhead to the several departments. The objective was to establish rates for each department and each item of road machinery, which could then be used in making future estimates. The departments included Garage, for by this time the firm had a number of autos and trucks, and Repair Shop, for breakdowns were common; metallurgy was less developed then and broken truck axels were far more frequent. Even heavy machines often still used bronze bearings rather than roller bearings, so the repair shop was always busy. Another department was called Barn, for the partners still employed horses and wagons. The Barn Account for one year showed the following figures which give some idea of the kinds of costs involved: labor - $291; hay - $701; grain - $421; medical - $19; harness repair - $125; miscellaneous - $92.

Although the partners had a fairly sophisticated system of cost accounting, the consultants came up with useful refinements, such as suggesting the establishment of a reserve account "to cover unexpected depreciation." Another suggestion was to consider the fixed charges, taxes and interest, on the land which underlay the firm's buildings and equipment storage yard as burden or rent to be set against each item of equipment, steam shovels, stone crushers, concrete mixers, etc. stored there. Such proposals made the process of estimating on future contracts more comprehensive and closer to reality.[25]

The consultant's report also included an inventory of the partners' property, which affords an interesting contrast with the inventory of 1910, showing how the firm had grown in 10 years. More significantly, the itemized inventory gives a clear picture of the kinds of equipment highway builders of the time required: two steam shovels, an Erie and a Thew; an industrial narrow gage railway consisting of one 30 hp steam engine and one 20 hp engine, plus dump cars and flat cars and 25 miles of track and switches; three stone crushers and a storage bin with elevator; three concrete mixers, a Koehring paver, a Lakewood paver, and a Rex; two Buffalo steam rollers with scarifiers; three air compressors, one Ingersoll and two Westinghouse; five pumps; six steam boilers and engines; two hoisting engines; two derricks for quarry use and something called a boom swinger for traversing a derrick boom; five pneumatic jackhammers; five sprinkling carts primarily used for waterbound macadam; one tar spreader and one gravel spreader; six auto trucks, including three Packard six-ton trucks, one Packard three-ton, one Reo ¾-ton and a White ¾-ton. Included under "other equipment" were a Hupmobile auto, and an unspecified number of teams and wagons. In addition, there were various small tools, spares inventory, buildings and land, for a total value of $113,787, a miniscule sum when viewed from today's perspective, but apparently what it took to do the average annual $200,000 volume of business in which the partners engaged.[26]

Some miscellaneous accounting figures from 1923 offer further insights on the M & H partnership operation. For one successful contract on five miles of concrete highway from Torrington to Litchfield the State Highway Department agreed to a contract for $161,942. The partnership accounts show the following costs:

Labor	$52,106
Trucks	37,262
Hired teams	564
Equipment	4,171
Supplies	24,321
	118,731
Overhead	11,497
Total expense	$130,228

This makes a profit of $31,713 or 19.5%. The cost figures clearly reveal the upward trend in costs resulting from wartime inflation. The large figure for trucks includes truck rentals for vehicles to supplement those owned by the partners. And the small sum for hired teams indicates the partners were phasing down the "barn" account. Supplies involved for the most part purchase of cement and reinforcing steel.

The comfortable margin of profit on the Litchfield road was offset by a serious loss on a state contract for a concrete highway in the town of Kent, Connecticut, for $157,562. This job was further from the Torrington base of operations and ran into local difficulties. The presence of ledge rock that had to be blasted involved keeping a crew of workmen on site during the winter preceding the 1923 construction season. This crew was largely unsupervised and labor costs escalated beyond bid expectations. Further, the local civil authorities couldn't reach a decision on whether or not to authorize the removal of a memorial monument in the course laid out by the state, so M & H had to leave a gap until the issue was decided. This required hauling all their heavy equipment back to the site long after the rest of the job was completed. This ran up costs well beyond estimates. The resulting total costs came to $182,271, a loss of $21,226 or 13.18% on the contract. The two basic causes of this loss illustrate the typical unanticipated contingencies that beset highway builders.[27]

During the 1923 season, M & H performed on five major Connecticut highway contracts and several smaller municipal and private contracts. A tabulation of profits broken down by operating departments shows:

Construction contracts	$37,820
Jobbing	6,332
Renting out road equipment	20,820
Renting out company trucks	5,402
Commissary	1,682
Discounts	1,543
	$73,641

Against this gain there was a net loss on contracts of $4,876 which the partners had to share equally, deducting it from what they would otherwise have had in their drawing account of $13,882, leaving a net profit of $9,006 for 1923—a modest return for a partnership with a net worth in the year of $110,564 in a high-risk business.[28]

The gains of the operating departments tabulated above warrant comment. The figure for "jobbing" represents all local jobs such as installing a stretch of sidewalk or using a steamshovel to excavate the cellar hole for an office building. While small, these jobs served to keep both labor and equipment occupied between highway contracts, helping to offset the overhead which goes on whether or not the firm has active highway contracts. Also noteworthy are the substantial amounts received by renting out equipment. If a concrete mixer is standing idle between jobs, it is better to rent it to a rival contractor rather than let it sit idle. There were three or four highway contractors in the city of Torrington during many of the years M & H were operating, so there were opportunities for mutual advantage in reciprocal renting of heavy equipment.[29]

The firm of Mascetti and Holley took pride in leading the way by introducing the latest technology. They recognized that while steam engines had impressive power, the problems of providing coal and water at remote job sites was always bothersome. So in the winter of 1922–23, the firm acquired the first gasoline-powered shovel in the state of Connecticut. It came disassembled and had to be put together by Andrew Oneglia, the partner's master mechanic aided by 22-year-old Osvaldo Mascetti, who learned how to control the shovel by helping assemble it, then later practicing with it in the yard during the winter so as to be ready to use it on the Torrington to Litchfield contract when the construction season opened in the spring.[30]

While the gasoline-powered shovel proved to be a great success, not every effort of the partners in the transition to gasoline power turned out so well. Enthusiasm for the new shovel suggested that they could build a smaller version in their own shop. This they called a truck shovel, which appears to have been some sort of backhoe. The company books are filled with entries noting every item of cost that went into this project; every gear wheel, girder, or pulley is mentioned, but no set of drawings survives. Unfortunately, the truck shovel was not a success. The 1923 accounting shows the project was charged off as a $3,500 loss. The lesson was obvious: highway contractors should stick to what they know best, road building, and leave constructing road machinery to the manufacturers.[31]

The partnership of Mascetti and Holley grew from its small beginnings in 1910 to become one of the leading road builders in western Connecticut and New York state east of the Hudson. In a testimonial to the firm's excellence and integrity, Connecticut State Highway Commissioner Charles J. Bennett declared the state would willingly award contracts up to half a million dollars to the firm which had routinely demonstrated its ability to finish contracts on time and with the highest quality workmanship. Such praise would seem to indicate that the firm had a bright future. But it was not to be. The author's father suffered from a serious accident, which put him in a hospital for a year, and subsequent years of convalescence forced him to withdraw from the partnership. And a few months later, at age 50, Mr. Mascetti died unexpectedly after a three-month illness. Neither partner had children old enough at the time to continue the business. The machines and other resources of the firm were sold, some of it contributing to the future major contractors, O & G.[32]

One cannot say that the firm of Mascetti and Holley was typical of road builders all across the United States. However, the experience of this partnership made available by the chance preservation of a few of their records does serve to illustrate some of the problems confronting those who engaged in the high-risk business of highway construction. Even the limited glimpses afforded by the partners' experiences offer insights on the difficulties of technological transitions from horses and wagons to steam power and to gasoline engines, as well as the financial problems and difficulties arising over estimating probable costs. One can only wish that the remaining record had provided fuller insights on the human problems of wagon drivers becoming truck drivers. How readily did the pick and shovel men adapt to the advancing technology?[33]

CHAPTER 7

THE LONG ROAD FROM ASPHALT STREETS TO ASPHALT HIGHWAYS

Before asphalt paving for interurban highways became commonplace in the United states, the use of asphalt passed through a painfully slow evolution as a medium for surfacing city streets. The denser population in urban areas meant there was not only a greater desire for the convenience and comfort of paved streets but also a sufficient tax base to justify the expense. There were several alternative forms of paving from which town and city dwellers could choose. Cobblestones, one of the earliest paving materials employed, suffered from several drawbacks. They were bumpy and noisy under the screech of steel-tired wagons, and far more importantly, they gave poor purchase to horses' hooves. Injuries to falling horses were a common occurrence on cobblestoned streets. Granite paving blocks offered a smoother surface, which gave better traction, but they too were noisy and gave poor footing to horses. What is more, they were more expensive to construct than cobbled streets. Some communities experimented with wood block paving. Wood was quieter than stone paving and offered fewer hazards to horses, but it tended to disintegrate in a very few years in the absence of suitable chemical preservative.[1]

In areas of the country where stone was scarce but clay plentiful, brick would seem to hold considerable promise as a paving material. Because brick had long been used as a building material, by the middle of the 19th century there were not only large numbers of brickyards, but also a wide range of steam-powered machinery had been developed to mix, press, and cut bricks efficiently so as to turn them out relatively cheaply. Unfortunately, the bricks long used for building were relatively soft, and when used for paving failed to stand up under the stress of traffic. Not until the industry developed a hard, vitrified brick impervious to water did brick become widely used for paving, and even then its smooth surface gave less than ideal footing for horses.[2]

When 19th-century communities began using coal gas for heating and il-luminating purposes, the by-product coal tar provided a potential topping for urban streets. It was readily available, cheap, and was useful in dust abatement. Since many municipal streets were either graded dirt or water-bound crushed stone macadam, a spraying of coal tar, while not exactly paving, made such streets more impervious to water as well as less dusty. But narrow-tired wagon and carriage wheels soon cut through the tarred surface.[3]

Given the drawbacks of these several alternative paving materials, munic-ipalities cast about for a more satisfactory form of paving. And just after the Civil War, they began to experiment with asphalt, which had been highly de-veloped in France and then in England as a paving material. Asphalt is com-posed of a hydrocarbon found in nature, usually in combination with some mineral substance such as limestone or clay. There were numerous deposits of asphalt scattered all over Europe, in Italy, Germany, France, and Switzer-land. The asphalt most commonly used to pave the streets of Paris came from Val de Travers in Neûchatel canton in Switzerland, a rock asphalt consisting of bitumen, the Roman term for the hydrocarbon, and limestone.[4]

When word of the success achieved with asphalt paving in Paris reached New York, the municipal authorities decided to put an asphalt topping on the noisy granite block paving of Fifth Avenue. Unfortunately, the experiment was not a success. Within a few weeks the granite was showing through the topping, and workmen were busy patching. The following year, Newark, New Jersey, laid down some asphalt streets with great success. The contrasting performance in the two cities offers two important insights. To begin with, the contractor who applied the asphalt in New York had no experience with this novel material. In Newark, the work was supervised by a Belgian-educated chemist, E.S. de Smedt, who had a good deal of experience abroad in working with asphalt. Further, a perceptive engineer pointed out that the two cities had used asphalt from different sources. It was to take several years before those who tried to pave with asphalt came to appreciate that this novel material was not homog-enous. Deposits in different locations contained varying percentages of bitu-men as well as differing mineral constituents, which sometimes substantially altered the behavior of the mixture. After the New York fiasco, the editors of *The New York Times* rather shrewdly observed that the municipal authorities in Paris had prescribed rather demanding specifications which controlled the *methods* as well as the *materials* the French paving contractors were to employ. The history of asphalt paving in the United is the story of the gradual mastery of *methods* and *materials* by those working with asphalt.[5]

In Washington, D.C., President Grant, encouraged by the Newark experiment and disgusted by the rapid deterioration of the woodblock paving which had been laid in the capital at considerable expense, set in motion a competition. This eventually narrowed down to two bidders, one offering French rock asphalt from Val de Travers and the other sponsored by the chemist, de Smedt, using asphalt from the Caribbean island, Trinidad, which proved to be the better of the two.

An enterprising Howard University professor, Amzi L. Barber, who was impressed with the potential of asphalt as a paving material, soon managed to secure control of the Trinidad source. This consisted of a 115-acre asphalt lake formed in the collapsed throat of an ancient volcano. Workmen armed with mattocks could walk on the surface and hack out chunks of asphalt, but the lake was viscous enough to fill in the excavations in a few hours. Originally the material was moved in lighters to schooners standing offshore, but Barber promptly had a railroad built to the coast, where a steel pier was constructed to dump loads directly into freighter holds. These steps made it possible to lower the cost of the asphalt delivered to New York, giving Barber an edge over imports from France. Moreover, Trinidad asphalt, largely composed of bitumen and clay, proved less slippery than the French product, consisting of bitumen and limestone. To exploit the Trinidad asphalt, Barber organized the Barber Asphalt Paving Company, which promptly earned a reputation for quality work in many cities across the United States. In time he built up a nationwide organization.[6]

The notable success of the Barber company led potential competitors to undertake an aggressive search for asphalt deposits in the United States in hopes of lowering the cost below the imported Trinidad. California's pitch beds had long been known. There, hydrocarbons ranging from liquid petroleum to a soft, putty-like bitumen were widely distributed, but the cost of shipping barrels of the latter to eastern and Midwestern cities where most of the paving was taking place inhibited the sale of California's asphalt. A limestone rock, rich in bitumen at 23%, found in Kentucky, and an even more extensive deposit discovered in the Indian reservations of Utah stimulated several efforts at competing with the Barber firm. The Pennsylvania oil fields produced a type of petroleum in which the residue after the lighter oils were distilled off was parafin, rather than asphalt, and thus useless for paving.[7]

While the several efforts to develop asphalt sources in the United States were going on, other nearby foreign sources turned up in Cuba, Mexico, and Venezuela. Of these, one of the more promising was the Bermudez deposit in Venezuela. Imports from this rich source threatened to undercut Barber's virtual monopoly, so the well-capitalized Barber interests moved to gain control of the Bermudez deposits where competitors threatened his Trinidad monopoly. The economic advantage of Barber's assured supply of quality asphalt is evident in the following figures. In 1893, Barber was delivering crude Trinidad to New York at $13 the ton as opposed to Cuba's $28 the ton and Utah's $60.[8]

While a favorable price on crude asphalt did indeed give the Barber Asphalt Paving Company a decided advantage, it is only fair to add that the firm turned out a high quality paving. Trinidad clay-based asphalt proved to be both durable and stable under heavy traffic. As a result, many cities offered testimonials as to the firm's workmanship. Competent supervision and years of experience also contributed to the firm's ability to lay successful pavings. These factors, taken all together, allowed Barber to charge high prices, ranging up to $5 a square yard for paving, although $3 a yard was more typical. In some communities where competition threatened, the company would shave the price to $2.50 or even lower, which tended to prevent potential competitors from investing in an asphalt plant in a given city.[9]

As more cities and towns sought asphalt paving, many local contractors were tempted to enter the business. These men not only lacked experience in dealing with asphalt but often failed to realize that asphalts from different sources behaved quite differently. As a consequence, failures were frequent. Pavements laid by these contractors all too often suffered from the common faults of this novel substance: it would remain sticky in summer, resulting in pedestrians tracking black footprints into buildings, and turning brittle and flaky in winter.[10]

Clearly there was a crying need for scientifically informed understanding of the chemistry and physical properties of bitumen in its various guises in asphalts of differing composition. Larger cities with an ample tax base began to establish municipal laboratories to deal with the problem. Brooklyn, N.Y., was among the first to do so. A competent technician would sally out from the lab armed with testing equipment to check on the efforts of contractors. He would use a thermometer to measure the temperature of the mix being spread, as laboratory studies and experience had shown that overheating was a major cause of paving that turned sticky in summer and brittle in winter. On-site tests by the lab technician also detected the contractor who skimped on quality by using only 4% bitumen when a contract specified 8%. But even the best equipped laboratory and highly competent technicians could not guarantee fully satisfactory pavements. Too many other factors were involved. These included the proportioning of the mix and how the contractor's laborers actually laid it. Each of these impacted on the resulting pavement.[11]

Beginning in 1901, the Department of Agriculture provided a laboratory for rural counties lacking a sufficient tax base to sustain such research on their own account. The Office of Road Inquiry, described in an earlier chapter, established a lab that offered free testing of road construction materials, including asphalts. In 1905, Congress substantially increased the organization's funding and changed its name to the Office of Public Roads.[12]

Assisted by the OPR's free testing, state and county specifications became more demanding and as contractors acquired more experience, they laid better pavements. This made for greater competition for the nationwide Barber paving company. But the greatest stimulation to such competition came from a technological development. Hitherto, when a contractor wished to construct asphalt pavements in a given community, he had to erect a local plant capable of delivering asphalt hot and viscous to the streets being paved. This involved a considerable outlay of capital. However, in 1896, several firms began to produce portable plants mounted on a couple of railroad flat cars. Among these, the best known was that of the Hetherington and Berner Company of Minneapolis, Minnesota. Soon, orders were pouring in from contractors eyeing the lucrative small-town market throughout the United States. Now any town on a railroad could have access to asphalt paving.

When Amzi Barber saw his near monopoly of the paving business threatened by the burgeoning competition made possible by the appearance of portable rail-car mounted mixing plants, he resolved to form a trust. To secure capital, he sold $30 million worth of bonds with 5% coupons and used the money to buy up all the small competitors he could persuade to join the trust. In doing this he made a serious tactical blunder; he paid far too much for the small firms he took in, and the new corporation soon went into receivership when it proved unable to pay the annual bond interest. In the resulting reorganization Barber was squeezed out of the successor firm, the General Asphalt Company, but his operating unit, the original Barber Asphalt Paving Company, continued to function.[13]

Although the reorganized trust continued in operation, it engaged less in paving contracts and increasingly in supplying asphalt to the many local contractors who entered the paving business in mounting numbers, thanks to the availability of railroad mixing plants. A number of factors contributed to their frequent successes in laying pavements. One such was the appearance of a helpful textbook, *The Modern Asphalt Pavement* in 1905. As one commentator remarked, there was no excuse for failure when laying asphalt if one heeded Clifford Richardson's volume. Apparently contractors agreed with this assessment, for the book appeared in several editions over the next decade and sold thousands of copies.[14]

Another factor assisting inexperienced contractors in achieving sound asphalt pavings was the increasing number of trained engineers recruited by state highway commissions and city street departments. As more university engineering schools offered courses in road construction, engineers capable of closely supervising contractors were beginning to appear in ever larger numbers. Also important in producing successful pavings was the appearance of more carefully devised standardized specifications. In this effort the Office of Public Roads played a significant role by urging the American Society for Testing Materials to establish a committee to formulate standards for evaluating road materials.[15]

One problem that continued to vex contractors was the difficulty in securing the right quality of sand. Even when a contractor scrupulously followed the prescribed specifications and was careful not to overheat the mixture of sand and bitumen, the resulting pavement sometimes showed a distressing tendency to creep or slip, indicating that the mixture was unstable. In addressing this problem, a member of The Warren Brothers Company of Boston, a major paving contractor, performed an interesting experiment. Starting with a box containing a solid cube of stone, he broke the stone into two-inch particles and found he could only get half of the original stone cube back into the box. Next, he broke the residue into progressively smaller fragments, carefully weighing each lot being infiltrated into the ever smaller interstices. Eventually, he found he could return 90% of the original stone cube to the box.[16]

Warren's experiment demonstrated that slight differences in the size of the grains of sand made a great difference in the extent of surface to be covered by bitumen. A very fine 200-mesh screen produced grains with 30 times the surface area of grains passing a 20-mesh screen. The fewer the voids, the more compact the mixture. Warren patented the precise proportion of each particle size and called the result a "bitulithic" macadam, a highly stable paving material. The soundness of the bitulithic concept of carefully sized sand and aggregate led the Warren Brothers Company to nationwide success, with branch offices in major cities across the United States.[17]

For many years, California's large beds of liquid petroleum were regarded as unfit for asphalt production. But as more laboratories were established, the chemists' enhanced understanding of hydrocarbons led them to realize that California petroleum could be successfully manipulated to produce an excellent asphalt for paving. At the same time, a development in the technology for transporting asphalt also played a critical role in creating a market for the California product; the railroads designed tank cars for shipping asphalt. There were many problems to be solved. Some contractors continued to favor shipments in barrels because of the difficulties encountered with the early tank car designs. In cold weather, the asphalt hardened in the tank. This caused delays and added to demurrage charges. The rail firms became irate when some contractors built fires under the tank cars to soften the contents. The response to this was to design cars with internal steam lines, which could be supplied by a contractors' steamroller. Many contractors bought junked tank cars to park on a siding to store asphalt until needed, thus saving on demurrage by returning the railroad's car as soon as unloaded. Improvements such as these lowered the cost of California asphalt in the East and Midwest, where the greatest demand existed.[18]

Although the Hetherington and Berner portable asphalt plant mounted on two railroad flat cars stimulated a marked increase in municipal paving projects, the pace was pushed still further with the appearance of more compact and less expensive plants mounted on one flat car. And, in time, this was followed by one mounted on a steel-wheeled vehicle drawn by a traction engine, and eventually a mixing plant mounted on a motor truck became available. These latter developments made it possible for small towns not on a rail line to consider asphalt paving. So the scope of the industry widened still further.[19]

In many of these towns where asphalt paving became available, the streets and adjacent highways were virtually all waterbound macadam or merely dirt, graded and crowned perhaps but no more. When contractors undertook to pave such roads with asphalt, they first had to provide a stable foundation. For waterbound macadam, they could scarify the surface with a steam roller and then spray the surface with molten bitumen. This was called the penetration method. The bitumen would seep down into the existing crushed stone foundation. The drawback of this method lay in the superficial penetration of the bitumen and its failure to coat all the particles of stone completely, giving a poor bond and allowing moisture to enter the foundation course and freeze there in winter. Poor penetration was probably inevitable when the penetration method was first tried. The bitumen arrived in wooden barrels, was heated in kettles, and then applied by men with hand pots, sprinkling cans, which they waved back and forth over the surface of the rolled aggregate.

Some improvement appeared when contractors took to using the horse-drawn water sprinkling carts, such as had long been used to puddle waterbound macadam. Sprinkling carts gave a more even coverage but did little to insure a thorough penetration. To offset the defects in these early methods of distributing bitumen, enterprising manufacturers came up with a major improvement, a pressurized steel tank mounted on a wagon equipped with a small steam boiler. This produced a substantial increase in the depth of penetration, but still left the coating uneven below the uppermost layers of aggregate. While better than handpot distribution, the pressure method was still defective in offering control over neither the temperature of the materials sprayed nor the rate of travel of the horse pulling the wagon. This made it difficult for a superintending engineer to be sure that each square yard received the desired one or two gallons of bitumen.[20]

Gradually, it became clear that the solution was to mix the bitumen and crushed stone *before* it was laid down. At first this was done by hand. Men with shovels would turn the dumped stone and bitumen over and over on a wooden platform until they could see that all the stone was thoroughly coated before it was raked to spread it evenly before being rolled. Hand mixing in time gave way to mixing in a powered drum not unlike a conventional concrete mixer. Bituminous macadam by the mixing method, as the resulting road foundation came to be called, was more expensive than the penetration method, but it produced a far better road.[21]

By 1910 or 1912 the art of paving urban streets with asphalt was well developed. But by this time the agitation to "get the farmers out of the mud" had begun to bear fruit. The Good Roads movement and the many demonstrations of The Good Roads Trains staged by the Office of Public Roads had begun to persuade at least some states to begin improving highways as well as urban streets, although the problem of financing such efforts continued to be debated.[22]

A number of Eastern states with higher per capita income levels were beginning to provide waterbound macadam highways throughout much of their road network. Massachusetts, for example, in 1908 could boast of having macadamized 95% of her highways and was spending about $100 a mile on annual maintenance. This was fine for rural horse-drawn traffic, but, as the editors of *Scientific American* observed, autos traveling at "excessive speeds" would probably require the application of tar or asphalt toppings to the macadam highways. In 1900 there were only 8,000 automobiles in the entire United States, but ten years later there were 458,000 and the tally was mounting rapidly. This posed a serious problem for highway commissioners. As Logan W. Page of the Office of Public Roads observed, "We can build a road that will perfectly suit horse traffic, or we can build one that will perfectly suit motor traffic, but no type of construction has been devised for satisfactorily meeting both classes of traffic."[23]

Although Page fully expected that the automobile would one day replace the horse he had good reason to believe that day was in the rather distant future. While auto registrations were mounting, the horse population of the

United States was rising even more rapidly. Between 1900 and 1910, the horse population rose by 20% from 13 million to 23 million. So those who had to make decisions on highway construction had to give consideration to horse-drawn traffic. Asphalt paving seemed to offer something of a comprise between waterbound macadam, which provided the ideal purchase for horses' hooves, and the harder forms of road surfaces. But consideration of asphalt turned the issue back to the question of cost.[24]

A Maryland highway engineer offered a possible solution to the problem of financing paved highways. He reported that Maryland was spending as much as $5,300 per mile for improved highways. But against this seemingly high cost, the state over the past 10 years had been spending at least $500 per mile to maintain such highways. Given such expense, he argued that it would be sound policy to invest in permanent paving, which would last 20 years with minimum annual maintenance. Others echoed this line of reasoning. The editors of *Engineering Record* deplored that much of the money currently being spent on roads was not being wisely spent for lack of skilled engineers. In Iowa, which was still building nothing but gravel roads in 1907, the Highway Commissioners saw the day was coming when the state would pave its highways as "the Eastern states are doing."[25]

One of the ways the Eastern states were helping to pay for their highway paving projects was with sums raised by fees for auto licenses. Connecticut by 1908 was already taking in $57,500 by this means, and the rapidly rising number of automobiles held promise of much higher subsidies from this source. At the Good Roads convention in 1908 the subject of license fees for highway construction was a topic of lively debate.[26]

As the need to meet the demands of auto traffic became more acute, increasing attention was devoted to deciding just what asphaltic treatment would suffice. Logan W. Page of the Office of Public Roads wrote an article in *Scientific American* in which he described the difficulties being encountered. Even when multiple layers of stone coated with bitumen were laid down and rolled, the road surface continued to crumble under traffic. He frankly admitted that the causes underlying such failures were not fully evident. Experiments in several states produced a wide range of answers. A New York highway engineer argued that light oil on a top dressing of screenings laid on a sound waterbound macadam base was "nearly ideal" in dry weather but turned to oily mud in wet weather and was "ruinous to clothing." A pavement of heavier bituminous macadam he rated as excellent, but only if closely supervised during construction.[27]

The quality of supervision was a critical factor in determining success or failure. As one engineer complained, there were no approved specifications for applying asphalt to highways. They were "according to the whim of the engineer in charge" and often resulted in failures. One jurisdiction in Pennsylvania indicted its highway commissioner for the failure of a highway pavement. The editors of *Engineering News* doubted the efficiency of this approach, since it would tend to discourage able men from seeking positions as commissioners. In many states, highway commissioners were objects of political patronage. In Missouri, the professional engineers protested when the governor appointed a lawyer with no known technical competence. To avoid the favoritism of appointees, some states resorted to electing commissioners as did New York. But this meant that every election which brought a different party to power introduced a new commission with loss of continuity in policy making. Whatever defects there may have been in the mode of securing commissioners, those states which had commissioners were no doubt better off than states such as Alabama, which as late as 1913 still allowed taxpayers to work off their taxes by labor on state highways. That rural constituencies which clung to the discredited system of "working out" taxes still had political clout is evident in the practice of calling highway engineers "superintendents" because the term "engineer" roused distrust among local farmers.[28]

While engineers debated the best means of applying asphalt to highways, some voices were raised against the extravagance involved in paving rural highways. Surprisingly, the editors of two leading engineering journals deplored the excessive bond issues launched for highway construction. "The burden of debt we are shouldering on the next generation ... is a mistake." This concern for the national debt found numerous supporters in engineering society discussions. One critic deplored the spending of public money on rural highways where "a good dirt or gravel road was all that economic considerations justified." Another pointed out that a study of Missouri mail carriers found only 29 days in the year when their routes were "impassable." He admitted the highways were extremely bad in midwinter, "but we could trot the horses much of the time."[29]

Despite the naysayers who professed concern over the national debt, the rising numbers of automobiles reflected a powerful lobby for paving rural highways. When a delegate to the American Road Builders Convention in 1912 suggested that waterbound macadam roads were "no longer of any use," he raised a storm of protest from his fellow delegates. Many of the Northeastern and Midwestern states had invested heavily in such highways and were loath to abandon what they had built up at great cost over many years. For example, while Ohio had 14,168 miles of gravel roads, there were 9,687 miles of waterbound macadam that could be used as a base for an asphalt topping. The lure of salvaging the sunk cost on such a significant proportion of state highways proved decidedly attractive.[30]

Massachusetts, as the state with the highest proportion of waterbound macadam highways, began a series of experiments for consolidating these roads with applications of asphalt. The cheapest solution was to employ the penetration method, spraying the surface with two coats of less than a gallon each per square yard and topping it off with a quarter-gallon finishing coat. A more expensive approach, the layer method, involved putting down a course of small crushed stone, sprinkling with bitumen, rolling, then adding another layer in similar fashion, topping it off with a layer of fine crushed stone and spraying with a gallon of bitumen per square yard of highway. Experienced engineers assured adequate performance. The issue then became one of whether to use the cheaper penetration method and stretch the available funding to pave more highways or build more durable pavings on fewer miles of highway.[31]

Unfortunately, many states lacked the accumulated expertise and technically competent engineers of Massachusetts. The variability in asphaltic oils proved to be particularly disturbing. In California, this variability was especially acute, with the asphalt content from different sources ranging from less than 2% to more than 57%. Some of these hydrocarbons ranged from virtually no asphalt to highly viscous oils which could be used for road material with virtually no refining. In New York state, as auto traffic began to ravel the surface of waterbound macadam and topping coats of macadam were added, the raveling ceased, but the bitumen soon bunched up into gobs on the surface, which made for rough riding. Poor quality asphalt accepted by ill-informed "politically appointed inspectors" lay behind many such failures. As a consequence, the public, failing to distinguish between a poorly constructed asphalt highway and one soundly built, began to distrust asphalt as a suitable material.[32]

When Massachusetts began using bitumen on waterbound macadam in 1907, the cost was only $.08 more a square yard. But after five years of experience it was evident that this thin coat was poor economy. As soon as a road was treated with asphalt, it attracted more traffic. And as traffic increased, the highway surface was more seriously stressed. This led to a decision to resort to the penetration method, costing $.20 more a yard. But increasing traffic, and the appearance of heavier trucks, led the Highway Commission to consider going the next step by introducing the "mixing method" to establish a sounder foundation for highways. This would increase the cost to an estimated $.75 a yard. The more costly mixing method had proved to be a sound economy for city streets, but would the public be willing to foot the increased cost for highways?[33]

By 1916, when the condition of New York state highways had almost reached a crisis status, a Highway Commission engineer published an extensive analysis of their condition and how they got that way. The problem, he declared, was the revolution in traffic which had taken place over the previous 15 years. When there was only horse traffic, deterioration of waterbound macadam was very slow. Even where a surface raveled, slow traffic often self-cured the problem. Mounting auto traffic, however, began to cause serious difficulties. Even a slight imperfection in the surface causes a fast moving vehicle to bounce and then come down with a thump, pounding the surface in a way that 3 or 4 mph horse traffic never did. To cope with this problem, the Highway Commission in 1907 began applying asphalt to the waterbound macadam. This led to a political outcry, especially from the rural interests, that the state was incurring needless expense by catering to these automobile owners. By 1912, the autoists had become so numerous they constituted a powerful political lobby. Once asphalt began to be laid, maintenance which had been left to politically appointed inspectors was no longer feasible. Smoothing out raveled sections of waterbound macadam had been readily within the scope of politically appointed local patrolmen.[34]

In short, there had been a revolution in highway traffic between 1900 and 1916, which no one had rightly anticipated. Now heavy trucks and omnibuses were using the highways on regular schedules regardless of weather. When it had been only private automobiles, touring cars, drivers usually waited until the spring thaws were over and highways had dried out. Now, however, heavy traffic was churning up the highways even as the spring thaws were making them most vulnerable. The damage being done was such that many of the state's highways would need to be virtually rebuilt. The excellent roads constructed prior to 1911 simply were not built for the current traffic.

If motor traffic was going to require rebuilding the existing state highway system, the cost for the taxpayers would become an issue of vital concern. The New York Commission engineer's study offered insights on why these costs would be inescapable. He cited as a practical example a 5 ½ mile stretch of highway in Herkimer County built in 1906 at a cost of $11.65 per mile. But in the six years following its construction, the state had paid $7,294 per mile to maintain the highway. Such costs, he observed, placed a burden on the taxpayers that was clearly "insupportable." The solution was to invest in a more permanent paving, at greater cost to be sure, but without the prospect of staggering annual charges for maintenance. At prices current in 1916, he laid out the options: the state could build brick highways at $2.70 the square yard. It could lay down a solid bitumen road at $2.50 the yard; it could build cement concrete highways at $1.50 the yard, or it could apply a bitumen carpet to existing roads at $1.50 the yard. He seemed to favor an asphalt solution, for he went on to say that the state had found it could maintain asphalt by applications of a light bitumen called "cold oiling" every other year. This approach he suggested had the added advantage that it could be done with locally available equipment.

Would such a solution provide the state with adequate highways? Only time would tell, but it was almost certain that the voters would go for the least expensive treatment. And the least expensive solution was the penetration method, which had proved to be inadequate when employed on urban streets. The debate might well have gone on for several years had not the war years, 1917–1918, brought the problem to a head.

CHAPTER 8

GASOLINE POWER AND
HIGHWAYS, 1908–1918

Because automobiles—passenger vehicles and trucks—have so completely replaced horse-drawn vehicles, it is easy from the perspective of the 21st century to see the triumph of gasoline over animal power as inevitable, but in the first decade of the 20th century it was by no means so obvious. Some, like the president of the carriage builders association, may have been sure that the auto was just a rich man's toy, a fad which would fade as rapidly as did the bicycle craze of the 1890s. But even more far-sighted people who anticipated a great future for the auto were reluctant to dismiss the horse. This was especially true of those who had to think in dollars and cents about the relative efficiency of hauling by horse or by motor trucks. In the first decades of the 20th century the comparative merit of these two forms of hauling was still an open question.

That the superiority of the truck over the team was not conceded by many is evident in the amount of effort expended in the engineering journals to arguments in favor of the trucks. An extensive study by the Massachusetts Institute of Technology reported in *Scientific American* contrasted the economics of trucks vs. teams. A two-horse team traveled 10 to 20 miles per day whereas a truck averaged 40 to 60. The team could haul 48 to 60 ton miles per day while the truck hauled 165 to 275 ton miles. The team cost $8.50 per day but the 5-ton truck cost $15.00. However, this works out at 17.7 cents per ton mile for the team while the truck cost 7.42 cents per ton mile. This meant one truck did the work of 3.5 teams. Using figures from Chicago, the MIT study indicated that the use of horses was declining about 15% a year while trucks were increasing at 120% a year. Sometimes it seemed that the study was leaning over backwards to make the stronger case for trucks. This seemed to be so when reporting that baled hay and oats sufficient to feed a team for one month required 100 cubic feet of storage, whereas a barrel of gasoline for a truck involved only 20 cubic feet![1]

The editors of *Scientific American* gave the impression that they were determined to persuade the horse advocates that they were backing losers.

Horses, they pointed out, eat daily, while trucks use fuel only while working. In an effort to be objective, they did point out that horses when idle eat 19% less oats. And trucks did suffer from the defect that springs strong enough to cushion a full load made riding empty painful for the driver and wracking on a truck, which was at that day still equipped with solid rubber tires. Complex leaf springs that engage additional layers as the load increases had not then become commonplace.[2]

The editors of *Engineering News* continued the drive to tout the inferiority of team hauling. They offered a table of costs that seemed to favor the horses: when interest on investment, depreciation, and maintenance were all figured in, the comparative costs were

Teams	$.50 an hour
Trucks	$2.00 an hour
Tractors	$3.00 an hour (pulling trailers)
Railroads	$4.00 an hour (narrow gage industrial railroads).

Against these figures several factors had to be taken into account: length of haul, rate of travel, time lost loading, time lost due to bad roads, capacity of vehicle per trip, and cost of operation. Given 2.5 mph for teams, 3 mph for tractors, and 10 mph for trucks and trains, and capacity of vehicles averaging 2 tons for wagons, 5 tons for trucks, 15 for tractor with trailers, and 20 tons for railroads, along with time lost in loading at 18 minutes for teams, 6 minutes for trucks, and 30 minutes for railroads, the inferiority of team hauling seemed self-evident.[3]

Road builders continued to rely upon horse hauling because teams were reliable and trucks were not. To be sure, when in good running condition trucks were far more efficient than teams, but when they broke down, which was often, they were a liability to the contractor racing to complete a road job in the short working season. Trucks appeared in the 1890s soon after the earliest automobiles, but these were light vehicles, commercial bodies mounted on automobile chassis. Truck sales in 1904 amounted to no more than 411 vehicles in the entire United States. Four years later truck sales reached 1,500 units. When the war in Europe generated a demand for trucks, sales in 1914 jumped to 25,375, but this was a limited production when compared with the 543,679 passenger cars sold in that year. [4]

The design of trucks of the sort required for road construction was largely conditioned by the miserable condition of the roads they had to travel. Given the deep ruts and boulders commonly encountered, trucks had to have heavy frames, and the heavier the truck itself, the lower the load capacity, given the limited engine power available. Year by year improvements were introduced as auto makers came increasingly to rely upon specialized parts vendors or suppliers turning out forged axles, radiators, ignition equipment, and brakes for numerous manufacturers. In 1917, there were 144 automakers in the United States; the shakeout of weaker firms and the merging into a few major producers took many years. By supplying parts to many automakers, the specialized firms with longer production runs and lower costs could invest more in improved designs.[5]

Despite the continual improvement in components, trucks were still, by present-day standards, marginal performers. A heavy truck meant 3- to 5-ton capacity. In 1908, the International truck was still a two-cylinder vehicle. In that year the newly formed General Motors Corporation turned out its first gasoline-powered truck as carburetors became available. In 1913 trucks still had right-hand steering, chain drives were the standard transmission, and Bendix introduced the self-starter. In short, heavy-duty trucks had to prove they were up to the challenge presented by the national highways. To this end in 1908 a Packard truck with a three-ton load made an epic journey from New York to San Francisco, but it took 46 days to get there.[6]

The first decade of the 20th century saw automobile traffic increase so rapidly that the nation's road system began to suffer from serious decay. Waterbound macadam was an ideal road surface for horse traffic. It was hard and smooth enough to shed water yet allowed a horse's hooves to get a sure footing. But auto traffic began to ravel the surface of waterbound macadam roads. Increasingly there were complaints about the clouds of dust raised by "scorchers" racing along at 15 mph.

Contemporary pictures of autoists in ankle-length linen dusters, elaborate headgear and goggles testify to the dust menace. Adjacent property owners complained that the clouds of dust lowered their property values. An advertisement in the journal *American City* deplored the "Dust Disease Death," supposedly arising from infections spread by the dust stirred up by speeding autos. The dust in question was not just mineral but "organic dust," the polite term for horse manure. The solution proposed was to oil macadam roads. "Any neighborhood can do it," an advertisement proclaimed with a cut showing a man with a hand pump and a barrel of oil spraying a road surface. It further claimed, somewhat dubiously, that Boston streets sprayed with oil had since 1906 produced a steady decline in tuberculosis.[7]

The engineering journals began running articles or the subject as it became evident that auto traffic was forcing a change in road construction. Engineers began casting about for a more durable road surface, especially "petroleum in some form." While oiling might lay the dust, it was becoming increasingly clear that "a firmer and more durable surface was certainly needed to resist the extraordinary wear produced by fast and heavy motor cars." The Office of Public Roads was looking into the possibility of employing bitumen, a petroleum product, as a substitute for "the fines," the flour-like particles of crushed stone in the cementation process. "Given the complexity of the bituminous compounds," *Engineering News* warned, the problem "is not an easy one to solve."[8]

Highway departments experimented with many alternatives. One, which promised ease of application, was the scattering of deliquescent salts which, it was hoped, would hold the mineral particles together by the surface tension of the moisture produced by hydroscopic action. This did indeed hold down the dust briefly, but as a binder it was a failure. By successive oilings and applications of bitumen, the road builders hoped they could build up a solid surface, but in these efforts also they were disappointed. The truth was they simply didn't fully understand the chemical and mechanical properties of the materials they employed.[9]

In 1912, there were more than two million miles of roads in the United States, but only slightly more than 8% of them were hard surfaced, and most of these were in built-up urban areas. The rapid increase in "autobilism," as Logan W. Page, the director of the Office of Public Roads termed the rise of auto traffic, fairly demanded an answer to the problem of how best to make highways that would stand up to auto traffic. New York State alone had more autos than Germany and France combined. Rural highways in 1912 were confronted with ten times the traffic they had experienced ten years earlier. And as trucks began to replace horse-drawn wagons, the highway problem was sure to get worse. This plea for proper appreciation of the need for some kind of surfacing of highways had, of course, political implications. Paved highways would consume large amounts of tax money. To placate those rural areas that needed roads but would not see auto traffic in any considerable volume for years to come, Page reminded his readers that the natural dirt road would play an important part in the future. If well drained and crowned, he declared, it could prove to be "a comfortable road during a large part of the year." In the past, dirt roads had not been "scientifically cared for." If properly maintained, dirt roads "can be kept in splendid condition," he assured his readers, "except in the very worst weather." This was obvious political hedging to keep the farmers off his back for seeming to favor city folks with their expensive automobiles.[10]

Why did autos damage waterbound macadam roads? It was easy to blame excessive speed without understanding the actual mechanics involved. Some observers suggested that suction caused by the tires was the culprit. Studies by the Office of Public Roads disproved this hypothesis when films showed that it was the rear wheels only which produced the dust and tore into the road surface. This suggested that it was the shear action of the powered rear wheels, not suction, which caused the damage. These findings led to experiments with applications of bitumen to build a solid surface or the use of concrete grouting to consolidate the wearing surface of macadam roads.[11]

Better road surfaces held out promise, but some officials, concerned with the tax burdens better paving would involve, sought to preserve the surface of waterbound macadam roads by restrictions on automobiles. The British practice of limiting the speed of vehicles by their weight class (heavy trucks 5 mph; light passenger autos 20 mph) was sure to be a non-starter in the United States, as enforcement would be virtually impossible. A study of wheels and tires offered a more promising line of consideration. Back in 1861 the British manufacturer, Aveling, demonstrated the first practical steam-powered traction engine at the Royal Agricultural Society's show at Leeds. The smooth steel wheels provided traction only because of the massive weight of the engine. In 1868 Bill Thompson fitted solid rubber tires to a steam engine's driving wheels and achieved much greater traction, which allowed him to reduce the weight of his engine by half. Thompson's experiments with tires eventually led to pneumatics, but the difficulties encountered in trying to design a pneumatic tire strong enough to support a heavy truck made the continued reliance on solid rubber trucks tires seem unavoidable.[12]

The failure to produce a suitable pneumatic truck tire led one journal editor to conclude that only light passenger vehicles could enjoy pneumatic tires; trucks would have to be content with solid rubber, which did provide traction but, unfortunately, tended to wear down very rapidly. The more a solid rubber tire wore down, the rougher the ride. Changing a solid tire out on the road away from specialized tools was virtually impossible, at least until 1907, when Firestone developed the demountable rim.[13]

Tire manufacturers began experimenting with what they called cushion tires, solid rubber sculptured with voids to provide a capacity for shock absorption by means of distortion of the rubber. Where conventional solids had sides slightly tapered toward the bearing surface, cushions cut away some of the rubber. One form had concave sides that allowed the tire to bend as well as compress. Alternatively, the solid was grooved along the centerline of the bearing surface and the bottom attached to the rim. Configurations such as these offered some improvement in reducing the wracking experienced with conventional solid rubber tires, but the improvement in ride was modest. In

1911 the United States Rubber Company brought out a pneumatic design which it claimed to be suitable for use with trucks, but it was more than a decade before pneumatics were sufficiently developed for widespread use on heavy vehicles.[14]

The continued desire to avoid having to face up to the expense of surfacing roads led to many suggested alternatives. One such was a proposal to widen the tire tread so as to distribute the load over a greater surface. Since this presented greater resistance due to friction there was a practical limit to widening the tread surface. Abuses by truck drivers offered yet another approach to blaming the vehicle rather than the highway. Over-loading beyond a truck's specified capacity was an obvious target. So too was speeding, because greater speeds increased heat and heating tended to increase disintegration of the rubber. Wheels out of alignment and the damage done by tire chains could also be seen as culprits.[15]

The debate between those who would put the burden on trucks and their drivers and these who argued that paved highways would solve the problem might have gone on for years had not World War I intervened. By 1914 there was a number of well-established firms turning out trucks. The five Mack brothers had founded a wagon company in Brooklyn, New York, in 1890. After experimenting with electric and steam models, in 1900 they concentrated on gasoline-powered trucks. Although they sold their company to the International Motor Company the name Mack was retained. Another well-established firm was the White Motor Company of Cleveland, Ohio, selling both automobiles and motor trucks. The success of its trucks purchased by the U.S. Army for use in China and Mexico gave it a reputation in military orders, so when war broke out in Europe in 1914, the French government placed an order with White for 500 trucks. This was big enough to induce White to drop manufacturing passenger autos entirely to concentrate on truck production. Later orders from the French brought White's total for France up to 18,000.[16]

When the United States entered the war in 1917, the U.S. Army placed orders for 10,550 trucks with the two firms mentioned above and four others big enough to handle large orders. Although most of these trucks were destined for shipment overseas to the American Expeditionary Forces, many were assigned to training camps scattered about the nation. During 1914 the nation's truck builders sold 25,375 trucks. By 1917, they were selling a record number of trucks, 128,157 in all, so highways were subjected to a radical increase in heavy traffic.[17]

The increased volume of heavy truck traffic almost immediately began severely stressing the few paved arterial highways leading to the major production centers. Efforts to keep these highways repaired were inhibited by a government ban on using railroad gondola cars to transport road building materials such as crushed stone in order to save freight capacity for war needs. This was especially disruptive in the midwestern states, where stone suitable for highway construction often had to be shipped in by rail. So just at the time when prompt maintenance measures were needed to preserve the highways, government wartime priorities deferred the effort. As truck production accelerated, manufacturers found themselves living virtually hand to mouth on daily deliveries of parts. A casting firm some 30 miles outside of Cleveland was making overnight deliveries to the White Motor Company by truck. As the highway disintegrated the journey became more difficult and delayed deliveries threatened to disrupt White production.[18]

The high volume of wartime business rather quickly began to overload the railroads. Terminals became clogged with undelivered freight, and manufacturers who normally depended upon the railroads to provide their shipments of components and raw materials found themselves running short. To sustain production they began to use trucking freight lines or, in many instances, purchased their own fleet of trucks to sustain the flow of needed parts. And this compounded the stress on the highway system. As this problem reached crisis proportions in the fall of 1917, the editors of *Engineering News Record* sent telegraphic queries to large numbers of firms to elicit information on the impact decaying roads was having on their business. As expected, most of the negative responses came from the Midwest.[19]

There were horror stories from elsewhere; the manager of a lumber firm supplying the Army in New Jersey reported that the highways were disintegrating so badly under truck traffic that he expected to revert to the use of horses to make his deliveries. One revealing result of the editors' investigation was the recognition that trucks were indeed relieving congestion on the railroads, but were also making inroads on the railways' traditional business. Trucks were not only making overnight deliveries but offering door-to-door service, cutting out the usual drayage charges on both ends of conventional freight.[20]

If the condition of highways adversely affected the delivery of supplies to manufacturers, the situation was no less troublesome for the truck builders delivering their finished products. While the Army took title to its purchases at the factory door, it still had to get them to East coast ports for shipment to France. Some of the roads between Detroit, Michigan, and Newport News, Virginia, were paved, but some were deep mud. Colonel Chauncey Baker in charge of Army transportation urged the Highway Transportation Committee of the Council of National Defense to investigate and put in shape the highways he was about to use for the first of many Army truck convoys to follow from Detroit to the coast.[21]

Decaying highways were already an acute problem in the winter of 1917–18 but promised to be even worse when the spring thaws set in. Colonel Baker was probably being unrealistic in looking to the Council of National Defense for a prompt cure. The problem was almost certainly too complex for such a hastily assembled group of wartime advisors to resolve immediately. This seems evident in the paper prepared by the widely respected and broadly experienced Connecticut State Highway Commissioner C.J. Bennett, titled "Hard Surface Pavements for State Highways."[22]

Bennett was emphatic in asserting that while the surge in truck traffic on the nation's highways required well-constructed highways, limited experience made it imperative to avoid dogmatism in deciding what kind of paving to provide. Existing pavements, he said, were simply not adequate for heavy truck traffic in all seasons. The solution lay, he declared, in modifying both road and truck design. States should build highways with the same care they devote to city street pavements. This, he realized, would involve both greater initial cost and subsequent maintenance costs. As for the trucks, Bennett envisioned weight limits as inevitable. He suggested a five-ton maximum on four or six rubber-tired wheels with no more than 700 pounds pressure on the road surface per inch of tire width. The way to go beyond five tons was to add a trailer. Bennett favored concrete over asphalt highway paving simply because more was known about concrete than asphalt, but having expressed this preference, he was careful to point out that no scientific data existed to indicate the superiority of one or another paving material.[23]

The use of one or more trailers pulled behind trucks was adopted by a number of firms during World War I when there was little hope of substantial improvement the highway system given the acute shortage of labor. While some firms used three or even more trailers to hold down the pressure on the road surface, there was a decided limitation when the truck and trailers encountered deep mud, which was not infrequently the case. Given the limited horsepower available in five-ton trucks of the period, the only way to get through muddy stretches was to unhitch the added trailers and pull them through the muddy stretch one at a time.[24]

So long as trucks and trailers used solid rubber tires, even when staying within the prescribed weight limits, trucks continued to damage highway surfaces. Moreover, they were limited to approximately 15 mph if they wished to avoid the brutal vibration suffered by the driver and the excessive wracking of the truck itself. There was, however, a potential solution, or at least a partial alleviation, of the difficulty on the horizon. While pneumatic tires for automobiles had been widely available for many years, building pneumatics sufficiently strong to cope with the weight of heavy trucks continued to elude the tire manufacturers. If pneumatic truck tires could be perfected, they would make possible greater speeds with greater comfort to the driver and less strain on the truck. At the same time pneumatics would drastically reduce the damage to lightweight paving on highways. So there was a powerful incentive for tire manufacturers to develop pneumatic truck tires, an incentive reinforced by the record sale of more than a quarter million trucks in the United States during 1918.

The automobile tire evolved from the bicycle tire perfected back in the 1880s by J.B. Dunlap in England. In the United States, Firestone produced solid rubber tires for buggies. As its volume of business grew, the firm licensed Goodrich to use its patents. Firestone moved early into making auto tires, single-tube inflatables similar to bicycle tires. The next step was adding an inner tube. But even pneumatic tires for use on relatively light autos tended to have a short life. They were constructed with laminations of fabric and rubber; the warp and woof of the threads in the fabric crossed each other at right angles. As such tires flexed in use, friction where the "square woven" fibers crossed one another tended to heat the fibers of the fabric to the point of destruction. Tires which were only marginally satisfactory on autos were manifestly unsuited for use on heavy trucks. In an effort to accommodate heavier trucks, Firestone produced solid rubber tires with treads eight to fourteen inches wide, but even these failed to reduce the destructive vibrations experienced by trucks attempting to go faster than 15 mph.[25]

Another invention dating back to the bicycle era was a patent issued in 1892 to J.F. Palmer of Riverside, Illinois, which substituted cord embedded in the tire rubber replacing the square cut fabric with its propensity to friction producing destructive heating. Palmer's "all warp and no weft" single-cord construction worked by twisting the cord helically, so as to impart a capacity for stretching. This gave the tire greater flexibility under compression without inducing heat. Goodrich acquired the Palmer patents in 1910 and cord tires began to replace square cut fabric plies. Firestone began experimenting with cord construction in 1915.[26]

When the great surge in truck traffic came during World War I, virtually all heavy trucks were riding on solid rubber tires. When tire makers attempted to thicken the rubber to minimize vibration, the increased mass only heated up faster. And as it heated it wore down faster. Cord construction offered an

out. With cords, which avoided the heat producing sawing motion encountered with square-cut fabrics, tire manufacturers could add ply upon ply without inducing excessive heat. Firestone by 1918 was producing pneumatics for
trucks with as many as 16 plies, yielding tires fully capable of carrying trucks
of five tons or more.[27]

Unfortunately, for the war effort, the fabrication of effective cords required
very strong long staple cotton, and the boll weevil infestation had driven this
type of cotton out of production. In 1916 the Goodyear company sold only
2,141 pneumatic truck tires as opposed to 124,000 solids. Moreover, pneumatics cost more than solids, so the tire companies had to push promotion
vigorously to persuade buyers to accept the better tires. There were added difficulties; many trucks lacked clearances to accommodate the larger dimensions
of the pneumatics, and this involved buying smaller wheels. Finally, some of
the less well known tire makers rushed into manufacturing pneumatic tires
before fully mastering the technology and turned out inferior tires which gave
pneumatics a bad name. As a result, the major change over to pneumatics did
not take place until after the war. Once begun, the switch took place rapidly.
Farmers hauling hogs to market in trucks equipped with pneumatic tires
found their hogs lost less weight than they did when the trucks had solid tires.
Heavier hogs sold for more and readily paid for the tire conversion.[28]

Truck users were slow to convert to pneumatic tires for good reason. At
first, pneumatic tires were suited only for use on trucks up to 3 ½ ton capacity, even if well constructed by the better tire companies. On average, solid
tires had much less down time than pneumatics. Moreover, there were uncertainties with pneumatics. Could drivers on long intercity highways always
be able to find pumps offering up to 100 psi pressure to inflate faltering pneumatics? On the other hand, if pneumatics could be developed to sustain loads
of five or more tons, there were decided advantages: greater traction, more
comfortable ride, greater speeds, and fewer truck repairs. Some truckers com-
promised by installing pneumatics on the front wheels to get a more comfortable ride while retaining solids on the rear wheels to accommodate the
load. Because of the many uncertainties about pneumatics, solid rubber truck
tires dominated sales until 1926. By 1930 they were down to one-tenth of the
sales of pneumatics.[29]

Back in 1907, the *Cycle and Automobile Trade Journal* predicted that vehicles weighing more than 3,000 pounds could never be developed since it was
"impossible to make pneumatic tires of any materials which will withstand
this strain." The tire companies in fierce competition began aggressive research
and development programs that soon demonstrated the folly of making this

and most other negative predictions. As radically improved pneumatic truck tires appeared on the market, the debate turned increasingly from the need to secure better tires to the need for better road surfaces.[30]

As the debate developed, commentators sought to establish the true costs of truck transportation. Should it include highway construction charges? Trucks, most of them still using hard rubber tires, were manifestly wrecking the existing highway system. In wartime it obviously was impractical to banish them from the highways. Should strict weight limits be imposed on trucks? Should truck license fees vary according to horsepower? Should vehicles with solid rubber tires pay higher fees? What was obvious to all was that inter-urban trucking was here to stay. Where railroad costs averaged only 4.3 mils ($.043) per ton mile, trucking lines averaged $.12 to $.25 per ton mile, but the faster service, reduced crating, and door-to-door delivery more than justified the added cost for large numbers of shippers, at least on other than very long distance runs.[31]

Even before the war ended highway officials realized that hundreds of miles of highways would have to be reconstructed. Early in 1919 the Bureau of Public Roads took stock of the situation. Prewar engineers had favored the idea of bituminous topping for macadam-based highways, but after the experience of the war years they were not so sure. The unusually severe winter of 1918, the sudden vast increase in highway truck traffic, and the wartime restrictions on highway maintenance combined to produce widespread collapse of the nation's highway system. Engineers were shocked by the suddenness with which the roads disintegrated. Almost overnight what had been excellent bituminous surfaces became impassable. This large-scale failure forced the engineering community to reconsider the whole question of bituminous pavings—not just the wearing surface but the entire road structure.[32]

Horror stories of bituminous macadam highway failures appeared on every hand. One such told of an eleven-ton truck which broke up a bituminous highway from one end to the other in a single trip. Bureau of Public Roads tests revealed that the culprit was not just truck gross weights but the impact of solid rubber tires. As truck speeds increased, the damaging impact rose from 10 to 100%. With pneumatics, as speed increased the impact rose from 0 to 10%. Moreover, as solids wore down, their impact was greater and more damaging. Since it was evident that some years would pass before pneumatics entirely replaced solid tires, the issue became one of deciding what kind of road surface would stand up best.[33]

By the end of the war well over half a million trucks were in use in the United States. While not all of these traveled extensively on inter-urban highways, it was evident that decisions on what kind of highway construction to

Figure 8.1   A truck bogged down on a seriously degraded bituminous macadam highway between New York and Washington. The road failed due to a combination of heavy traffic and inadequate drainage during spring thaws. Source: 118 *Scientific American* (13 April 1918) 353.

employ were needed. Moreover an upsurge in the number of trucks manufactured was anticipated throughout the nation. Although asphalt had been used with considerable success in paving city streets, the widespread failure of this form of highway construction gave it a bad name. So highway departments in one state after another turned to concrete as a promising alternative. Reports of how well an experimental concrete highway of eight-inch slab had held up under heavy traffic in Michigan impressed many engineers. So many states turned to concrete when the end of the war once again made labor and materials available for highway contracts.[34]

Concrete highways, while ideal for truck traffic, promised to be far more expensive than the existing waterbound macadam highways. The 1916 federal highway legislation which had provided funding for state highways did not underwrite heavy paving for highways suitable for truck traffic. Three-quarters of those federal funds went to waterbound macadam, sandclay, and even gravel roads. What is more, under that earlier legislation, construction was spotty, doled out to individual counties in short sections designed to "get the farmers out of the mud." Little thought had been devoted to developing trunk lines for through traffic. The conflicting objectives of rural interests who wanted feeder highways to get into towns and cities on the one hand and industrial and tourist interests favoring interstate trunk lines was reflected in the congressional debates looking toward additional federal highway funding. Support for federal funding was universal, but there was considerable disagreement over just how such funds were to be applied.[35]

The compromise eventually worked out in Congress in the Federal Highway Act of 1921, which provided 75 million dollars for 1922. It specified that only 7% of the allocated funding could be used for trunk or interstate systems. The Post Office Appropriation Act of 1922 authorized $190 million supplementing the initial $75 million to cover the years 1923, 1924, and 1925, giving state highway departments the continuity needed for long-range planning. An earlier measure passed by Congress had a significant impact on the way states made use of the federal money. It included authorizations for expenditures for maintenance as well as initial construction, specified standards such as 18-foot widths for all federally funded roads, and strengthened the authority of state highway departments over individual counties in decisions on construction.[36]

The provisions enhancing the authority of state highway departments were of vital significance. Under the initial 1916 Federal Highway Funding Act, individual counties were to come up with the matching funds for highways within their jurisdiction. As critics pointed out, this favored the wealthy counties, giving them an economic advantage and denying it to the already poorer counties who had a greater need for an economic boost. On the analogy that wealthy states' taxes paid to the federal government were used to assist the poorer states, the critics proposed that wealthy counties should be willing to have their tax dollars paid to the state to be used to enhance the highways of the poorer counties. This was decidedly sensible proposal not only for financial reasons but also because states were far better prepared to administer and supervise highway contracts than were county governments.[37]

Although the federal acts strengthened state highway departments, the tug of war over how the newly available funds were to be distributed continued. Where Congress set a maximum of $20,000 per mile of highway, rural interests favored a ceiling of $4,000. That way the available money could be stretched to cover more miles of road. Political pressure from the counties was manifestly successful. In 1922, for example, more than 10,000 miles of highway were improved using federal funds, a large gain over previous years. But because of county interests most of these miles were low-grade gravel, sand-clay, or merely graded earth construction rather than paved highways suited to heavy traffic. The logic behind this, especially in western states where distances were great and traffic light, was that it seemed better to lay down a stable base for most highways and defer paving until later.[38]

There were, however, strong lobbies for paved trunk routes. The American Automobile Association, the AAA, with its touring Blue Books built up a national network of chapters urging paved highways. They were supplemented by the so-called "trail associations" backing such projects as the east-west Lincoln Highway and the north-south Dixie Highway fostering tourist traffic. The sheer numbers of automobiles operated to favor paving. By 1921 there were more than ten million autos in the United States and registration fees produced more than $122 million for the states to spend on highways. Moreover, beginning in 1919 gasoline taxes began to produce significant dollars for highway construction.[39]

Despite the pulling and hauling amongst rival interests, more money than ever before became available for state highway departments to let paving contracts. Increasing numbers of relatively small urban street and sidewalk contractors ventured into the more difficult and large-scale business of highway construction. The flow of state and federal funds provided a stimulus to innovations in construction machinery. This trend was accelerated by the inflation of wage levels brought on during World War I. Improved machinery that cut down on costly labor held promise of virtually paying for itself from savings on payrolls. And nowhere was the development of labor saving machinery more spectacular than in the wide variety of equipment perfected to produce concrete highways. Given the perceived failures of bitumen asphalt paving during the war years, concrete became the paving of choice in the boom years of the 1920s. But before addressing the story of how concrete highways were built, it may be useful to consider the background of cement, concrete, and the evolution of powered mixers.[40]

CHAPTER 9

·CEMENT, CONCRETE, AND MIXERS

The story of cement goes a long way back in antiquity. The Roman architect, Vitruvius, speaks of Greek authors who describe forms of cement used in building. The Romans perfected a cement that remained hard under water by using pozzolano, volcanic ash mined near the town of Pozzuoli. More than twenty centuries later, some of these Roman-cemented structures are still standing. In 1759, the great English engineer, John Smeaton, found by practical experiments that lime, when combined with ground-up bricks, could be used to make a cement which he employed in constructing the underwater foundation of his famous Eddystone lighthouse. He achieved this result by sintering, that is, heating, the lime and clay. Joseph Aspdin, a Yorkshire man, carried the process a step further in 1824, when by experiment he discovered that by sintering the lime and clay at very high temperatures in a kiln, he produced clinkers with which, when pulverized to a fine powder in a mill, he could make a concrete hard enough to resemble Portland limestone. The name Portland thus became synonymous with high quality hydraulic cement.[1]

In the United States, cements employed in building the locks on the Erie Canal in 1818 marked the initial significant use in this country. These were natural cements made by grinding a local stone found near Fayetteville, New York, and in other scattered locations. The beginnings of the cement industry in the United States centered on a wood-burning kiln and water-powered mill erected in 1828 at Rosendale in Ulster County, New York. In time the name Rosendale became synonymous with natural cement. These natural rock cements would not harden under water unless, following the British discoveries, combined with certain clays. Portland cement emulating Aspdin's development didn't appear in the United States until 1876, when David Saylor of Copley, Pennsylvania, erected a vertical kiln for sintering. A major step forward in the production of cement came in 1899 when the first horizontal kiln was erected in the United States, copying a British design invented 44 years earlier by Frederick Ransom. The horizontal rotating kiln vastly increased productivity by providing continuous feed rather than the batch processing that had characterized the earlier vertical kilns.[2]

Unfortunately, in the absence of close scientific analysis of the many cements which appeared in the U.S. market during the latter years of the 19th century, there was little standardization or quality control. As a consequence there were numerous instances of failed concrete. Engineers and contractors became skeptical of locally produced brands. This is reflected in Austin T. Byrne's textbook, *Highway Construction*, published in 1893: "All cement furnished must be of some well and favorably known brand," he warned, and should be subjected to tests to insure quality. Because of this, most of the cements used in the United States were imported until the mid-1890s. After 1900, imports fell off sharply. Domestic production rose from less than six million barrels in 1900 to more than 16 million barrels a mere two years later. Clearly the delayed development of domestic production arose out of the tendency of engineers to specify the imported products, mostly from Germany and Britain, whose quality they trusted.[3]

While standards of quality were slow to develop, the standard container for shipping emerged early on: because it was crucially important to keep cement dry, wooden barrels became the universal form of packaging. A wooden barrel containing 375 pounds of cement would gross at about 400 pounds, an excessively heavy weight for manhandling when loading into a horse-drawn vehicle. There were marked differences in the cements produced at different locations. "Western" Rosendale ran only 265 pounds net to the barrel, while "Hudson River" Rosendale ran 300 pounds net to the barrel. Such differences suggest wide variations in the strength of concretes produced, not to mention the difficulties confronting contractors and engineers estimating requirements for a particular job.[4]

In the last decade of the 19th century, the inconvenience of handling 400-pound barrels led to an agitation in favor of cloth bags weighing 94 pounds when filled, or roughly one-quarter of a barrel, a size far easier to manhandle. The barrels were frequently broken up and used for fuel for a contractor's steam engine, a needless waste according to critics. Overseas shipments continued to be by barrel, and cement firms continued to offer customers a choice of bags or barrels for at least two decades into the 20th century. As evidence of how slowly long-established business practices persist, even when shipping bags to a customer, the cement manufacturers continued to bill by the barrel. By 1915, some firms were offering a choice of cloth bags or multi-ply paper bags. The paper sacks were non-returnable, but contractors could get a refund on undamaged cloth sacks returned in bundles of 50. Some cement firms sold non-returnable cloth bags at five cents more, contending that such sacks could stand five or six times as much rough handling as paper.[5]

The economics of cement bags offer an interesting insight on a contractor's profit margins. Which was the better buy, cloth or paper? In 1912, cement makers charged $.10 for each cloth bag, a charge refunded if the bags were returned. But contractors soon learned that not all the bags were returned. Workmen used them for aprons and as sacks to carry things, so up to 20% of the invoiced bags were not recovered. Moreover the contractor had to pay the labor cost on shaking out the bags; cloth bags routinely retained up to 1.5% of their contents in the fabric when dumped for mixing. Paper bags involved no such costs. Cloth bags had to be untied to dump, a time-consuming process. Paper bags could be hastily slit open. On the other hand, even multiply paper bags sometimes tore open. Cloth bags tended to have greater losses from absorbing moisture than did paper bags. When a contractor returned cloth bags in bundles of 50 as required, he had to trust the cement manufacturer's count of the returned bundle. Usually the contractor bought cement through a middleman dealer, not directly from the manufacturer. Occasionally an unscrupulous dealer would take returned bags bearing the advertising logo of a reputable manufacturer and refill them with an inferior brand of cement, thereby causing the buyer to lay down, quite unwittingly, inferior concrete. Meanwhile, when charging $.10 per cloth bag, the cement firm was buying them at $.07 to $.09 apiece, so he made a profit of at least a penny each time the bag was shipped. In time, contractors came to realize that however vulnerable paper bags were to tearing, they were a better buy than cloth bags. What is surprising is how long it took users to recognize this fact.[6]

Until the end of the 1890s, natural cement dominated the domestically produced market. However, by 1900 U.S. production of Portland exceeded natural for the first time. From then on consumption of Portland rose rapidly, at least in part because the use of horizontal rotary kilns made possible the greater efficiencies of continuous flow production and lower costs. As demand for Portland increased, more producers were encouraged to enter the field. And as more firms began to produce, variations in the quality of the product mounted. As one commentator at a meeting of cement producers remarked, the industry was expanding so rapidly, "there is danger of its product being misused and its value undermined in popular opinion." The American Society of Civil Engineers began a study of cement in 1906 and found a pervasive lack of reliable data. One important finding of the study was the frequently ignored observation that laboratory tests were often not comparable to experience with actual construction in the field.[7]

From the earliest days in the 19th century, when cement began to be used, contractors recognized the need for ways to judge the strength of concrete comparable to the measurement of strength in iron and steel. Lacking such, failures in applications of concrete were painfully frequent. The American Society of Civil Engineers appreciated that different applications called for different specifications; the requirements for a concrete building foundation differed from those for the arch of a bridge. Even when standards were established and tests devised to implement them, there remained the need for qualified people to conduct such tests. It also gradually became clear that more than suitable cement was involved. The sand mixed with the cement was equally a consideration.[8]

Against this background of slowly evolving understanding of cement in the making of concrete, the idea of using concrete for pavings raised a host of new problems. The first attempt at paving a highway with concrete appears to have been a stretch laid down in 1865 at Inverness in Scotland. The first concrete highway in the United States was a short 220-foot experimental section in Bellefontaine, Ohio, during 1884. Some fifteen years later, it was still in good condition. However, an engineer writing about pavements rather off-handedly dismissed it, saying that horses found it slippery just as they had granite block pavements. This writer concluded, "very few people now advocate their construction, brick and asphalt having the preference." A great part of the difficulty lay with the scanty information generally available to contractors experimenting with concrete.[9]

Several states experimented with concrete paving around the turn of the century. A contractor in Chicago achieved considerable success with it. He overcame the objection that horses found it slippery when wet by grooving the surface before it set. Nonetheless, *Scientific American*, as late as 1914, claimed that concrete highways were "virtually unknown" less than five years earlier. In reporting that New York State had adopted standard specifications for highways built with Portland cement, the editors went on to mention a litany of objections to the material. Some critics claimed that concrete highways would lame the horses traversing them. Other complaints, such as the allegation that the eyesight of drivers would be injured by the glare of the white surface in the sun, seem absurd from today's perspective. Still, other critics more reasonably noted the tendency of concrete to crack under temperature changes. Ira O. Baker's influential 1903 textbook, *A Treatise on Roads and Pavement*, saw little future for concrete other than as a foundation for asphalt, "This form of road surface is not likely to come into general use owing to its cost and slipperiness...."[10]

Despite such criticisms, some states, especially Michigan with its many automobile manufacturers in the Detroit area, pressed ahead with experiments in concrete highways, trying varying mixes, combinations of cement, and crushed stone. These early gropings were often off the mark. For instance, in 1912 one Detroit specification called for a ratio of one part cement to one-half part clean, sharp sand, to three parts broken stone, a mix using far less sand than subsequent practice found desirable. The requirement for "clean, sharp sand" was sound, as builders of waterbound macadam had found that rounded sand from river bottoms and the seashore was undesirable. Another stipulation wisely included in the Detroit specification called for continual inspection to insure that the requirements were actually carried out by the contractor.

California also experimented with concrete highways. There a distinctive feature was the ⅜-inch topping of "asphaltic sand" covering the concrete. This provided better footing for horses but was expected to wear off in about three years. However, it could be replaced relatively cheaply and had the added advantage of waterproofing any cracks which developed in the concrete. Although farmers continued to worry about laming horses, at least one admitted that concrete highways raised the value of adjacent property and permitted teams to haul at least double the loads they could pull on unpaved dirt roads.

These early state experiments with concrete highways turned up a whole series of problems with the material which had to be solved to insure success. When the initial efforts using a four-inch slab proved too light, an experienced building contractor suggested that highway slabs should use steel reinforcing the way buildings did. He favored 8- to 10-gage steel wire with a two-inch mesh. Another controversial issue was the expansion joint. Should they be added every 25 feet or could one lay slab for 100 feet before inserting a tar-filled joint? Should the joint be ¾ of an inch or less? The longer interval between joints would mean less thumping in driving, but only time would tell if 100-foot intervals were sufficient to forestall cracking. Should the two lanes of a road 16 or 18 feet wide be laid separately? If so, should there be a longitudinal expansion joint along the centerline? Would laying the two lanes separately affect the effort of crowning adversely? Clearly, there were dozens of issues to be confronted, but before concrete highways could be laid down economically, an efficient powered concrete mixer had to be developed.[11]

Power mixing of concrete has had a long, slow evolution with many fits and starts. In 1866, the London Metropolitan Board of Works specified that its contract for a new Thames embankment use concrete "mixed by machinery." In response to this mandate, the contractor's engineer, a Mr. Ridley, designed a mixer to do the job. It consisted of an inclined steel cylinder open at both ends and powered by belting from a steam engine. Sheet metal blades, described as "shelves" inside the rotating cylinder, served to stir the mixture. This invention was not a success because the contractor found that the labor involved in lifting the ingredients into the open high end of the mixer ran up costs, so it proved cheaper to mix by hand.[12]

Although the engineering journals mentioned one or two experiments with machine-powered mixers in the 1880s, there was little interest in the subject in the United States until the 1890s. Thomas Carlin's Sons of Allegheny City,

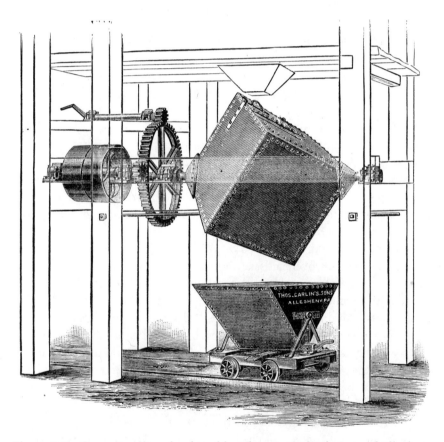

Figure 9.1   Concrete mixer developed by Thomas Carlins's Sons of Allegheny City, Pennsylvania, in 1890. 24 *Engineering News* (5 July 1890) 16.

Pennsylvania, designed a square metal box mixer, which hung in an elevated frame providing a gravity drop into a waiting vehicle below. This arrangement differed radically from most earlier machines in that it was a batch mixer rather than a continuous feed. This meant that the proportioning of cement, sand, and crushed stone could be carefully determined for each batch. For Ridley's continuous feed cylinder and similar designs, no such control was possible. However, the Carlin design suffered from the same fatal flaw as the Ridley in that charging the elevated box was inconvenient and involved excessive labor costs.[13]

In 1893 Austin T. Byrne's widely used engineering textbook, *A Treatise on Highway Construction*, pictured a continuous feed steam-powered mixer sold by the Cockburn Barrow and Machine Company of Jersey City, New Jersey. From this, it would appear that the Carlin concept of batch mixing, which allowed control over proportioning the ingredients, had not yet caught on, but a decade later there were several different mixers on the market, each repre-

Figure 9.2 Steam-powered concrete mixer of the Cockburn Barrow and Machine Company of Jersey City, N.J. This mixer was apparently designed to run on railroad and trolley tracks. Loading was awkward, since the materials had to be lifted by shovelers to the top opening where the revolving blades of the mixer are just visible. A.T. Byrne, *Treatise on Highway Construction* (New York, 1892) 607.

senting a different concept. As one observer listed them, they were cubical, drum, screw, and gravity, as well as what the writer called "dago," that is, Italian workmen using shovels and a mixing board.[14]

By 1905, Ira O. Baker's textbook, *A Treatise on Roads and Pavements*, was ready to declare that machine mixing was superior to hand mixing because it did so more thoroughly and quicker. Nonetheless, he observed that highway contractors usually mixed by hand. They did so, at least in part because of the difficulty of continually moving the mixer as the job progressed, clear evidence that the available machines were not really designed for highway work. Mixing by hand involved placing the sand and cement on a ten-foot square wooden or sheet metal platform and setting a gang of shovelers to turning the mix over and over before adding water. Although Baker tactfully attributed the reluctance to use mixers on highway jobs to practical obstacles, he may have been reluctant to insult those to whom he hoped to sell his book, engineers and supervisors. Ever anxious to avoid costly catastrophic failures, engineers tended to be conservative, sticking to tried and true methods. *Engineering News*, looking back to the recent past, observed that not many years had passed since conservative engineers regarded mechanical mixing as "a dangerous innovation." As late as 1907, a standard text on concrete with rare progressiveness admitted that "the best forms of mixers now on the market give results quite equal to the best hand work." This rather patronizing view was rapidly disappearing as engineers "tardily recognized that muscle cannot compete with machinery."[15]

Steam-powered batch mixers soon became the favored machine in the United States, but there was considerable variety in design. While most of them favored a rotating drum, there were many differences in detail. One manufacturer tilted the whole cone-shaped drum to discharge the mix; another substituted a chute projecting into the drum. Several of the drum-type mixers had ring gears about their circumference driven by pinions. One ingenious improvement involved the mixing blades inside the drum that stirred the ingredients. Where most manufacturers attached these across one full side to the drum, he attached the blades only at two ends, allowing water to scour the inside of the drum at the day's end, where clods of concrete tended to collect and harden at the edges of the blades. This might seem like a small improvement but the manufacturer's advertising made clear the advantage: "You don't have to pound our mixer to clean it."[16]

By 1909, with several efficient mixers available in the market, concrete began to be used increasingly for highway paving. The Koehring Machine Company of Milwaukee, Wisconsin, which had entered the field in 1907, soon became the leading manufacturer of mixers by virtue of aggressive innovations in design. In 1913, the journal *Engineering and Contractor* defined just what the requirements were for an efficient mixer by listing the refinements and features which one or another of the competing mixer manufacturers had introduced. These included a traction engine to move the mixer backward and forward and climb a 15% grade under its own steam power, although at the time this meant only about one mile an hour. The machine had to be steerable. It ought to be easy to charge with the piles of material, cement, sand, and aggregate deposited alongside the road under construction, and it should be capable of discharging the mixed concrete rapidly with minimal labor. A single workman should be able to stoke the boiler and handle the engine controls. In short, an efficient mixer should minimize labor costs in every way possible.[17]

Earlier mixers almost all involved heavy labor costs in charging. The usual procedure was to erect an inclined plank for men with barrows to dump their contents into the mixer. This was eliminated by the invention of the skip, the power-operated scoop. With its bottom on ground level in the lowered position, workmen with barrows could wheel directly from the roadside supply and tip their loads into the skip. The front edge of the skip was wide enough to allow up to three barrows to be tipped in simultaneously.[18]

At the other side of the operation, discharging the completed mix, one solution was a chute or tube which could be projected into the turning mixer drum to catch the mix and send it sluicing out to be deposited on the rolled sub base. At first, these chutes were rigidly hung from the mixer, so they deposited the mix along the centerline of the pavement being poured and workmen had to rake or shovel the mix to spread it evenly between the forms at the sides. Later chute designs were hinged to allow it to be swung from side to side, thus depositing the mix across the whole width of the sub-base, a substantial saving in labor costs.

A still later device for improved discharge of the mix provided a boom projecting as much as 20 or 25 feet out in front of the mixer. This swinging boom supported a bucket which received the contents of the mixer and, using a powered windless, could spot the concrete anywhere desired within the range of the boom. This device overcame the limitations of the short chute and the frequent difficulty of getting concrete to flow suitably. It also reduced the number of times the concrete mixer had to be moved to deposit a new area of slab.[19]

Mixer makers had much to learn from contractors as the latter acquired practical experience on the job. Complaints from users led manufacturers to

Figure 9.3 An early model of a steam-powered mixer manufactured by the Koehring Machine Company of Milwaukee, Wisconsin, equipped with a boom and bucket to distribute concrete over a wide arc. 42 *Municipal Engineering* (March 1912) 204.

replace conventional 4-inch steel wheels with 9-inch wide versions which functioned better on soft earth. By 1915, a mixer appeared in the market mounted on crawlers, caterpillar treads, which functioned even better on soft earth. Complaints from contractors working late in the fall or early in the spring confronted with frozen sand piles led Koehring to introduce a mixer with a heater, which could unfreeze sand or gravel in a minute. The T.L. Smith Company of Milwaukee came out with an automatic water weighing device which controlled the flow to provide precise amounts to the mix, a consideration belatedly attracting increasing attention from contractors.[20]

While improved concrete mixers did much to facilitate highway construction, contractors had a great deal to learn about the processes involved in laying concrete highway slabs. In 1912, the Office of Public Roads admitted that concrete for highways up to the recent past had not proved satisfactory. But now it seemed that success was "almost in sight," providing skilled supervision was available. While contractors had acquired considerable experience in laying concrete foundations for asphalt streets, they soon discovered that constructing concrete wearing surfaces posed a whole new set of problems. Within months after laying, concrete slabs developed hairline cracks, admitting water that froze in winter and consequently degraded the surface. When used as a foundation for asphalt, the concrete was promptly covered with bitumen, so the cracks didn't matter. Shrinkage and expansion of as much as three-quarters of an inch in concrete as a wearing surface, however, was manifestly unacceptable. The obvious remedy was to insert expansion joints, but how frequently, how wide, and what kind of filler?[21]

Only trial and error would answer these questions. Should the joints be three-eighths of an inch wide or half an inch? Wood, tarpaper, felt, and bitumen were all tried. Some contractors experimented with such alternatives as pavements of five-foot square slabs; others resorted to bricklike concrete cubes in the search for a way to beat the expansion and contraction problem.[22]

Far more elusive was the problem of proportioning, that is, determining the appropriate ratio of cement to sand and aggregate, usually expressed in the form 1:2:4. Many factors entered into the decision, depending on the objective sought: hardness, high tensile strength, density, etc. Concrete for a bridge or culvert arch calls for a different proportion than that suitable for a pavement slab. In 1907, a paper presented before an American Society of Civil Engineers meeting reported on a series of tests conducted to determine ideal proportions, claiming to have established the laws for proportioning concrete, "believed to be unknown hitherto." There were many variables to confound the conscientious contractor. For a durable pavement the stone in the aggregate had to have a coefficient of wear suited to the job, but this wasn't enough; the size of the stone mattered, for the amount of cement in the mix had to be sufficient to coat each particle to insure proper bonding. In short, despite claims to have established the "laws of proportioning," experienced contractors recognized that while proportioning might appear simple in theory, it was decidedly not so in practice. A good concrete wearing surface required uniformity, yet even the most conscientious application of an approved proportion could produce a bad pavement if the temperature at which it was laid was too hot or too cold.[23]

The spread between theory and practice calls for particular attention. While highway engineers almost certainly perused the professional journals conscientiously and benefited from the information found there, how many highway contractors subscribed to even one of the engineering journals? There is little evidence of their presence in substantial numbers within the readership judged by the paucity of letters to the editors from contractors. When improving and paving highways became a national concern, many, probably most of these individual firms which entered the field, came to it from small beginnings in urban street paving, where they acquired their competence from practical experience. An amusing confirmation of this is evident in the engineering journal report of a contractor who believed that a mix of 1:6 meant one bag of cement to 6 barrow loads of aggregate![24]

Even the contractor who was reading the professional journals and sensitive to the appropriate proportioning for a given job could go astray if he failed to inspect the aggregate he employed. Loam or dirt intermingled with the crushed stone could seriously upset the proportions. Some contractors tried to avoid this problem by hosing down each barrow load before it was dumped into the skips, using a barrow with a perforated bottom. An enterprising manufacturer developed a portable gravel washer to cope with this common problem, but even this had difficulty removing sticky clay from the aggregate.[25]

Proportioning and washed gravel were only two of the many items a contractor had to keep in mind. Quite apart from their impact on the quality of his work, they had a direct bearing on his costs and ultimate profit or loss. Alert contractors found it useful to heed one or another of Halbert P. Gillett's several manuals, which were filled with sound advice. After making his estimate at so much for a cubic yard of slab laid down, for which the state highway commissioners provided the final specifications, he learns that sand containing more than 2% of "dirt" must be washed. This might seem like a slight change, but washing the sand runs up his costs substantially. Similarly, the spec calls for crushed stone not over 1½ inches. This means that the daily output of his crusher is reduced by as much as 35%, since it produces stone up to 3 inches, and all the output over 1½ inches will have to be run through the crusher again, adding to costs. To give the slab sufficient strength to stand up to the pounding of heavy vehicles, states began specifying "well rammed" concrete. Ramming brought excess water to the surface and made for a denser concrete. But "well rammed" was an indefinite requirement on which a contractor could run up his labor costs alarmingly in that this involved hand labor in the prewar years.[26]

Contractors who had acquired their expertise in handling concrete in the building trades and in laying driveways, sidewalks, or even the concrete foundations for asphalt paving, had to learn that the wearing surface of a concrete slab highway required far more strength than the concrete they had been accustomed to mixing. If the aggregate was not thoroughly coated with mortar, it would creep under stress. The objective was to get enough mortar to insure that all facets of the crushed stone were coated, thus providing sufficient bond. Sensing this, contractors were inclined to add more cement, making a richer mixture. However, as an experienced road builder explained before a meeting of the American Road Congress, it mattered little whether the proportions of cement, sand, and stone were 1:2½:5; 1:2:4; or 1:1½:3, the resulting mortar will be about 50% in relation to the aggregate. So the solution was not to make a richer mortar by adding more expensive cement, but to provide a greater percentage of mortar in relation to the crushed stone. This could be achieved by proportioning 1:2:3½ instead of 1:2:4, thus attaining greater bonding without adding to the cost for cement.[27]

In short, state highway commissions, their engineers, and many contractors had learned a good deal about concrete in the years leading up to World War I, but there was much more that needed to be mastered when the postwar years confronted the 1920s boom in highway construction.

CHAPTER 10

CONCRETE HIGHWAYS: THE BOOM YEARS

As the previous chapter has shown, by 1914 concrete as a form of highway paving was making substantial headway. By then, well over 9 million yards of such paving had been laid in the U.S. and Canada. Cubic yardage, of course, tends to inflate the impression. When reduced to miles of completed highways, the statistics seem less notable. Connecticut, for example, one of the earliest states to perfect its highway commission on a non-partisan and efficient basis, had only 24 miles of concrete highway in 1914 in contrast to 923 miles of waterbound macadam, 128 of asphalt-topped macadam, and a little over one mile of brick. In Michigan, a much larger state, where its lively interest in automobile production offered a powerful incentive to improve paving, a single county could boast of 67 miles of concrete. But even this represented only a small fraction of the state's total highway miles.[1]

The momentum for turning to concrete was both stimulated and retarded by the nation's involvement in World War I. It was retarded by the wartime restrictions on highway construction resulting from diversions of the labor supply, the curtailment of railroad transportation of materials, and the demands of the military forces for a large portion of the output of cement manufacturers. On the other hand, the failure, the actual breakdown, of so many asphalt-topped crushed stone macadam highways gave asphalt, albeit unfairly, a bad name, which induced many states to look to concrete paving when highway construction began again after the Armistice. The New York State Highway Commission had had such bad experience with asphalt highways that failed that it announced that it would invite construction bids only for concrete paving.[2]

New York's all-concrete contract proposals attracted few bidders. One reason was the acute shortage of cement. The wartime shortage resulted largely from the difficulties experienced by the manufacturers in securing coal to fire their kilns. As a consequence, a number of cement producers dropped out of the business. Wartime discussions as to the feasibility of having state governments take over the manufacturing of cement certainly gave no encouragement to those firms driven to the wall for want of fuel, so the cement shortage continued for some months after the Armistice.[3]

Shortages were not the only problem roiling the waters for would-be purchasers of cement. In 1921, the state of New York indicted some 70 cement manufacturers alleging price-fixing and illicit division of sales territories in violation of the Sherman Anti-Trust Act. Other communities followed suit, charging 24 major cement firms in the Midwest with price-fixing. A Columbia University banking professor investigated the tax returns of 11 major producers and found that these companies averaged only 7.3% return on their total investment, so whatever their practices may have been, they were making far less than the average return on industrial enterprises. And the cement makers pointed out that their costs per barrel of cement had been sharply increased by wartime inflation in labor, fuel, and raw materials. However, contractors had complaints other than cost. Cement manufacturers refused to sell directly to contractors, forcing them to buy from local dealers, middlemen whose added profit figure increased the cost to contractors.[4]

Cement suppliers accused some contractors of over-ordering and then selling the cement they didn't need at inflated prices in a tight market. Contractors rebutted by saying that yes, they did order more than the total required, but only to protect themselves from cement suppliers' failure to deliver in timely fashion, causing delays that could bankrupt a contractor. What the contractors wanted more than anything else was guaranteed delivery dates.[5]

Until 1923 the major cement companies continued to bill contractors "by the barrel," although barrels had given way long since to sacks. Though many contractors insisted on ordering cloth sacks, paper sacks were becoming increasingly common. The suppliers offered a choice of cloth, paper, or bulk. Bulk, shipped in railway hopper cars, was cheaper for the contractor but involved more elaborate storage and handling equipment at the construction site. Although the standard 94-pound sack containing one cubic foot of cement was the most convenient for calculating requirements, some contractors favored half-cubic-foot sacks, which weighed about 50 pounds, because they were easier to manhandle. Against this advantage the increased cost of loading and unloading the greater number of smaller sacks dissuaded some contractors from buying them. Paper sacks gained adherents when they were made tougher with long fiber hemp, and because of the speed with which they could be slit open with the blow of a shovel.[6]

As contractors began laying concrete highways in the 1920s, they encountered all the problems which had plagued highway builders before the war. A

Bureau of Public Roads staffer enumerated the difficulties: shrinkage caused by the drying of excessive moisture in the initial mix; contraction and expansion resulting from temperature changes; warping caused by both temperature and moisture; bending caused by imposed wheel loads and bending resulting from uneven subgrade; and damage from frost action. In an article titled, "Should Cement Be Made Better for Highways?" the author speculated on whether or not improved fineness of cement might produce concrete of greater tensile strength. Fineness could be specified by reference to standardized testing sieves. The hope was that by specifying a cement of almost impalpable fineness, most of the shortcomings of the resulting concrete enumerated above, would be avoided. But these common difficulties were by no means all of the problems contractors encountered. One more was the need for a quicker-setting concrete. Cements which took considerable time to set tended to slump downward on even slight grades. While finer cement might produce concrete of a higher tensile strength, it was by no means clear that it would overcome all the problems encountered when pouring highway slabs.[7]

Contractors' concerns for the proper choice of cements were not confined to paving slabs. Before precast concrete pipe became readily available, masons laid up stone and mortar arched culverts where stone was at hand. Alternatively, they cast all-concrete conduits which posed different challenges from those encountered in laying slab. Concrete culverts had the advantage of permanence, but they were labor intensive to build and therefore expensive. Galvanized iron pipes offered a cheaper alternative available since about 1905, but even after 15 years of trial, contractors were uncertain as to just how long they would last. Because there was no simple test for the quality of the galvanizing, road builders concerned for their reputation hesitated to use galvanized iron culverts.[8]

The character of the sand no less than the quality of the cement largely determined the resulting concrete. Builders back in the 19th century, a whole generation earlier, had recognized that wet sand bulked larger than dry sand. And fine sand bulks larger than coarse. What is more, dry sand weighs more per cubic foot than wet. The deviations possible in the differences between wet and dry could wreak havoc on concrete, where proper proportioning was essential to success, so a contractor was under great pressure to exercise a continual watch over the supposedly carefully measured barrow loads of sand being tipped in to the skip of his mixer.[9]

The quality of aggregate employed in road construction also mattered. The Bureau of Public Roads laboratory testing had established an abrasion test to measure the durability of different kinds of stone employed as aggregate. But even the use of the same kind of stone could be misleading if gradations in size were allowed to pass unnoticed. Given an aggregate running from ¼-inch to two inches in size, the amount of water used per bag of cement would vary significantly. This difference could make a large variation in the strength of the resulting concrete. So consistency in the grading for size in the stone delivered by the crusher became of vital importance.[10]

The postwar boom in highway construction created a surge in demand for crushed stone. In 1919 half of all the stone quarried in the United States went to highway builders. Earlier efforts to find a cheaper substitute by crushing chunks of salvaged concrete proved disappointing, as the resulting aggregate was only two-thirds as strong as natural stone. In some areas, cheaper aggregates could be secured by exploiting tailing slopes from mines. Waste flints from zinc tailings in 1926 could be had sometimes free or for as little as $.05 a cubic yard, but in general quarries supplied the bulk of the aggregate employed by road builders.[11]

While contractors and state highway commission engineers were grappling with the various problems of raw materials for concrete highway construction, voters across the nation began to take an active interest in the kind of paving their tax money was buying. The New York Highway Commission, having come out in favor of concrete exclusively, felt obliged to defend its decision. Pointing to a claimed seven- to 10-year life of bituminous macadam, it made little sense to build such roads with 50-year bonds, which would mean buying the road at least five times over before the original bonds were retired. Skeptical taxpayers began to query the Bureau of Public Roads as to the relative merits of asphalt and concrete. Bureau spokesmen hedged in their replies, pointing out that both were durable but each had advantages and drawbacks according to local conditions, ending up saying it was best to follow the advice of an experienced local engineer.[12]

If Bureau of Public Roads officials were ambivalent about the relative merits of concrete and asphalt, it was increasingly evident that the nation was turning to concrete as the paving of choice for highway construction. For the asphalt interests this threatening trend called for action. In 1919 they formed an Asphalt Association, which promptly began a vigorous campaign touting the merits of asphalt construction in a series of circulars given wide publicity. To bolster the credibility of the campaign, the Association recruited two of the best known authorities on asphalt from the Bureau of Public Roads, Prevost Hubbard and J.E. Pennypacker.[13]

At first the Association built its case against concrete on the basis of its greater cost than asphalt pavements. For the period 1915–1917 it offered figures purporting to represent average costs:

	Average cost per mile	Average maintenance cost per mile
Waterbound macadam	$20,000	$976
Penetration method Asphalt macadam	$22,000	$464
Concrete	$35,000	$124
Brick	$50,000	$196

To minimize the appeal of the low maintenance cost claimed for concrete, the Association circular noted dismissively that concrete was so new that limited experience probably didn't reflect its true maintenance costs. Subsequent circulars issued by the Association deprecated concrete even further: "That a cement road needs a top to protect it from abrasive wear and the constant pounding and vibration of heavy traffic has practically ceased to be disputed."[14]

Another line of defense in favor of asphalt was taken by Mr. Pennypacker, the Association's executive director, and his highly competent research chemist Prevost Hubbard. They pointed to the need to preserve the heavy investment made by many states in what Pennypacker described as "time-honored waterbound macadam" roads. This could be readily accomplished by applications of asphalt if properly done by well-informed engineers and contractors. Appeals to economy were probably more effective than negative jibes such as caustic remarks about "the extravagant claims for the merits of cement concrete." The positive case for asphalt was undoubtedly more persuasive. Pointing out that asphalt paving could be opened for traffic the day after it was laid, whereas concrete required a curing period of many days, was sure to appeal to highway commissioners sensitive to public opinion.[15]

The defensive tone of the early publications of the Asphalt Association was misplaced. It reflected the postwar fear that bituminous materials would be replaced entirely by concrete after the breakdown of bituminous macadam highways during the war. In time, the Association became the most important clearing house for technical information on the application of asphalts. Association chemists largely replaced the Bureau of Public Roads laboratories as the source of ever advancing knowledge as to how to manipulate hydrocarbons to suit a wide variety of specialized needs and challenging environments. The best evidence of the long-term success of the Asphalt Association and its assistance to users of asphalt is manifest in the facts of U.S. highway construction. By the end of the 20th century, over 90 percent of the nation's paved roads had asphalt surfaces.[16]

Clifford Richardson, an employee of the Barber Asphalt Paving Company, widely regarded as a leading authority of bituminous materials, pursued a different approach in the debate over concrete versus asphalt. He offered a com-promise: why not use concrete as a foundation for asphalt wearing surfaces? If heavy wartime traffic had broken through the asphalt wearing surface laid on a bituminous macadam foundation constructed by the penetration method, the obvious answer for Richardson was to build a concrete founda-tion which, he asserted, "will last for all time." This was not an entirely new idea, for concrete foundations had been used for asphalt-topped city streets for a number of years. Its novelty lay in suggesting it for highway construc-tion. The obvious flaw in Richardson's proposal was cost. If a contractor were to bring out his full array of machinery to construct a concrete foundation, why not build the whole road with concrete rather than haul out a second set of machinery to top off the concrete foundation with asphalt? In the highly political arena of building public highways, cost containment is a must.[17]

In striving to sustain an impartial stance between concrete and asphalt, the Bureau of Public Roads placed its faith in a program of experimental testing. Early experiments showed that even a slight imperfection in a highway sur-face caused a heavily laden truck to bounce up and then strike the road sur-face with a considerable impact. The Bureau staff hypothesized that this im-pact was far more damaging to a road structure than much heavier static loads. To test this hypothesis they constructed an elaborate mechanism to measure the bearing power of different road surfaces. According to the test engineer, the Bureau was "making an earnest effort to place road building on a much more scientific basis than exists at present." This search for a "scientific basis" was a characteristic response reflecting the spirit of the Progressive Movement that culminated in the Wilson Administration.[18]

The Progressive faith in science and laboratory testing had adherents far beyond the confines of BPR. This is evident in the number of advertisements for laboratories and testing facilities for paving products in professional jour-nals in the 1920s. The appeal to "scientific testing" was useful in giving cred-ibility to a highway commission's decision in favor of one form of paving over another, but there were skeptics who questioned the efficacy of the pretense of scientific decision-making. A decade earlier one doubter had warned that the only conclusive test of a paving material was a road test under traffic over a period of years. "All the empirical or hurry-up tests may lead you into error." Testing the composition of a concrete or asphalt sample took no account of the methods a contractor employed, even if he used the best of materials.[19]

Concrete as a material for paving highways had a significant advantage over asphalt in that there had been substantial improvement in the design of effi-cient mixers in the prewar years. The war had run up labor costs alarmingly, so contractors had a powerful incentive to invest in machinery that promised to reduce the number of individual laborers required. A review of the various types of labor-saving equipment available in the 1920s should help make clear why the postwar years were seen as the golden age of concrete paving. Although mixers were the main item of equipment, there were many other items that improved the efficiency of contractors and the speed with which they were able to lay concrete slab. In a business where the working season was short, three to six months at best, the speed at which one could lay slab of acceptable quality was a vital factor in determining profit or loss.

The introduction of the power-operated skip or hopper was undoubtedly the most important improvement in mixer design, because it did away with the need for loading ramps. As long as loading was done by barrows running up a ramp to dump in the ingredients of the mix, there was an incentive to design mixers with the drum close to the ground to minimize the effort involved in climbing the ramp with a loaded wheelbarrow. But once the powered skip was introduced, mixers could be designed with the drum set higher. This facilitated delivery of the mixed concrete, whether by chute or boom, by providing a steeper angle for gravity discharge.[20]

Steam-powered mixers were favored by contractors because the care and operation of steam engines were understood by many workmen, but in the 1920s mixers powered by gasoline engines began to replace them. This trend was facilitated by the increasing number of automobiles, which led to larger numbers of workmen familiar with gasoline engines. There were significant advantages in this shift in power sources. Where steam required repeated deliveries of large quantities of coal and water during a working day, a single tank of gasoline would run the engine for a 10-hour shift.[21]

Another significant improvement was the introduction of self-propelled mixers. Earlier models had steel wheels, which meant only slow-speed hauling to the construction site was possible. Self-propelled mixers could move backward from each completed section of freshly laid slab without the need to be towed by truck or traction engine. One manufacturer experimented with continuous tread crawlers, which gave a decided advantage in soft or muddy earth but proved to be a disadvantage when moving over a highway to reach the construction site. The obvious answer to this was to provide pneumatic tires, which made it possible to increase road speeds. Pneumatic tires also reduced wear and tear on the mixer.[22]

With the loaded skip charging the mixing drum every minute and a half and then dropping back down to receive its next load, a mixer could be a dangerous place for workmen. To obviate the risk of the falling skip crushing an inattentive workman, the Chain Belt Company of Milwaukee, Wisconsin, introduced a simple but effective safety feature. This was a rod or railing hinged on the frame of the mixer and surrounding the three sides of the skip. When the skip went up, the railing came down and prevented anyone from walking under the raised skip. Contractors saw this ingenious device as a good way to secure lower insurance premiums.[23]

Under the spur of competition mixer makers introduced a stream of modifications in response to contractor complaints. Another Chain Belt Company innovation was a mixer with a folding top which permitted it to pass safely under railway and highway bridges built in the days of horse-drawn traffic. The T.L. Smith Company of Milwaukee developed a water tank to apportion the precise amount of water required for a given charge entering the mixing drum. There were many such innovations, not all of them successful. One of the latter was a mixer without blades in the drum. It relied entirely on centrifugal force imparted by rotating the drum at 80 rpm as opposed to the usual 20 rpm. The theory behind this design was that the greater centrifugal force would insure that every particle of the aggregate would be thoroughly coated.[24]

The best-known firm, and the most aggressive in developing improved models of mixers, was the Koehring Machine Company of Milwaukee. This firm took a leading role in organizing the industry by such means as sponsoring university lectures by authorities on cement and concrete. Efforts such as these eventually led to a movement by the trade organization, the Associated General Contractors, to establish design standards such as uniform capacity ratings for mixers, standard wheel sizes, pipe connection diameters, and the like. This action, the work of a committee representing both highway contractors and mixer manufacturers, offers significant evidence of the maturity of the mixer industry.[25]

Next to the highly developed mixer models, the most important innovation for highway contractors was the tamping and leveling machine which evolved just before World War I but didn't become fully perfected until the 1920s. As early as 1906 a German study revealed that freshly laid concrete could be made much denser and stronger if tamped to force excess water to the surface. However, this process had to be conducted with great care, for beyond a certain point such tamping *decreased* the strength of the slab. Contractors were continually tempted to make wet mixes because these would readily slide down a 20-degree slope in the discharge chute, but dry mixes required as much as a 45-degree slope to flow.[26]

The high cost of labor involved in hand tamping led to the development of a gasoline-powered tamper. This machine, developed by Pawling and Harnischfeger of Milwaukee, delivered 50 blows a minute. But tamping was only one problem with freshly laid slab. The concrete emerging from the mixer chute or boom bucket was roughly surfaced as workmen raked the dumped piles between the forms on either side. To level it, the original practice was to ride a plank or strike board along the edges of the side forms, pushing the excess concrete forward to attain a smooth surface. This plank could be contoured concavely to give the desired crown to the slab. So the next obvious step was to combine the tamper and the strike board into one machine.[27]

One version of the combined tamper and leveler took the form of a massive two-ton roller that squeezed out excess water as it pushed a wave of concrete ahead. A more successful model developed by the R.D. Baker Company of Detroit, Michigan, set the strike board tilted forward at a 60-degree angle to push along the excess concrete. But instead of tamping, it vibrated from side to side in a 1½-inch stroke that surfaced excess water as effectively as tamping. By this time steel side forms had largely replaced the wooden planks originally used, so the combined machine rode on flanged wheels resting upon the forms as a track. Clearly this use of the side forms as a track for the leveler put a premium on meticulous accuracy in having their surfaces conform to the state engineer's grade stakes on either side of the roadbed. The great advantage of such leveling machines for a contractor lay in the fact that he no longer had to run a wet mix to prevent voids in his slab. The machine operated much faster than hand tamping, which required a wet mix to allow sufficient time before the concrete began to set or harden. With the drier mix now possible, contractors could lay more slab in a working day. One observer pointed to 600 feet of slab per day with hand tamping as opposed to as much as 1,000 feet with the leveling machine.[28]

To give the concrete slab a smooth surface contractors developed a number of simple devices. One of the earliest was the float, a smooth board mounted on a long pole so the workman standing to one side of the newly laid surface could polish it as the mixer was being moved back to lay yet another section of slab. These floats were clearly just a modified version of the hand smoother workmen had long used in working the surface of sidewalks. An alternative to the float was the roller at the end of a pole or ropes to opposite sides which workmen could run to and fro over the newly laid slab. Still another version of the float was the canvas strap or belt which workmen on either side of the slab pulled back and forth to achieve the desired finish.[29]

Where detours were not feasible, contractors in the 1920s began laying half-width slab to allow one-way traffic to continue operating on the other side. This was an idea brought back from France by U.S. soldiers returning from the war. This arrangement was more expensive for the contractor, but it was popular with the public, who appreciated having the road open to traffic during construction. On the other hand, laying half-width slab created a serious problem for finishing machines which were usually designed for the full-width 18-foot pavement. To avoid requiring the steel forms to be moved repeatedly, one manufacturer devised a nine-foot-wide leveling machine with a flanged wheel to ride on the outside form while the middle wheel was flat to ride on the finished slab. Another firm decided to produce only the full-width machine, but this would not permit one-way traffic when in use. Yet another indication of the growing maturity of the highway machinery industry was the success of the Associated General Contractors organization in persuading a finishing device manufacturer to license the use of his patented invention on generous terms.[30]

With the war over and the public clamoring for paved highways, Congress lavished millions in matching appropriations for state projects. Improved models of the major machinery required for laying concrete slab promised greater output and lower costs. As the year 1919 began there was a prevailing atmosphere of anticipation for the many miles of construction that lay ahead. The editors of *Engineering News Record* surveyed the large building firms of the nation to determine their interest in taking on highway contracts. The response they evoked suggested that the big firms wouldn't be interested unless states offered contracts for projects of large mileage, 15 or 20 miles or more, rather than the shorter 1- to 5-mile projects typical of the prewar years. Only multi-year contracts, some argued, will justify the heavy capital investment in mixers, levelers, industrial railroads, and similar equipment needed to fulfill large-scale contracts.[31]

The threat of competition from heavily capitalized building firms stirred a response from experienced contractors already in the highway business. The argument that the economies of scale favored the big contractor rang hollow. Shorter contracts allow the owner-contractor to supervise the job in person. "Each piece of work requires constant, resourceful supervision personally," a kind difficult if not impossible to hire. Moreover, since highway work is seasonal, retaining high-priced supervisors over the winter is decidedly uneconomic.[32]

Another approach to defending the experienced contractors' turf was the litany of lament over the paucity of profit to highway contractors. With millions of dollars available, why is contracting so precarious? The proffered reply listed the many hazards confronting contractors: the short construction season, lost time due to bad weather, excessively rigid specifications drawn up by inexperienced state engineers, shortages of materials, breakdowns of machinery, lack of spare parts and lack of skilled mechanics on site to speed repairs, (as labor stands by idle, wage costs continue relentlessly). Without long experience in estimating, it was painfully easy to suffer from unexpected costs. An unexpected rainstorm can do serious damage to a finished subgrade and require expensive regrading before starting on paving. Pity the poor contractor who doesn't realize that earth shrinkage has altered the level of the state engineer's all-important grade stakes. The list of such hazards goes on and on.[33]

One of the complaints the small contractors leveled against the large heavily capitalized firms concerned the bidding practices some of them employed. States letting contracts on large numbers of miles (in 1919, for example, New York state accepted bids on 600 miles of highways) tended to break the jobs down into some large and some small. This was done in hopes of attracting the largest possible pool of bidders to insure maximum competition. The smaller firms complained that the big contractors bid unrealistically low on the short mileage contracts to drive out the small firms, then bid excessively high on the longer stretches too big for small firms to tackle with their existing capital and limited machinery. The smaller firms suggested that the way to stop this was to rule that whenever the bid of a contractor on any one section was less than the average price on all sections, it should be considered the low bid for all his increments.[34]

There is little evidence that the malpractice in bidding attributed to the large-scale firms was widespread, but the protest reflects the fears of the typical highway contractors. By far the large majority of such firms entered the field grading and paving urban streets. Moving out into the country to construct highways, especially concrete highways, confronted them with a host of problems to master. Tracing the progress of such contractors as they learned from experience will illustrate what these problems were and how they were resolved.

One of the initial problems many contractors first confronted when venturing to move from urban paving to highway jobs was the matter of grading. In cities the grading required was often minimal, a bit of scarifying to loosen the surface followed by the use of a grader to obtain a proper surface. Highway work, on the other hand, often involved large-scale cut and fill operations. The task was defined by the grade stakes posted by the state engineer and his survey party. If a fill was adjacent to a cut, it might be possible to do the work with slips or fresnos. For more distant fills, wagon teams or trucks might be required. Should these be loaded by shovelers or by steam shovel? Estimating probable costs such as these was difficult for inexperienced contractors. Grading involved scarifying, shaping, ditching, dressing slopes, grubbing out tree stumps. Unless a contractor had kept careful records of the costs involved in each of these operations, he was almost certain to submit a faulty bid.[35]

If the fill was a deep one, the contractor might wish to do the cut and fill in the off season in order to let the fill settle and benefit from rainstorms. Failing to insure a solid footing, he would need to bring in his steamroller to compact the fill at various stages as the level rose. With the subgrade established to his satisfaction he would then haul in crushed stone for a foundation. If stone was locally available, he needed to select the most economical site for his crusher, bearing in mind the cost of hauling to all parts of the highway. If stone had to be imported from a distance by rail, the contractor had to make a decision as the most economical form of hauling. In the 1920s, as teams were phasing out, the choice was increasingly between trucks or industrial railroad. In sandy soil, horse-drawn wagons were out of the question and trucks were little better, so the industrial railroad was the obvious solution. One clear advantage of the railroad lay in its location parallel to the roadbed, where it did no damage to the subgrade. Trucks, on the other hand, if still equipped with solid rubber tires, tended to tear up the crushed stone foundation that had been carefully compacted to the specifications set by the state engineer. Trucks with pneumatic tires could safely ride on the subgrade or the stone foundation. Trucks of large tonnage were more flexible and more economical than the railway, but in wet weather they tended to bog down in the mud, so a contractor had to balance the higher cost of lighter trucks making more runs, but usable in all weathers, against the greater economies of larger trucks, which imposed delays in bad weather.[36]

With the grading finished and the crushed stone properly compacted, the contractor was ready to bring on his concrete mixer to begin laying slab. The early practice was to spot supplies of aggregate, sand, and bags of cement at intervals at the side of the road to be ready for loading into the mixer skip as the mixer gradually advanced along the prepared stone base, leaving a ribbon of freshly laid paving behind. There were inherent difficulties with this approach. Bags of cement spotted at the roadside in advance were subject to theft, and a night watchman meant extra expense, even though he couldn't hope to guard all the piles on several miles of road. Putting off delivery until just before the cement was needed risked imposing delays on the whole mixer crew. Moreover, sacks of cement had to be securely covered with tarps to keep dry, another item of expense subject to theft. Finally, to keep the skips properly filled every couple of minutes meant keeping several men with barrows busy shoveling up sand and aggregate. Unless they were careful, soil under the bottom of the pile found its way into the barrows and adulterated the mix. Sometimes this was sufficient to weaken the resulting concrete.[37]

As long as contractors continued to use cement from cloth sacks, there was some loss from the cement which remained in the sack when it was dumped into the skip. Given the split-second timing of the mixing cycle, there were few seconds available in which to shake out the last particles of cement. Cost-conscious contractors began to fabricate dust bins in which to have a workman salvage what he could of the lingering contents. These bins were designed to minimize the clouds of dust inevitable during the shaking. One firm claimed to have recovered the equivalent of 11 bags of cement from a total of 1,500. Another firm reported that a bundle of 60 well-shaken empty sacks being returned to the dealer weighed only 25 pounds, as opposed to 50 to 75 pounds for unshaken sacks. Savings on salvaged cement and the lower cost in returning lighter bundles, the contractor claimed, amounted to a $1,000 savings on the contract.[38]

Cost conscious contractors soon found ways to avoid the multiple handling of materials deposited by the roadside. Especially in the Midwest, where crushed stone frequently had to be brought by rail, it proved practical to provide hoppers at the railroad siding from which trucks could be loaded by gravity. The exact desired proportion of aggregate, sand, and cement could be dumped into a truck body provided with two or three dividers. This allowed a single truck to dump two or three charges into the skip for successive cycles of the mixer, a far more efficient procedure than charging by barrows.

Getting the truck to the skip posed some difficulties. The truck had to have pneumatic tires if it hoped to avoid disturbing the carefully prepared stone foundation. Further, since the men setting forms had to prepare them behind the mixer in anticipation of its next move back to lay a new section of slab, the truck driver would have to back his vehicle carefully for some distance to avoid harming the forms. To simplify this process a turntable was developed so the truck could drive ahead facing the skip, and roll up on the turntable. The driver would dismount, manually swing the roller bearing turntable reversing the truck's position, unlatch the tailgate and then tilt his truck body to dump the first of his measured charges into the skip. Not every firm enjoyed the efficiency of trucks in loading the skip. Many contractors in the 1920s were still using teams. It takes little imagination to sense the difficulty, if not the impossibility, of employing wagons to load the skip without disturbing the crushed stone and the forms.[39]

When contractors began using heavy tamping and leveling machines, it soon became evident that the wooden forms traditionally used would have to give way to steel forms that would serve as a track on which the machines could ride. Economics alone would have favored steel forms. These could be rented at $.30 a foot versus about $.03 a foot for wooden forms. But wood was worthless after three or four uses. Before the war, steel forms could be purchased for $.45 a foot.[40]

As in so many areas of highway construction machinery and equipment, the development of steel forms illustrates the virtue of competition in pushing improvements. In 1923 the Blaw Knox Company of Pittsburgh introduced a much heavier style of steel form with a lock-joint to insure better alignment. The slightest irregularity in the level of the forms tended to produce a wavy surface in the resulting slab. Two years later the Dravo Equipment Company of Pittsburgh came out with forms with square sockets to accommodate square stakes. These provided greater contact between stake and form, giving added stability. A wedge pin locked the stake to the form. But no matter how superior the form, a careless workman backing a truck into the form or dropping a heavy object could press the stake into the soil and ruin the horizontal alignment.[41]

One of the virtues of the industrial railroad was that it ran parallel to the road bed and thus had no occasion to harm the alignment of forms. While the normal procedure was to lay the narrow gage track parallel to the road, some contractors, when laying slab one side at a time in order to allow one-way traffic in the other lane, found it convenient to place the track on the newly laid slab after it was cured. They did this because the pavement offered a superior roadbed for the track and reduced the number of derailments which not infrequently happened when the rails had been laid on unnoticed soft spots alongside the highway. Efficient contractors, aware of this tendency, found it economical to have a workman patrol the line daily to look for sagging sections of track betraying soft spots.

Contractors employing industrial railroads on highway jobs found that a 20-horsepower engine could haul 10 or 12 loaded cars and 12 to 16 empties, providing there were no grades of more than 4 or 5 %. They also found it was desirable to use a mule to switch empties to convenient sidings to free the engine for heavy hauling. Using rail cars was substantially cheaper than horse hauling, but the faster tempo of rail cars was no less significant. Instead of spotting sand, cement, and aggregate at intervals along the road layout, the rail cars could deliver ingredients directly from the source, a gravity feed bin located at the crusher site or main railway bringing in gondola cars of materials. Batch boxes of properly proportioned ingredients, three to a flat car, could be brought to the mixer, where a power-operated boom or derrick, newly added to the mixer, lifted the boxes over the skip, allowing their contents to be dumped directly. This eliminated the need for workmen with barrows to load the skip, and made it easier to sustain a two-minute or less cycle time for the mixer.[42]

Some contractors experimented with centralizing the mixer at a point adjacent to the bins used for loading material into batch boxes. This saved significantly on hauling and induced some to order cement in bulk, that is, in gondola cars covered with tarps. Spoilage from rain and difficulties in handling bulk cement with clamshell buckets led to a return to paper sacks. One disadvantage of the centralized or fixed location of the mixer was the tendency of the mixed concrete to segregate as it made the journey, whether by truck or tilt-body rail car from mixer to the pouring site. When dumped at the construction site, the wet concrete lay all at one side of the road. This meant that the puddlers, the men who performed the brutally hard labor of spreading the concrete evenly between the forms, had to push the mix across the width of the roadbed. When employing a portable mixer using either a swivel chute or a boom and bucket rig, the heavy wet concrete could be distributed over most of the desired area, sharply reducing the amount of physical labor involved. For this reason, many if not most contractors favored the portable mixer over a centralized stationary plant. The puddlers' task was the most disagreeable and hardest work, so laborers tended to seek easier positions unless induced by higher wages. Even when the swivel chute or boom and bucket were used to distribute the mix, a foreman had to drive his men hard to keep up with a two-minute cycle of batches.[43]

Clearly, the gravity loading bin used to drop the proper charge of aggregate, sand, or cement into a waiting truck or railcar was an important piece of machinery, although it has been largely neglected in the engineering literature. There were portable all-steel bins available from construction machinery dealers, but many contractors fabricated their own bins of heavy timbers and planking. These locally fabricated bins were often less well designed than they should have been, with too little attention given to the pitch or slope of the floor, which determines the speed of discharge. And given the frequency of moves from one contract to another, bolting the sections rather than spiking, along with the provision of lifting lugs, would have made these cumbersome structures more readily moveable.[44]

Another problem confronting contractors laying concrete slab is the matter of water supply. Producing slab creates a prodigious demand for water. In sandy soil as much as 100 gallons per yard may be required to wet the subgrade to prevent it from absorbing excessive moisture from the freshly poured concrete. The mixer could use 50 gallons for each cycle of the mix, which is to say 50 gallons about every two minutes. After the slab begins to harden, as many as 80 gallons per yard may be required to facilitate curing. Given 230 gallons for each cubic yard to concrete turned out, this means 1,900 pounds of water, nearly a ton for every cubic yard of mix. It should be evident that this volume would soon prove too difficult for tank trucks to supply if the source of water was at a distance.[45]

Contractors early on resorted to pipelines from the most convenient source of water, normally a 2-inch pipe, to minimize friction as the distance grew longer. In some waterless areas contractors had to import water in railroad tank cars of 8,000-gallon capacity. This involved freight charges, and demurrage for two or three cars a day. If the water came from a city source, this too meant additional expense. Why buy from a city water supply? Why not just pump from a stream or pond? There was sometimes a fear that mineral content or organic matter in a local supply would produce inferior concrete, although tests revealed that these fears were not always warranted. In rare cases a contractor might have to run pipe 10 miles to insure his water supply, but typically pipelines were much shorter. An electric or gasoline-powered high-pressure pump was required to push water for long distances through a 2-inch pipe. A 3-inch pipe would have reduced the friction but would have added significantly to cost, and the 2-inch pipe became more or less standard when contracts for concrete paving were for much shorter distances than those let in the 1920s.[46]

The higher the pump pressure, the greater the probability that it would produce leaks at imperfect joints in the system. To insure ready access to water as the paver moved along the subgrade, contractors added taps and valves every 250 or 300 feet along the pipeline. By attaching 175 feet of high-pressure wirebound hose to one of these outlets, workmen could provide the required water as the mixer made its incremental moves. A high-pressure hose 175 feet long required several men to drag it from one outlet to the next, an operation of several minutes. Given the two-minute mixing cycle, when it came time to move the mixer, precious time could be lost with expensive labor standing around idle while waiting for the hose to be moved. Efficient contractors provided two hoses, so one could be moved to the next nearest outlet while the mixer was still being supplied at the end of the hose already attached.[47]

Getting water to the mixer was one problem, but determining just how much water to add to the mix was quite another. The goal was to discharge concrete which had both the desired workability and strength. Workability was a rather unscientific judgment; the mix had to be dry enough so the aggregate wouldn't sink to the bottom and wet enough to flow readily when filling the forms. Strength was conventionally determined by a slump test. This consisted of placing a sample of the mix in a conical mold and measuring the time it took to slump. Such tests revealed that variations in water content could yield major variations in strength. Finding precisely the right amount of water to inject into the mix was difficult, since "water content" was not just a function of water deliberately added, but varied with the moisture content in the sand and the aggregate, which could readily differ from one batch to the next.[48]

One perceptive observer writing in an engineering journal suggested that the problem of determining the amount of water needed for an optimum mix reminded him of what the English say about how cocktails are mixed in the United States, "a little sugar to make it sweet, a little lemon to make it sour, a little whiskey to make it strong, and a lot of water to make it weak." How, the writer inquired, can water be kept to a minimum but the charge still fluid enough to mix properly? Perhaps, he suggested, there should be a three-stage mixer: the first to mix cement and water, a second stage to mix in the sand and a third to mix in the aggregate. Since this proposal would almost certainly have slowed down the mixing cycle, he found few if any takers. However, he did suggest another "reform" which might well have been adopted to the benefit of all. In the extended debate over proportioning, the conventional form was to express the proportion of cement, sand and stone was, say, 1:3:5. But the amount of water to be added was not specified, even through it played a critical part in the mixture produced. The writer suggested that it would be useful to add water content to the form: water, cement, sand, and aggregate, say ½:1:3:5. Like so many seemingly good ideas, this one appears not to have caught on.[49]

One of the prewar problems which continued to vex contractors in the 1920s was the appearance of hairline cracks soon after slab had been laid. Every effort to eliminate these cracks had met with failure, different proportions in the mix, better subgrade. Every step taken to eliminate these tiny cracks ended in frustration. Contractors finally concluded that hairline cracks were inevitable and unavoidable. About the best one could hope for was to keep the cracks from enlarging and admitting enough water to be a serious menace in winter freezes. Coupled with the presence of hairline cracks was the rapid increase in heavy truck traffic. To minimize the menace of enlarging cracks and coping with heavier traffic loads, state highway commissions began specifying various forms of steel reinforcement.

Warm days and cool nights caused pavements to warp. Thickening the outer edges of the slab seemed to give some relief, and a few states began to specify the addition of ¾-inch reinforcing bars running along the outer edge on both sides of the pavement. Where the two sides of the slab had been laid separately, they specified such reinforcing bars along the longitudinal center joint. Where many states had specified light wire mesh before the war, in the 1920s they increasingly specified much heavier bar stock. Placing steel reinforcement two inches below the surface was a labor-intensive task that added significantly to the cost of laying slab.[50]

As each day's run of slab was completed, it had to be prepared for curing. In principle, this meant preventing the slab from drying out too quickly, which led to cracking. When contractors failed to recognize the importance of curing and simply let the newly laid slab air dry, the resulting concrete was significantly weaker than when properly cured. Some contractors contended that misty, moist or slightly rainy weather yielded a satisfactory cure, but such arguments may have been an attempt to avoid the considerable added labor expense of curing.[51]

The curing process began soon after the forms were removed, which was done as soon as the slab was firm enough to stand on its own. Contractors usually wanted to remove forms as soon as possible in order to have them available to set in place ahead of the mixer as it backed away from the just completed section of slab. Forms represented a considerable outlay of capital and required quality labor to be placed with the exactitude demanded by the supervising state engineer.

There were several alternative methods of curing. One was to spread sand or loose dirt about 2 inches thick on the finished slab not later than a day after the forms were removed. In order to obtain the maximum possible density, this covering was sprinkled daily for about two weeks to retard the drying out of the slab. The duration of the curing process depended on the weather. Concrete sets faster in warm weather than in cold. In colder weather, some advocated curing for as much as 30 days, but the public, ever anxious to get a road open to traffic, tended to put pressure on the supervising engineer to open the road sooner. To cut labor costs when putting the earth coat on the finished slab, some contractors plowed or scarified the soil along the edges of the highway and then used a continuous belt of buckets loader to lift the loosened earth to the slab, where it could be readily raked to the desired thickness.[52]

An alternative employed by some contractors was called "ponding." This involved building earth dikes along both sides of the slab and covering its enclosed surface with water. This reduced the labor costs of daily sprinkling, but it suffered from the obvious drawback that it wouldn't work where there were considerable grades. Then even transverse dikes would be insufficient. Other contractors used burlap or canvas to top the slab, employing a reel or roller mounted on the forms. But this had the disadvantage of leaving the forms in place longer, so they weren't available for laying fresh slab. Manifestly, the cost of extra forms would offset some of the economies obtained by reducing the cost of applying the fabric. Where readily available, moist hay or straw offered another form of curing in the continual search for a less expensive way of achieving the desired quality of concrete.[53]

As early as 1916 the U.S. Bureau of Standards conducted a series of experiments to determine if adding salt and sodium chloride to the mix water would accelerate the hardening of concrete without having to resort to the various forms of curing. These tests showed that adding salt did indeed lead to denser, harder concrete in 24 to 48 hours, but the salt added a cost of $.12 to $.15 a yard to the finished product. In the 1920s a few states picked up the idea of using salt to hasten curing, arguing that the sooner the concrete highway was opened to local traffic, the greater the economy for haulers, who reckoned in ton-mile costs. While the added salt did attract moisture from the atmosphere by hydroscopic action, some engineers feared the presence of salt would induce a retrogression in slab hardness over time. Other engineers blamed salt as the cause of scaling which sometimes afflicted concrete slab. Investigation eventually revealed that the scaling resulted from excessive tamping.[54]

With the curing completed, only one job remained before the final clean-up and removal of all the contractors' equipment. This was grading or dressing the shoulders. Some states required more than just backfilling against the edges of the slab, insisting on a crushed stone macadam shoulder, three feet wide with a two-inch slope for drainage, filled with fines and compacted. The objective was to provide a sound bearing surface to support the outer wheels of a vehicle. Experience had shown that when an automobile traveling at high speed strayed off the edge of the slab where the shoulder consisted of nothing more than earth fill, wet and soft, a wheel sinking into the mud could cause a serious accident, even flipping over an automobile.[55]

By the mid-1920s, the golden age of concrete road building was in full swing. Great progress had been achieved over the previous dozen years or more. The process had been one of continual trial and research. Many mistakes had been made: faulty design, unsuitable materials, inadequate preparation of the sub-base, faulty proportioning, and inexperience. But at least by 1925, while there were still many problems to solve, there was a pervasive sense of confidence, of mastery, a feeling that at last many if not most states understood how to specify sound practice, and many contractors were available to perform with assurance that the pavement produced would be a durable one good for many years of service. Moreover, that many states now embraced concrete as desirable paving is evident in the miles of concrete they laid down. By 1925 California had 3,465 miles of concrete highway, Illinois had 4,104 miles, Michigan had 2,042 miles, and New York had 2,794. Of course the poorer states, especially in the South, lagged behind. Alabama had only 48 miles of concrete. But the editors of *Engineering News Record* could point with pride to the fact that road building had become "one of the nation's great industries." The American Road Builders Association convention in Chicago was deemed "a commercial triumph" and "the greatest ever," with 185 manufacturers of road-building equipment displaying their latest models. In 1927 Thomas H. Macdonald, the Bureau of Public Roads chief, could declare, "For the past eight years, highway building has been the greatest single public activity in the United States."[56]

To get some perspective on what had been accomplished, the sheer scale of the concrete paving operation, it may be useful to consider what a mile of concrete highway involved. At an average cost of about $30,000 a mile in the mid-1920s, the state purchased 2¼ acres of concrete, some 2,000 cubic yards of mixture. This consumed 3,400 barrels of cement on 17 carloads. Some 11,000 cubic yards of sand required 32 carloads to deliver; 1,600 yards of crushed stone required 40 carloads. If the needed 300,000 gallons of water had to be brought in by rail, this would require 38 tank cars. If the 3,400 barrels of cement came in cloth sacks, that would mean 13,000 sacks of one cubic foot each. That number of sacks required 13 bales of cotton to manufacture. Highway building in 1923, some 7,600 miles under contract, required some 600,000 freight cars to transport the needed materials. And this didn't include the railway cars needed to provide the 390 tons of coal consumed by the cement makers' kilns in producing the cement for a mile of concrete highway.[57]

CHAPTER 11

RETROSPECTIVE ON
A REVOLUTION

The foregoing chapters, a series of essays in roughly chronological order, should help the reader to understand the "highway revolution" of 1895–1925, or how the nation's highways got out of the mud. A brief retrospective on those chapters may pull them together.

The first great over-arching problem was financing. The traditional urban practice of making abutters pay for the streets that enhanced the value of their properties broke down when applied to the long frontages of highways abutting farm and other undeveloped rural properties, where the relatively high cost of road building ran well beyond the yield of the properties. The reluctance of prosperous urban dwellers to pay taxes for rural highways was matched by the cash-strapped farmers' preference for "working on the roads" in lieu of paying taxes in cash. The mid-19th century development of railroads largely dampened what little sentiment there was in favor of highway building.

Dismal as the prospect of support for highway construction may have appeared, there were forces at work gradually gathering momentum in favor of funding highway construction. The farmers needed surfaced highways to reach urban markets or railroad terminals if they hoped to maximize the yield of their acreage. The railroads needed surfaced highways as feeder lines to increase the volume of their freight from more distant farms. Finally, when first bicycle riders, and then automobile drivers, began to clamor for surfaced highways, interest in Congress began to move toward the payoff point. The income from auto license fees available for road building gave an added push to the move for Federal appropriations to match state funds. The culmination came when Congress passed the multi-million dollar road act of 1916.

The United States in 1916, it is well to remember, was still a horse-powered nation. The horse population had been increasing faster than the number of automobiles. So the move to surface rural highways had to accommodate horse traffic. Fortunately an ideal model was available from foreign sources: the road designs of British road supervisor John Loudon McAdam. His 1816 treatise, *Remarks on the Present System of Road Making*, provided a virtual textbook for road builders. The great secret of McAdam's method lay in the use of crushed stone in which the sharp fractured edges tended to lock together. When the voids between the pieces of crushed stone were filled with fine stone dust and repeatedly sprinkled and rolled to insure adequate penetration, the result was a surface firm enough to shed water, but flexible enough to provide a suitable footing for horses. This was called waterbound macadam.

The high cost of labor in the United States would undoubtedly have inhibited any widespread use of waterbound macadam for road building. The practice of breaking stone by employing men with hammers would have been a serious impediment, were it not for Eli Whitney Blake's 1852 invention of the steam-powered stone crusher, which drastically reduced the cost of broken stone.

Even the best waterbound macadam construction will rut and ravel under heavy traffic. Steel tires of heavily laden wagons will ultimately disturb the surface. And the iron-shod hooves of horses will in time begin to disintegrate the water shedding surface. The obvious problem was lack of maintenance. Communities in the United States were slow to recognize the lessons long since learned in Europe. French roads were superb because they enjoyed well-organized and continuous maintenance. In the United States there developed the all too common practice of relying upon local property owners to work off their taxes by maintaining the highways. Lacking suitable supervision, this form of maintenance was seldom satisfactory.

After the debacle of the turnpike movement, road building had come to be regarded as a local problem, a responsibility of county governments. Since most county governments were minimal at best and almost universally lacking in professional staff of any sort qualified to supervise construction, it is hardly surprising that the nation's rural highways in the 19th century were wretched. In the post Civil War years, when the nation was still saddled with heavy war debts, Congress was understandably reluctant to appropriate funds for highways, even though common sense suggested that a national system of highways would contribute significantly to national prosperity. This hesitancy on the part of Congress is evident in the decidedly modest funding granted to support the Office of Road Inquiry, whose placement in the Department of Agriculture was clearly a bid for the farm vote—at the lowest possible cost. But, as experience had shown, a government office, once established, takes on a life of its own. All that was required to make it grow was some grass roots support.

The prosperous state of Massachusetts, with its ample tax base, led the way because some exceptionally able individuals, men of vision, took the initiative. As a propagandist for good roads, one of the most notable was bicycle manufacturer Albert Augustus Pope. He saw clearly that little would be accomplished until road construction became a concern of the state government. Further, he recognized that highway construction called for technical competence, which men working out their taxes and part-time county supervisors simply did not have. By 1892, Pope's stream of publications secured enough momentum to nudge the Massachusetts legislature toward establishing a state highway commission, the first in the nation. The fortunate selection of Harvard geologist Nathaniel Shaler as one of the commission members reinforced the momentum of Pope's campaign. Shaler's book, *American Highways*, was virtually a textbook on sound construction. It stressed the importance of investing greater funds on initial construction in order to cut down on wasteful annual maintenance, an able appeal for waterbound macadam highways. Although Shaler thought in terms of highways for horse-drawn vehicles, he was broad-minded enough to advocate the use of steam-powered stone crushers and steam rollers, which had been perfected to construct urban streets.

The success of the Massachusetts Highway Commission soon inspired a number of eastern states to follow its example, but the rest of the nation was much slower to establish such commissions. The appearance of several textbooks on road construction beginning in 1892 had considerable impact, if the appearance of successive editions is to be taken as evidence of their influence. But the practice of the Massachusetts Commission in constructing short "demonstration" segments of highway brought the virtues of waterbound macadam to widely scattered communities. By this means, limited annual appropriations by the legislature reached the largest number of people. The concept of "demonstration" sections of highway was picked up by the president of the National Good Roads Association, who persuaded a railroad to provide an eleven-car train to transport a road show on highway construction from community to community. Flat cars laden with heavy equipment such as graders and steamrollers contributed by manufacturers were used to construct a half-mile of local road before audiences, frequently numbering in the thousands from the vicinity. Under the rubric that "seeing is believing," the demonstrations seemed to be more effective than endless reams of written instructions issued to local road builders by state commissions.

Throughout the 19th century and well into the first quarter of the 20th century, road building required a large volume of manpower—pick and shovel men. But horsepower did pick up much of the burden in three basic areas:

scraping, rolling, and hauling. Scrapers, whether in the form of the simple horse-hauled scoop or skip or any one of the many varying types of wheeled graders, relied upon horses. Although the damage done to a rolled surface by horses' hooves was an unavoidable drawback with the horse-drawn roller, still it was animal power, not manpower, that did the work. When it came to hauling, however, both horse and man shared the stress. Horses pulled the load to be sure, but when it came to loading and unloading a horse-drawn wagon, manpower did the job. Loading a wagon with shovels involved heavy lifting, and until the introduction of powered machinery, this burden could seldom be avoided. Unloading a wagon could be done by shoveling, but at least a hundred years of ingenuity went into the effort to find a satisfactory way to use gravity to unload a wagon.

Even the contractor's simplest wagon, the two-wheeled cart with a tilt body box, involved no little muscular effort to get it started. The heavier load of a four-wheel wagon posed an even greater challenge. For readers of the present generation, for whom engine power tilts a 10-ton load with ease, it may be difficult to appreciate the amount of effort, imagination, and ingenuity that went into trying to find an efficient solution to using gravity to unload a wagon. Every combination of doors and pivots had some serious drawback until the final solution appeared with the centerline dump-bottom wagon developed in the 1880s by the Watson Wagon Company and widely copied thereafter.

In the age of gasoline and diesel-powered engines, it is sometimes difficult to recall how important steam-powered machines were well into the first quarter of the 20th century. So too the continued importance of the horse in the same period should remind us of the significant role played by waterbound macadam highways, so nearly ideal for horse-drawn traffic. And it was Eli Whitney Blake's invention of the steam-powered stone crusher that made macadam highways economically feasible. But the crusher would not have found such prompt adoption were it not that the portable steam engine was already available as a source of power for threshing and woodcutting in a still largely agricultural society.

To be fully effective, a crusher had to be combined with an elevated bin for gravity loading of wagons, an elevator consisting of an endless chain of buckets to lift the crushed stone to the top of the elevated bin, and a cylindrical screening device to separate the crushed stone by size. Here again, the elevator was already available when the need arose because it had been perfected to lift coal into gravity bins for loading at railroad sites. So too the steam-powered stone drill, originally developed for use in constructing railroad tunnels, was already available when the need for stone to feed the crusher arose.

Next to the stone crusher, the most important steam-powered machine for road building was the steamroller. Originally a French invention, it was the British firm of Aveling and Porter that had the greatest influence on roller design in the United States, until native manufacturers began turning out near-copies. When equipped with scarifiers of one design or another, these massive machines could tear up a raveled macadam road cheaply to prepare it for re-rolling. Contractors soon discovered that road rollers could be used as powerful traction engines capable of extracting wagons seemingly hopelessly bogged down in deep mud.

When highway builders needed steam-powered shovels to do heavy excavations, a number of these tools were already well developed for use in constructing railroad lines. Starting with William Smith Otis's original patent shovel in 1837, their machines were designed to operate on rails. By the time contractors wanted steam shovels for highway construction, they had been vastly improved, capable of self-propelled travel, 360-degree rotation, and able to "crowd" or dig parallel to the surface of the ground. Although steam shovels represented a large capital outlay, they were an important time-saver where there were substantial grades to cut down in a short working season. But the faster loading capacity of a steam shovel would be negated unless adequate hauling capacity were made available to carry away the spoil. This could involve either more teams and wagons, a traction engine hauling a series of wagons, or a narrow gage industrial railway.

Because most highway contractors were small firms that had gained their experience paving city streets, it is not surprising that comprehensive accounts of who they were and how they went about the business are exceedingly scarce. To build several miles of highway is a far more complex undertaking than paving a few blocks of city streets. On any contracting job, estimating probable costs is the crucial factor in determining future profit or loss. Highway work added many new variables, even for the highly experienced firm with ample practice on urban streets. Not least of a contractor's problems was the need to borrow funds to rent needed equipment, buy materials such as cement and reinforcing steel in advance, and meet weekly payrolls. Only a contractor who had earned the confidence of both his banker and a bonding company could hope to borrow the necessary working capital.

One of the hardest lessons for contractors to learn was the vital importance of record-keeping to insure adequate cost accounting as a basis for estimating. Because highway construction often involved more extensive grading, cuts, and fills than one encountered on urban contracts, many road builders ran into difficulty in estimating grading costs. This difficulty was eased somewhat when state highway commissions began accepting bids based on unit costs rather than lump sum figures for an entire contract. Units such as square yards of slab laid down or cubic yards of soil excavated could be paid on the basis of work actually done rather than on estimates prepared in advance.

The great loophole in most highway contracts was the typical provision that work should be "satisfactory to the supervising engineer." This opened the door to endless disagreements unless the engineer was not only broadly experienced but an individual with a fine sense of equity and fair play. That many contractors and many supervising engineers employed by state highway commissions suffered from inexperience may well have explained why profit margins on highway contracts were so low. To encourage greater competition, some states introduced the Cost Plus Fixed Fee contract, which reimbursed a contractor for all his costs. This was a great improvement over the Cost Plus Percentage of Costs form of contract used during World War I which gave contractors a positive incentive to inflate their costs, thereby increasing their profit as a percentage of those costs. But even the CPFF contract was flawed: even though it limited profit to a fixed amount, it exercised little or no discipline over costs.

As the federal government began pouring millions into highway construction, the number of highway contractors increased rapidly. Trade associations such as Associated General Contractors and the American Road Builders Association provided forums for the exchange of useful ideas and increased professionalism. Unfortunately, many of the smaller and medium-sized contractors failed to join these organizations. And while conclusive evidence is lacking, what scanty indications are available strongly suggest that many if not most of the smaller contractors were not subscribing to the several engineering journals which offered a wealth of information on road building. On the other hand, state highway commission staffers and supervising engineers do seem to have been taking advantage of these most useful sources of the practitioner's art.

Before asphalt was used as a paving material for highways, it had the signal advantage of a long history of development as a material for paving urban streets. The asphalt initially imported from Europe or the Caribbean was a bituminous hydrocarbon mixed with clay or limestone and could be applied as a paving material with little manipulation. But the bitumens found at various sites in the United States differed greatly in their chemical composition. Municipalities whose engineers and contractors had little technical knowledge of asphalt experienced erratic results in their paving efforts until chemists working in laboratories developed a better understanding of the hydrocarbons that they employed.

The successful use of asphalt as a paving material hinged not only on the better understanding developed by chemists, but also on the appearance of large firms such as the A.L. Barber corporation, which early on mastered the art of laying high quality asphalt pavings. The Barber company enjoyed a near monopoly on asphalt paving when it built up a nation-wide organization with branch offices in major cities. The Barber company's grip on the asphalt business began to be undercut when a portable asphalt plant mounted on two railroad flatcars became available. Better trained engineers employed by municipal authorities, and the good work of the Office of Public Roads in providing standardized specifications perfected by the American Society for Testing Materials, served to improve the quality of workmanship turned out by local contractors competing with the Barber and other similar national organizations. The development of railroad tank cars made it possible to provide the relatively less expensive petroleum-based asphalt from California, Texas, and Mexico to paving contractors in the industrial East.

By 1912, the rapidly increasing number of automobiles in the United States had begun to make it clear that something had to be done to inhibit the damage autos were doing to the previously excellent waterbound macadam streets of the nation's towns and cities. Initial efforts at spraying bitumen on macadam roads, the "penetration method," proved unsatisfactory. But superior results could be obtained if macadam surfaces were scarified and the bitumen thoroughly mixed before being rolled and compressed, the "mixing method." Urban communities with an ample tax base could afford the more expensive mixing method for street paving, but when it came to applying asphalt to rural highways, the expense of the mixing methods seemed insupportable, so the trend was to revert to the penetration method for highway applications. For states like Massachusetts, which had macadamized 95% of its highways, using the less expensive penetration method made it possible to salvage a good part of the heavy investment already made in waterbound macadam highways, minimizing the damage being done by auto traffic while still providing a highway suitable for horse-drawn traffic.

The extreme difficulty tire companies had in developing pneumatic tires capable of supporting five and ten-ton trucks had a direct impact on the decay of asphalt topped macadam highways. When the volume of heavy truck traffic mounted sharply during World War I, it seriously stressed these asphalt topped highways in a way that might have been minimized, if not avoided, had pneumatic tires been commonly available. The 1916 federal legislation, which unleashed a flood of matching funds for state highway commissions, did not immediately solve the problem of financing stronger paved highways for truck traffic. Much of the money was doled out to counties for short sections of highway "to get the farmers out of the mud." Three-quarters of the federal money went to building waterbound macadam, sandclay, and gravel roads rather than to paving trunk lines. The agricultural lobby was still powerful, and well into the 1920s most of the federal money went for improvements other than paving by asphalt or concrete.

Although natural cements were manufactured in the United States early in the 19th century, variations in quality led contractors to rely largely upon imported British and German cements until the end of the century. Lack of reliable tests to determine the strength of concrete delayed its use somewhat. A greater deterrent was the prevailing uncertainty as to what constituted the optimum mix or proportions of cement, sand, and aggregate. Despite these obstacles, a few states experimented with limited stretches of concrete slab highways, but as long as the horse dominated highway traffic there continued to be a pervasive opposition to concrete paving, which was hard on hooves and gave precarious footing.

Until the first decade of the 20th century, a major factor inhibiting the use of concrete as a material for paving highways was the lack of an efficient machine for mixing. Soon self-propelled steam-powered mixers were widely available. Two major modifications made the mixers into a highly efficient machine: the power-operated skip for loading the mixer and the power driven discharge boom and bucket for spotting the mixture at any point up to 20-odd feet out in front of the machine.

Better understanding of proportioning, efficient mixers, the advent of federal funding, and the breakdown of penetration method asphalt pavements under the stress of wartime truck traffic all combined to launch a trend toward concrete highway construction at the war's end when the rapidly escalating number of automobiles was beginning to make concern for horse traffic less and less relevant in highway construction.

Wartime inflation in wage rates put a premium on the introduction of machines to cut labor costs. The timely appearance of the powered tamping and leveling machine, which rode on the steel forms at either side of the newly poured slab, was no less important than the powered mixer in this respect. With the two machines working in tandem and two- and three-minute mixing cycles, concrete road construction became a fast paced exercise, turning out hundreds of feet of paving in a day. The development of pneumatic tires for heavy trucks made it possible to feed the mixer skip with three to five carefully proportioned mixes partitioned off in the body of the truck to sustain the pace of two- or three-minute mixing cycles.

In short, highway construction by the 1920s had become a high-tempo industry increasingly mechanized with a wide range of labor saving devices. To be sure, the "revolution" didn't exactly end in the '20s. New and improved machines continued to appear, and greater knowledge of materials and how to work them led to ever greater efficiencies, but the revolution that got the nation's highways out of the mud had developed the momentum which would carry it for a generation. The elements of the revolution are evident: federal and state funds; federal and state organization; an impressive array of technological developments, the machines of the trade; knowledge of materials and methods, scientific and practical; educated engineers and contractors with the practical experience required to apply their learning; skilled laborers to operate the increasingly complex machinery; and taxpaying citizens sufficiently persuaded that the high cost of paved highways was fully justified by the economic advantages. These factors, taken together, added up to the highway revolution of 1895–1925.

What were the considerations that gave highway contracting as an industry its unique configuration? There were several. One such was the short operating season. This put a premium on small organizations; otherwise a contractor would have to pay talented and expensive employees during extended periods of winter idleness. Similarly, the capital costs of large quantities of machinery would continue in idle off-season months. Smaller firms with limited amounts of machinery could better find non-highway jobs, such as excavating cellar holes and laying sidewalks. A second factor was the ready availability of contractors with experience in building urban streets when the need for highway contractors first appeared. To be sure, constructing highways brought many challenges beyond those encountered in street work, but contractors who had developed effective teams of skilled workmen on city streets enjoyed a distinct advantage. And finally, the number of machines, such as the portable steam engine and the traction engine developed for the agricultural market, and the steam drill and steam shovel developed for railroad construction, neither of which were generally used in building city streets, were ready, waiting in the wings, when needed for rural highway contracts.

The importance of city street construction in advancing the development of highway machinery should not be overlooked. Contracts for city street construction, usually relatively short distances, served not only as a training ground that produced experienced contractors and skilled laborers, but also provided an incentive for the development of machinery, notably the equipment for asphalt paving. No less important, however, was the contribution of city street building to the perfection of heavy-duty wagons with provision for various types of dumping bodies, a major technological advance in its day, even if largely forgotten today.

The indebtedness of street and highway machinery to prior development in external industries was extensive. The speed with which manufacturers in the United States turned out clones of the Aveling and Porter steam roller derived from on the existing capability for production of the traction engines so popular with western farmers for threshing wheat. The portable link-belt loaders, so useful in cutting costs loading sand and gravel into wagons and trucks, were direct descendents of coal loading equipment developed years earlier. And coal loading was indebted to still earlier devices for lifting pond ice into storage buildings.

The role of components and ancillary items in road building equipment should not be overlooked. Early models of powered equipment such as steam-rollers and steam shovels employed bronze bearings. These tended to wear quickly under rough duty and breakdowns were frequent. Out on rural highway construction sites far from maintenance shops, such stoppages could be costly in idled labor. Prudent contractors provided on-site spare parts and mechanics to minimize delays. The development of roller bearings radically reduced such equipment breakdowns, significantly reducing down time and subsequent wasted pay for idled wage earners. A similar improvement in metallurgical knowledge during the period covered by this study assisted greatly in advancing the efficiency of road-building equipment. In dozens of ways improved metallurgy resulted in fewer breakdowns. Where broken axels and drive shafts were by no means uncommon in the early days of automotive trucks for heavy construction work, the advent of specialized steels for such applications virtually abolished this form of breakdown.

The statistics presented by the chief of the Bureau of Public Roads for fiscal year 1926 clearly spell out the highway revolution that had taken place in the U.S. since 1895. By the middle 1920s, the federal program had assisted the construction of more than 55,000 miles of highway. Of these, some 4,800 were asphalt and nearly 12,000 were concrete. What is more, the states found that putting up the funds required to match the federal contribution was no great burden, because gasoline taxes and license fees were already bringing in six times as much revenue as the federal subsidy.[1]

There were still many miles of unpaved highways in the United States in the middle 1920s, and it would take a generation before most of them were paved. But the revolution in highway construction had taken place. Funding procedures were established, state and federal organizations were well developed. Highly efficient heavy construction machinery was available and a substantial industry of suppliers was continuously developing ever-improved designs. In short, by the mid-'20s the infrastructure was in place and ready to provide the nation with the magnificent highway system it enjoys at the opening of the 21st century.[2]

The author's objective in writing this volume was to provide a short but comprehensive overview of the highway-building story. His intended thesis is to demonstrate the impressive complexity that characterizes the process involving so many inter-related factors: the fundamental problem of financing, reconciling the conflicting demands of horse and motor traffic, developing suitable machinery, mastering the difficulties of new and untried materials such as asphalt and concrete, perfecting suitable forms and procedures for contracting, as well as acquiring well-trained state and municipal engineers to supervise construction and insure quality. All of these were further complicated by the multiplicity of jurisdictions, federal, state and municipal, each reflecting the wide differences in resources, geography and attitudes in this far-flung nation.

NOTES

Chapter 1
To Get Out of the Mud: Who Pays?

1. Karl Raitz, ed., *The National Road* (Baltimore, 1996); Norris F. Schneider, *The National Road* (Columbus, Ohio 1975), 10–13.

2. Roger N. Parks, *Roads and Travel in New England: 1790–1840* (Sturbridge, Mass., 1967), passim.

3. 92 *Transactions of the American Society of Civil Engineers* (1928): 1193.

4. 92 *Engineering News Record* (17 April 1924): 685–86.

5. Clarkson H. Oglesby, *Highway Engineering* (New York, 1975), 6; for a description of U.S. highways during the first half of the 19th century by a British visitor, see Henry Howe, ed., *Memoirs of the Most Eminent American Mechanics* (New York, 1842), chapter titled, "Road Making," 367 ff.

6. 11 *Engineering News* (23 February 1884): 85; 14 *Engineering News* (14 November 1885) 314; "The Passing of the Road Boss," 47 *Municipal Engineering* (Aug. 1914): 155–56.

7. 17 *Engineering News* (9 April 1887): 237.

8. Austin T. Byrne, *A Treatise on Highway Construction* (New York, 1893), 11.

9. 21 *Engineering News* (18 May 1889): 449.

10. 23 *Engineering News* (8 February 1890): 122.

11. William C. Hilles, "The Good Roads Movement in the United States," Duke University MA thesis, 1958, for this and the two following paragraphs, pp. 24–35.

12. Albert Augustus Pope, *Road Making as a Branch of Instruction in Colleges* (Boston, 1892), and *The Movement for Better Roads* (Boston 1892); 27 *Engineering News* (27 February 1892): 210.

13. Hilles, *supra* note 11, 37–42.

14. Dennis S. Nordin, *Rich Harvest: History of the National Grange, 1887–1900* (Columbia, Mo. 1997), 235.

15. Hilles, *supra* note 11, 47.

16. 13 *The Forum* (March 1892): 115–19.

17. 75 *Scientific American* (26 December 1896): 455.

18. Bruce Seely, *Building the American Highway System* (Philadelphia, 1987), 11 ff.; U.S. Government Serial Set 3216, part 6, 1893, p. 76; *Statistical Abstract of the United States* (Washington, 1916), 278.

19. 52 Cong. 2 Sess. Serial Set 3216, part 6, 1893 p. 585 ff.

20. 55 Cong. 3 Sess. Serial Set 3651, part 6, 1897, p. 173 ff. For an extended discussion of steel roads, including trials in Europe, see Ray Stone's article in *The New York Times*,

1 Feb. 1903, p. 27; 74 *Scientific American* (30 May 1896): 347; 74 *Scientific American* (14 August 1897): 98; and 74 *Scientific American* (16 October 1897): 248.

21. 79 *Scientific American* (8 October 1898) 230; Hilles, *supra* note 11, 67.

22. 41 *Engineering Record* (26 May 1900): 489; for a similar criticism some years later see Ira O. Baker, *A Treatise on Roads and Pavements* (New York, 1905), 20, dismissing the Office of Road Inquiry statistics as "ridiculous."

23. Seely, *supra* note 18, 17–27.

24. Hilles, *supra* note 11, 170. For an account of a typical legislative proposal, see 34 *Cosmopolitan* (Jan. 1903): 355–56. For examples of opposition to federal financing of highways, see "Notes on a New Pork Barrel," 26 *World's Work* (May 1913): 27, and "Who Shall Pay for Highway Construction?" 23 *Municipal Engineering* (Feb. 1902): 96.

25. A.B. Hurlbert, *The Future of Roadmaking in America* (Cleveland, 1905), 15–16; John H. Bateman, *Highway Engineering* (New York, 1934), 7.

26. Hurlbert, *supra* note 25, 26, 50, 125.

27. 2 *Engineering Index* (1892–95): 356; 43 *Scientific American* (16 January 1895 Supplement): 17555.

28. Seely, *supra* note 18, 28; 35 *Engineering Record* (19 January 1907): 83.

29. Hilles, *supra* note 11, 92–96.

30. Seely, *supra* note 18, 67. By 1924, motorists had paid 30 million dollars in gasoline taxes at rates ranging from $.01 to $.03 a gallon, and more than half of this went to road construction, 68 *Good Roads* (July 1925): 165.

31. 39 *Statutes at Large* (Part 1): 355–59. For some of the problems encountered in securing passage of the measure, see Representative Browne's defense of his committee's report, *Congressional Record* 64 Cong. 1 Sess. (1916): 1269–83.

32. *Congressional Record* 64 Cong. 1 Sess. (1916): 1274.

33. For a summary account of the highway movement, 1916–1935, see F.L. Paxon, 51 *American Historical Review* (1946): 236–256.

Chapter 2
What Kind of Road? The Macadam Era 1816–1916

1. Curiously, while reference sources in the United States give extensive coverage to Tresaquet, similar French sources all but ignore him. See *Encyc Brit* 11:915 and 26:321; *World of Invention* (Detroit, 1994), 524; M.F. Alphandéry, *Dictionaire des Inventeurs Français* (Paris, 1962), 327 identifies him briefly.

2. Alexander Gibbs, *The Story of Telford* (London, 1935), 175–176; Lawrence Maynell, *Thomas Telford* (London 1957), 15. For a detailed account of why Telford's construction was so excessively expensive, see Henry Low, *Rudiments of the Art of Constructing Roads* (London 1850), 102.

3. John Loudon McAdam, *Remarks on the Present System of Road Making*, 4th ed. (Baltimore, 1821), 37, 50. Note that I cite the 4th edition, published in Baltimore. The original edition was published in England in 1816.

4. For insights on cementing values of broken stone, see A.S. Cushman, "Testing Cementing Values of Road Materials," 31 *Municipal Engineering* (Dec. 1906): 457–62; also 53 *Engineering Record* (23 June 1906): 760–62.

5. For a concise account of the National Pike, see H. Trombower, "Roads," in *Encyclopedia of Social Sciences* (New York, 1937) VII:406 and 31 *American Highways* (Jan. 1952):

36–37. For the agitation to build the missing link, see William Hollins, *Remarks on the Intercourse of Baltimore with the Western Country with a view of the communication proposed between the Atlantic and the Western States*, (Baltimore, 1818); Sherry H. Olson, *Baltimore: The building of an American City* (Baltimore, 1980) 47; Clayton H. Hall, *History of Baltimore* (New York, 1912) 462–63; Jared Sparks, "Baltimore," 20 *North American Review* (January 1825): 132; Department of Transportation, *America's Highways* (Washington, D.C. 1976), 36.

6. 31 *American Highways* (January 1952): 35–37.

7. *Encyclopedia Britannica* (Chicago, 2005), 26:321–22.

8. Mary H. Mitchell, *History of New Haven, Connecticut* (Boston, 1930), 637–38. James H. Macdonald, [Connecticut] *Highway Commissioner's Biennial Report, 1901–2* (Hartford, Connecticut, 1902), 244–47; the New Haven Colony Historical Society has a Blake crusher in its collection. Joseph W. Roe, *Connecticut Inventors*, Tercentenary Pamphlet #33 (New Haven, Connecticut, 1934), 22–23.

9. 8 *Transactions of American Society of Civil Engineers* (December 1879): 375.

10. 4 *Engineering News* (7 July 1877): 176–77; 34 *Scientific American* (29 April 1876): 275. Even in England, the adjustable Blake crusher was seen as "an improvement of great value," 30 *The Engineer* (London, 2 Sept. 1870): 149.

11. Charles F. Johnson, "The Good Roads Movement," 28 *Overland Monthly* (September 1896): 247; 54 *Engineering Record* (27 October 1906): 455.

12. 52 *Engineering Record* (14 October 1905) 441; American Highway Assn. *Good Roads Yearbook: 1914* (Washington, D.C. 1914), 67; 41 *Engineering Record* (10 February 1900): 122.

13. 53 *Engineering Record* (1906): 424; 40 *Engineering Record* (27 January 1900): 81; 99 *Scientific American* (24 October 1908): 274; Austin T. Byrne, *A Treatise on Highway Construction* (New York, 1893), 466.

14. 79 *Scientific American* (24 December 1898): 407; 50 *Engineering Record* (3 December 1904): 642.

15. The American Highway Association, *Good Roads Yearbook 1914*, (Baltimore, 1914), 113–15.

16. The American Highway Association, *Good Roads Yearbook 1917*, (Baltimore, 1917), 281; 54 *Engineering Record* (17 November 1906): 555.

17. The American Highway Association, *Good Roads Yearbook 1914*, (Baltimore, 1914), 110.

Chapter 3
Educating Rural Highway Builders: Getting out the Word on Construction Methods

1. *Dictionary of American Biography* (N.Y. 1935) 15:74–75. For Pope's many publications, see *The National Union Catalog: Pre-1956 Imprints* (London, 1968–1981) 465: 310–11.

2. Nathaniel Shaler, "Betterment of Our Highways," 70 *Atlantic Monthly* (Oct. 1892): 505–14. See also his article "The Common Roads" 6 *Scribner's Magazine* (Oct. 1889): 473–83.

3. Nathaniel Shaler, "The Move for Better Highways" 38 *Harper's Weekly* (6 Jan. 1894): 15.

4. Roy Stone, *Dept. of Agriculture Year Book 1894*, 501.

5. George A. Perkins, "State Highways in Massachusetts," 1894 *Yearbook*, 505–12.

6. Nathaniel Shaler, *American Highways* (New York, 1896), 188.

7. *Ibid.,* 190, 254.

8. *Ibid.,* 210, 151–2.

9. *Ibid.,* 198–99.

10. *Ibid.,* 200.

11. *Ibid.,* 200–207.

12. *Ibid.,* 229.

13. *Ibid.,* 250, and 23 *Engineering News* (8 Feb. 1890): 137.

14. Earl May, "A Good Road a Good Investment" 2 *World's Work* (Oct. 1901): 1285–89; Bruce Seely, *Building the American Highway System,* (Philadelphia, 1981), 29. The good beginning made by the Massachusetts Highway Commission is evident in the *Instructions to Engineers* published in 1899, copy in Smithsonian National Museum of American History, file "Roads."

15. Connecticut Highway Commissioner's Office, *Forty Years of Highway Development, 1895–1935,* Tercentenary Pamphlet #46 (New Haven, 1937), 6.

16. Austin T. Byrne, *A Treatise on Highway Construction* (New York, 1892). For Byrne's career, there is a skimpy obituary in *The New York Times,* (26 May 1934) 17:5.

17. Byrne, *supra* note 16, 326.

18. *Ibid.,* 522–23.

19. *Ibid.,* 548–49.

20. Ira O. Baker, *A Treatise on Roads and Pavements* (New York, 1903); *The National Union Catalog: Pre–1956 Imprints* (London, 1968–1981) 31:36.

21. Baker, *supra* note 20, 185.

22. *Ibid.,* 149, 178, 191.

23. *Ibid.,* iii, 7–10.

24. *Ibid.,* 146, 174–75, 248.

25. Arthur H. Blanchard and Henry B. Drowne, *Textbook of Highway Engineering* (New York, 1913). *The National Union Catalog Pre-1956 Imprints* (London, 1968–1981) 60:349–50.

26. U.S. Department of Commerce, *Historical Statistics of the United States* (Washington, D.C., 1975), 140 and 710.

27. Baker, *supra* note 20, 42.

28. 94 *The Engineer* (London, 24 Oct. 1902): 380; 52 *Engineering Record* (8 July 1905): 47.

29. 50 *Engineering Record* (19 Nov. 1904): 604; 54 *Engineering Record* (25 Aug. 1906): 205; 56 *Engineering Record* (19 Oct. 1907): 441.

30. The publications of ORI and OPR can be tracked in the *Government Printing Office Monthly Catalog,* 1893–1918.

31. *Government Printing Office Monthly Catalog,* 1910, 6.

32. U.S. Department of Transportation Federal Highway Administration, *America's Highways, 1776–1976* (GPO, Washington, D.C. 1977), 48–49; 2 *Worlds Work* (July 1901): 956–60.

33. *America's Highways, 1776–1976,* 76; 106 *Scientific American* (16 March 1912): 232; 17 *Technical World Magazine* (June 1912): 448.

Chapter 4
Horse-Drawn Road Machinery

1. For the two-wheel one-horse cart, see pictures in Chapter 2.

2. Austin T. Byrne, *Treatise on Highway Construction* (New York, 1892), 570–75; I.O. Baker, *A Treatise on Roads and Pavements* (New York, 1905), 96–101. For the development of wheeled scrapers see James L. Allhands, *Tools of the Earthmover* (Huntsville, Texas, 1951), 71–75, 88–90.

3. Oliver Evans, *The Abortion of the Young Steam Engineer's Guide* (Philadelphia, 1805), 78–79.

4. 93 *Engineering News Record* (10 July 1924): 80–82 for this and the previous four paragraphs. For illustrations of the adjustable axel and tilt wheels, see I.O. Baker, *supra* note 2, 108–109. See http://www.volvograders.com/history.html for additional history of the Pennock grader.

5. Baker, *supra* note 2, 105 and illustration on 108; James L. Allhands, *supra* note 2, 58–67, illustrates earlier attempts to perfect elevating graders, none as effective or widely used as the Edwards machine marketed by Austin. For an illustration of an early elevating grader, see Baker, 110.

6. Allhands, *supra* note 2, 87.

7. Arthur H. Blanchard, and Henry B. Drowne, *Textbook on Highway Engineering* (New York, 1913), 163–64; 40 *Engineering News* (29 Sept. 1890): 205–06.

8. 28 *Engineering News* (1 Sept. 1892): 212; 13 *Scientific American* (22 May 1858): 289 reports on an earlier effort to produce a dump body, but this does not appear to have been put into production. It involved two separate body boxes, each centered over an axel to be dumped as easily as a two-wheel cart.

9. 33 *Engineering News* (14 March 1895): 165. Illustration.

10. 47 *Engineering News* (8 May 1902): 376. Illustration.

11. 53 *Engineering News* (11 May 1905): 498. Illustration.

12. Blanchard, *supra* note 7, 163.

13. 8 *American City* (March 1913): 322; 9 *American City* (August 1913): 198; 17 *Municipal Engineering* (July, 1899): 47–48. See various advertisements for drop-bottom wagons, especially that of the Watson Wagon Company stressing quality of lumber used, 4 n.s. *Good Roads* (6 July 1912): 43. For a brief history of the Watson Wagon Company see http://www.conastotalibrary.org/watson.html.

14. 8 *American City* (March 1913): 347; 7 *American City* (July 1912): 91; 6 *American City* (May 1912): 768.

15. 9 *American City* (October, 1913): 368; 6 *American City* (June 1912): 908; 7 *American City* (September 1912): 278; 53 *Engineering News* (11 May 1905): 498.

16. 66 *Engineering News* (21 December 1911): 770.

17. 33 *Engineering News* (3 Jan. 1899): 16; 29 *Engineering News* (6 April 1893): 334.

18. 12 *American City* (June 1915): 543–44; 39 *Engineering News* (5 Feb. 1913): 150.

19. 30 *Engineering News* (30 Nov. 1893): 430; Baker, *supra* note 2, 250; 58 *Engineering Record* (31 Oct. 1908): 523–24.

20. 37 *Engineering News* (18 March 1897): 165.

21. 39 *Engineering News* (31 March 1898): 213; 66 *Engineering News* (17 August 1911): 199.

22. Byrne, *supra* note 2, 616; Blanchard and Drowne, *supra* note 7, 256. Of the textbook writers, only Baker, *supra* note 2, 23–25, 126–28, offers a fuller discussion of the tire width problem.

23. 56 *Engineering Record* (27 July 1907): 85.

24. Baker, *supra* note 2, 223.

25. 39 *Engineering News* (3 March 1898): 142.

26. 43 *Engineering and Contracting* (27 Jan. 1915): 67; 6 *Public Roads* (April 1925): 25 and (May 1925): 45.

27. Donald T. Critchlow, *Studebaker* (Bloomington, Indiana, 1996), 45.

Chapter 5
Steam-Powered Machinery for Highway Building

1. *Connecticut Highway Commissioner's Biennial Report, 1901–1902*, 244–47. The New Haven Colonial Historical Society has a Blake crusher on display with its flywheel missing. For further details see 44 *Chronicle of Early American Industries* (Sept. 1991). Blake's 1858 patent was extended in 1865 for 7 years. At the time of the extension, Blake had sold 509 crushers. (Letter, Bacon, Greene and Milroy Co. of Hamden, Conn. 11 Feb. 1985, to Norman Wickstrand of Salisbury, Conn.) This firm manufactures the Farrel-Bacon crushers.

2. 25 *Engineering Record* (7 May 1892): 388; 29 *Engineering News* (9 March 1893): 220; 39 *Engineering Record* (10 Feb. 1898): 100–101. 6 *Paving and Municipal Engineering* (June 1894): 286 illustrates a portable horse-drawn stone crusher.

3. Association of Engineering Societies, *Descriptive Index to Engineering Periodicals: 1883–1887* (New York, 1893).

4. Austin T. Byrne, *Textbook on Highway Construction* (New York, 1893) advertising section pages 2, 4, 5, 12, and text pages 595–97; 30 *Engineering Record* (30 Nov. 1893): 436.

5. 38 *Engineering and Contracting* (11 Sept. 1912): 656; 39 *Engineering and Contracting* (15 Jan. 1913): 60.

6. Reynold M. Wik, *Steam Power on the American Farm* (Philadelphia, 1953), 18–24; Paul C. Johnson, *Farm Power in the Making of America* (Des Moines, Iowa, 1978) 48–50; Robert H. Thurston, *A History of the Growth of the Steam Engine* (Ithaca, New York, 1935), 353–354.

7. 1 *Public Roads* (May 1908): 35; Byrne, *supra* note 4, 4.

8. Jacques Besson, *Theatrum Instrumentorum et Mechanism* (Vincenti, 1585) figure 39, available in the Kress Goldsmith microfilm collection, N43 88, reel 20. The concept of the bucket elevator and cylindrical screen was previously developed in England. See *The Engineer* (London, 12 April 1872): 255 for illustration of the Dunston Engineering Co. version.

9. W.P. Blake, "Mining and Storing Ice," 86 *Journal of the Franklin Institute* (Nov. 1883): 355–69. Note especially woodcut of endless chain elevator p. 365; Frederick V. Hetzel and Russell K. Allbright, *Belt Conveyors and Belt Elevators* (New York, 1941), 6–7, 339; Richard O. Cummings, *The American Ice Harvest* (Berkeley, California, 1949), 42; Emil Pollak and Martyl Pollak, eds., *Selections from the Chronicle: The Fascinating World of Early Tools and Trades* (Needham, N.J. 1991), 77; Nathaniel J. Wyeth, "Ice Trade" in U.S. Commissioner of Patents, *Annual Report* (1848), 702; House Doc. 59, 30 Cong. 2 Sess.; Link Belt Engineering Company, *Modern Methods Applied to Elevating and Conveying* (Philadel-

phia, Pennsylvania, 1902) 9–17, 118. For a history of the Link Belt Company, see Josiah Seymour Currey, *Manufacturing and Wholesale Industries of Chicago* (Chicago, 1918), 2:25–29.

10. 1 *Public Roads* (May 1908): 35–39.

11. 78 *Engineering News* (3 May 1917): 260; 1 *Public Roads* (May 1908): 42.

12. Byrne, *supra* note 4, 174; Charles E. Singer, *et al.*, eds., *A History of Technology* (London, 1954), IV:538.

13. 47 *Engineering News* (27 March 1902): 258; Byrne, *supra* note 4, 174.

14. See illustration, Chapter 2.

15. 56 *Journal of the Franklin Institute* (1868): 3, 6; William Clark Hilles, "The Good Roads Movement in the United States," M.A. thesis, Duke University, 84; Byrne, *supra* note 4, 325.

16. 92 *Engineering News Record* (24 April 1924): 746; J.A. Allhands, *Tools of the Earthmover* (Huntsville, Texas, 1951), 317–24; 42 *Municipal Engineering* (Jan. 1912): 63.

17. 70 *Scientific American* (5 May 1894): 282.

18. Charles E. Singer et al., *supra* note 12, IV:537–38; 26 *The Engineer* (London, 17 Aug. 1866): 124; for the background on road rolling, see H.J. Collins and C.A. Hart, *Principles of Road Engineering* (London 1936), 33; 26 *The Engineer* (London, 13 Aug. 1866): 124 and 26 (London, 28 Dec. 1866): 515; see E. Purnell Hooley, "Origin and Use of Steam Road Rollers," 11 *Municipal Engineering* (August 1896): 75–82.

19. 28 *The Engineer* (London, 6 Dec. 1869): 476 and (17 Dec. 1869): 396. For an extended account of an early evaluation of the steam roller in the United States, see Prof. R.H. Thurston of Stevens Institute, "Traction Engines and Steam Rollers" in 95 *Journal of the Franklin Institute* (June 1873): 17–42.

20. 29 *The Engineer* (London, 8 April 1870): 217; 32 *The Engineer* (London, 8 June 1871): 313–14.

21. 22 *Engineering News* (7 Sept. 1889): 221.

22. 8 *Transactions of the American Society of Civil Engineers* (May 1879): 139 ff., Appendix III; 6 *Engineering News* (9 Aug. 1879): 251.

23. 30 *Engineering News* (30 Nov. 1893): 430.

24. 37 *Engineering and Contracting* (27 March 1912): 346. For a comprehensive survey of U.S. road rollers, see Raymond L. Drake and Robert T. Rhode, *Classic American Steamrollers: 1871 through 1935 Photo Archive* (Hudson, Wisconsin, 2001).

25. *Ibid.* Scarifying machines date back at least to the 18th century. See Gabriel Martin, *Machines et Inventions Appreuvées par l'Academie Royale des Sciences* (Paris, 1735), V, facing p. 37, reproduced in J.L. Allhands, *Tools of the Earthmover* (Huntsville, Texas, 1951), 24.

26. 37 *Engineering and Contracting* (10 January 1912): 36; 88 *Engineering News Record* (1 June 1922): 931; Arthur H. Blanchard and Henry B. Drowne, *Textbook of Highway Engineering* 250, 256–57, illustrates the earlier dragged scarifiers; see also 27 *Municipal Engineering* (August 1904): 142.

27. 74 *Engineering News* (16 Dec. 1915): 1199. *Scientific American* (28 Oct. 1916): 394.

28. 41 *Engineering and Contracting* (11 Feb. 1914): 180 ff.

29. 40 *Engineering and Contracting* (22 Oct. 1913): 455; 80 *Engineering News Record* (21 Feb. 1918): 377–378; 41 *Municipal Engineering* (Oct. 1911): 326; 50 *Municipal Engineering* (June 1916): 250 mentions Austin's large export sales.

30. Harold F. Williamson and Kenneth H. Myers, II, *Designed for Digging: The First 75 Years of the Bucyrus-Erie Company* (Evanston, Illinois, 1955), 23; Allhands, *supra* note 25,

95–96, illustrates Osgood's Land Excavator, a shovel powered by two horses on a tread-
mill. It was patented in 1852 just after the first steam shovel appeared, so it was manifestly
doomed from the start.

31. J.H. White, Jr., *A Short History of American Locomotive Builders in the Steam Era*
(Washington, D.C., 1982), 93–94; Williamsen and Myers, *supra* note 30, 23–24; 29 *Engineering News* (27 April 1883): 387, 409; 5 *Journal of the Franklin Institute* (1843) n.s.:
319–25 with annotated Otis shovel illustration explaining the functions of the parts. See
also Samuel Stueland, "The Otis Steam Excavator," 35 *Technology and Culture* (July 1994):
571–73. Stueland's contention that the Otis shovel could swivel or traverse only by means
of men pulling on ropes to either side may have been true of a very early model in development, but the fully developed Otis definitely traversed by steam power as the
Franklin Institute article clearly reveals. See also 23 *Cassier's Magazine* (Jan. 1903):
483–485.

32. 6 *Journal of the Franklin Institute* (1843): 175–177.

33. Williamson and Myers, *supra* note 30, 25–34.

34. 92 *Engineering News Record* (1 May 1924): 285–286. For a brief history of the Marion Company, see http://www.roundtripamerica.com/places/marion.htm.

35. Williamson and Myers, *supra* note 30, 75–76; 92 *Engineering News Record* (5 June
1924): 995; for a picture of the original Thew shovel, see Allhands, *supra* note 25, 197.

36. Ira O. Baker, *A Treatise on Roads and Pavements* (New York, 1903), 97.

37. 39 *Engineering and Contracting* (23 April 1913): 465; 80 *Engineering News Record*
(17 Jan. 1918): 136.

38. 57 *Engineering Record* (25 Jan. 1908): 84.

39. 43 *Engineering and Contracting* (7 April 1915): 327; 73 *Engineering News* (18 March
1915): 540–541; 74 *Engineering News* (16 Dec. 1915): 1184.

40. 74 *Engineering News* (21 Oct. 1915): 798; 60 *Municipal and County Engineering*
(Feb. 1921): 26 and 63 *Municipal and County Engineering* (April 1922): 15.

41. 90 *Engineering News Record* (4 Jan. 1923): 38–39; 73 *Engineering News* (21 Jan.
1915): 128; 62 *Municipal and County Engineering* (May 1922): 33 and (Jan. 1922): 15.

42. Orenstein-Arthur Koppel Catalog 910, 1914 p. 4; 55 *Engineering Record* (4 May
1907): 553. I am indebted to the Division of the History of Technology of the Smithsonian's National Museum of American History for copies of the Koppel catalogs. For a
view of industrial railways in the United States at large, see 65 *Engineering News* (20 April
1911): 493.

43. Koppel catalog 910, p. 5. See p. 20 for picture of V-dump car with friction brake
and p. 23 for Koppel engine. For transporting a 10-ton engine by trailer, see 55 *Municipal
and County Engineering* (Sept. 1918): 117.

44. 41 *Engineering and Contracting* (4 March 1914): 288; 43 *Engineering and Contracting* (7 April 1915): 306.

45. 10 *American City* (June 1914): 607; for other examples of moving industrial railroad engines by road, see 47 *Municipal Engineering* (Sept. 1914): 249 and 55 *Municipal and
County Engineering* (Sept. 1918): 117.

46. 45 *Engineering and Contracting* (23 Feb. 1916): 185; 43 *Engineering and Contracting* (7 April 1915): 326; 93 *Engineering News Record* (2 Oct. 1924): 565. A useful survey of
road-building machinery, 1915–1925, can be found in O.E. Kipp, "Evolution of Highway
Construction and Maintenance Equipment," 68 *Municipal and County Engineering* (Feb.
1925): 55–58.

Chapter 6
The Contractor

1. 92 *Engineering News Record* (17 April 1924): 664–66; for problems relating to surety bonding, see S.M. Williams, "Irresponsible Contractors Should be Eliminated," 69 *Municipal and County Engineering* (Nov. 1925): 232–34; R.L. Warren, "The Irresponsible Bidder," 69 *Municipal and County* Engineering (Oct. 1925 169–78; 67 *Engineering News* (15 Feb. 1912): 325–26 reviews one of the first books written on highway contracting; 92 *Engineering News Record* (10 Jan. 1924): 68–70 discusses bonding.

2. 59 *Engineering Record* (3 April 1909): 367. For problems of estimating, see T.I. Wasser, "Highway Contracting and Its Illusions," 66 *Municipal and County Engineering* (Feb. 1924): 63 and S.J. Clausen, "Taking Some of the Guess Out of Bidding," 68 *Municipal and County Engineering* (April 1925): 163–66 and 20 *Concrete* (June 1925): 189–91.

3. 39 *Engineering and Contracting* (11 June 1913): 649; 73 *Engineering News* (6 May 1915): 888.

4. 42 *Engineering and Contracting* (18 Nov. 1914): 471. For problems with depreciation, see R.E. Brooks, "Care and Maintenance of Contractor's Equipment," 66 *Municipal and County Engineering* (May 1924): 248; and 56 *Municipal and County Engineering* (June 1919): 213–14; 5 *Good Roads* (3 May 1913): 255–56; W.R. Smith, "Dominant Factors in Contracting," 14 *Highway Engineer and Contractor* (May 1926): 57–58.

5. 43 *Engineering and Contracting* (3 March 1915): 187; 92 *Engineering News Record* (28 Feb. 1924): 347–48.

6. 43 *Engineering and Contracting* (3 March 1915): 187; see also 90 *Engineering News Record* (19 April 1923): 725 and (7 June 1923): 998–99, which notes that state highway commissions were reluctant to pay for test borings prior to awarding contracts, leaving contractors in the dark as to the soil of an excavation, sand, hardpan, or ledge rock. On the need for contract clauses to minimize risks beyond a contractor's control such as weather, freight rates, etc., see 57 *Municipal and County Engineering* (Nov. 1919): 206; 84 *Engineering News Record* (4 March 1920): 457–58.

7. 40 *Engineering and Contracting* (6 Aug. 1913): 142.

8. 51 *Engineering Record* (1 April 1905): 366 and 505; 54 *Engineering Record* (19 Jan. 1907): 58; 46 *Engineering and* Contracting (22 Nov. 1916): 431; 2 n.s. *Good Roads* (2 Dec. 1911): 308–13; 68 *Good Roads* (May 1925): 129–30; "Defaulted Highway Contracts" 11 *Highway Engineer and Contractor* (Dec. 1924): 37; 13 *Highway Engineer and Contractor* (July 1925): 47. For a contractor's view of the difficulties encountered in contracting with a state government, see General C.R. Marshall Jr. of the Associated General Contractors of America, remarks, 14 *Highway Engineer and Contractor* (Feb. 1926): 55 ff.

9. 69 *Engineering News* (9 Jan. 1913): 80–82; 45 *Engineering and Contracting* (3 May 1916): 399; New York *Sun* (2 Jan. 1913): 5:3; *The New York Times* (15 Jan. 1913): 2:2; 10 March 1913): 1:6; (11 March 1913): 6:3; 91 *Engineering News Record* (15 Nov. 1921): 793–94; 85 *Engineering News Record* (2 Feb. 1922): 203; 42 *Municipal Engineering* (May 1912): 369–73; Henry B. Drowne, *Suggestions for Asphalt Paving Contractors* (Asphalt Assn., New York, brochure #13 n.d. [1926?]; "Making the Contracting Business Pay," 69 *Good Roads* (Feb. 1926): 59–61; 9 n.s. *Good Roads* (1 May 1915): 170; for a disillusioned contractor's view of the unlevel field in state contracts, "a short contract means a long lawsuit," see 16 *American City* (June 1917): 608; 40 *Engineering and Contracting* (15 Oct. 1913): 423; 9 n.s. *Good Roads* (1 May 1915): 170.

10. 95 *Engineering and Contracting* (17 Sept. 1925): 456. For an example of an attempt to cushion the losing bidders against total loss of the cost of preparing bids, see 73 *Engineering News* (6 May 1915): 901; 84 *Engineering News Record* (15 Jan. 1920): 122–23. For a survey of 700 contracts which led to 35 failures involving 21 contractors, see 68 *Municipal and County Engineering* (Jan. 1925): 3–7. For a discussion of often overlooked items in estimating, see 91 *Engineering News Record* (6 Sept. 1923): 391–93.

11. 75 *Engineering News* (23 March 1916): 567.

12. 75 *Engineering News* (6 April 1916): 644–645; 24 *American City* (March 1921): 233.

13. 91 *Engineering News Record* (13 Dec. 1923): 997. For contractor and supervising engineer relations, see Alfred Williams, "Conscience in Municipal Engineering," 47 *Municipal Engineering* (July 1914): 47–49; H.B. Bushnell, "Business Relations Between Contractor and Engineer," 49 *Municipal and County Engineering* (Aug. 1915): 73–74; W.C. Fraser, "The Municipal Contractor and Frequent Inconsistencies Met within Specifications," 58 *Municipal and County Engineering* (March 1920): 120–123.

14. 43 *Engineering and Contracting* (5 March 1915): 187; Halbert Powers Gillette, *Economics of Road Construction* (New York, 1901, 1906, 1908). See also his *Construction Cost Keeping and Management* (Chicago, 1909, 1916, 1922, 1927) and *Handbook of Cost Data* (Chicago, 1905, 1910, 1920, 1923, 1927). Gillette was the managing editor of the journal *Engineering and Contracting*.

15. Halbert Powers Gillette, *Construction Cost Keeping and Management* (Chicago, 1927), Chapter V. For problems in establishing "the lowest responsible bidder," see 91 *Engineering News Record* (15 Nov. 1921): 793–94 and 13 *Highway Engineer and Contractor* (Dec. 1924): 41–42.

16. Gillette, *supra* note 15, 121–25.

17. For excellent insights on the problems of estimating, see "Overlooked Items in Estimating Road Work," 91 *Engineering News Record* (6 Sept. 1923): 391–93 as well as 90 *Engineering News Record* (31 May 1923): 948–51. Especially helpful is Halbert Powers Gillette, *Earthwork and its Costs* (New York, 1912): 1–3, 7, a revision of the original 1903 edition.

18. 85 *Engineering News Record* (30 Dec. 1920): 1288–89; 93 *Engineering News Record* (7 Aug. 1924): 841; Burner, David, *Herbert Hoover: A Public Life* (New York, 1979), 160–73.

19. 91 *Engineering News Record* (6 Sept. 1923): 391–93; factors contributing to the difficulty of estimating for contingencies are extensively treated in 89 *Engineering News Record* (5 Oct. 1922): 548–51.

20. 23 *Cassier's Magazine* (Jan. 1903): 483–85.

21. 92 *Engineering News Record* (17 April 1924): 664–66. For an illustrative example of an Italian immigrant who became a successful contractor, see http://www.thetomassogroup.com/ttq/index.php?page=history.

22. For a brief sketch of Mr. Joseph Mascetti (1897–1925), see Raymond W. Mascetti (a nephew employed in the Connecticut State Highway Department), *A Pioneer in Connecticut Road Construction* (Torrington, Conn. 1994), 1–13.

23. Partnership agreement, 8 Nov. 1910, signed by Joseph Mascetti and Irving B. Holley, Torrington, Conn. Copy in Holley family manuscripts deposited in the Connecticut Historical Society archives, Hartford, Conn. Another copy is in the Torrington Historical Society archives.

24. "A New England Family: The Holleys of Connecticut," by I.B. Holley Jr., vol. I, chapter 15, "Mascetti and Holley; Road Builders, 1910–1925," copy in Torrington Historical Society.

25. Scovell, Wellington & Co., CPAs and Industrial Engineers, "Mascetti and Holley: Development of Burden Charges and Changes in Accounting Methods," 3 Dec. 1920. Copy in Torrington (Connecticut) Historical Society, M & H file; "The Holleys of Connecticut," vol. I, chapter 15.

26. *Ibid.*

27. Mascetti and Holley analysis for 1923, file in Torrington Historical Society, Torrington, Connecticut.

28. *Ibid.*

29. American Highway Assn., *Good Roads Yearbook: 1917* (Washington, D.C., 1917), 506. All of the four firms listed as bidders on road contracts, with the exception of the author's father, have Italian names, DiMichiel, Longi, Russi, and Mascetti, and three of the four worked at one time or another with the M & H partners.

30. Mascetti, *supra* note 22, 7–8.

31. Mascetti and Holley analysis for 1923.

32. Testimonial by State Highway Commissioner C.I. Bennett, 14 March 1923, is reproduced in Mascetti, *supra* note 22, along with obituary notices for Joseph Mascetti, *Torrington Register*, 18 March 1925.

33. For an extended account of contracting practices in the middle of the period covered by this book, see the series of articles by DeWitt V. Moore, "Contracting Practice," in 40 *Municipal Engineering* (May 1911): 393–395 and continuing each month thereafter until March 1912.

Chapter 7
The Long Road from Asphalt Streets to Asphalt Highways

1. William Fortune, "Street Paving in America," 46 *Century Magazine* (Oct. 1893): 878–903; Chelsea Frazer, *The Story of Engineering in America* (New York, 1928), 46; 1 *Paving and Municipal Engineering* (June, 1890): 3–4.

2. Edward Stabler Jr., "Vitrified Brick, the Roadway of the Future," 2 *Paving and Municipal Engineering* (Jan. 1892): 177; 41 *Engineering Record* (3 March 1900): 196–200.

3. 79 *Scientific American* (24 Dec. 1898): 407; 13 *Municipal Engineering* (Dec. 1898): 368.

4. W.A. Park, "A Brief History of Asphalt," 1 *American Asphalt Journal* (Aug. 1901): 10; 2 *American Asphalt Journal* (Feb. 1902): 5–6; Asphalt Assn., *Asphalt, A World Old Material*, brochure #2, n.d. [1916?]; "The Early History of Bituminous Materials," 72 *Engineering News* (30 July 1914): 236–37.

5. *The New York Times* (9 Oct. 1869): 4:7 and (14 Oct. 1869): 2:5; 19 *Engineering News* (21 Jan. 1888): 39; E.J. de Smedt, "The Origin of American Asphalt Pavements," 5 *Paving and Municipal Engineering* (Dec. 1893): 251; 8 *Paving and Municipal Engineering* (April, 1895): 199–200; G.W. Tillson, "Asphalt and Bituminous Pavements," 78 *Transactions of the American Society of Civil Engineers* (Dec. 1897): 822–25.

6. "Asphalts: Sources of Supply and Methods of Preparation," 37 *Engineering and Contracting* (12 June 1912): 661; 60 *Municipal and County Engineering* (Jan. 1921): 16–21. For the Barber company, see "The Men Who Manage the Barber Asphalt Company," 10 *Paving and Municipal Engineering* (May 1896): 331–45.

7. For California deposits, see 19 *The Engineer* (London, 13 Jan. 1865): 25; for Kentucky, see 20 *Engineering News* (11 Aug. 1888): 99; for Utah, see 29 *Engineering News* (6 June 1893): 540; for Pennsylvania, see 58 *Engineering Record* (31 Oct. 1900): 490–92.

8. Austin T. Byrne, *Treatise on Highway Construction* (New York, 1893): 43. For Barber's struggle to control the Bermudez deposits, see Brian S. McBeth, *Gunboats, Corruption and Claims: Foreign Intervention in Venezuela, 1899–1908* (Westport, Conn., 1908).

9. 52 *Engineering Record* (9 Sept. 1905): 285 and (30 Sept. 1905): 383–385. For testimonials, see 14 *Municipal Engineering* (May 1898): 297–298.

10. A.W. Doe, "Failures in Asphalt Pavements and their Causes," 18 *Municipal Engineering* (Jan. 1900): 18–29; 8 *American City* (June, 1913): 636.

11. George W. Tillson, "One Year's Work with a Chemical Laboratory for Testing Asphalts," 13 *Municipal Engineering* (Nov. 1897): 271–74; 14 *Municipal Engineering* (May, 1898): 350.

12. Secretary of Agriculture, *Annual Report* (GPO, Washington, D.C.) for 1893 and following years, especially 1901, p. 243 describing laboratory beginnings; Bruce E. Seely, *Building the American Highway System* (Philadelphia, 1987), 27.

13. For the trust story, see *Municipal Engineering* for the years 1901–1911, especially volume 28 (Feb. 1909): 99–101, which has a chronological summary. An authoritative account can be found in Joseph Rock Draney, "Asphalt Origins, History, Development, and its Relation to Petroleum," 35 *Americana* (April, 1939): 196–221; and Brian S. McBeth, *Gunboats, Corruption and Claims: Foreign Intervention in Venezuela, 1899–1908* (Westport, Conn., 2000), 43–44. For a typical protest against the trust's high prices, see "Asphalt Robbery," 1 *American Asphalt Journal* (April 1903): 6.

14. 30 *Municipal Engineering* (Jan. 1906): 60.

15. 52 *Engineering Record* (8 July 1905): 47; Logan W. Page, Director, ORI, to A.B. Fletcher. Massachusetts Highway Commission, 16 Nov. 1903, Bureau of Public Roads, letters sent by Division of Testing, National Records Center, Record Group 30, box 2.

16. 23 *Municipal Engineering* (Feb. 1903): 115–17.

17. F.J. Warren, "The Development of Bituminous Pavement…" 27 *Municipal Engineering* (Sept. 1901): 164–68; G.C. Warren, "History of Warrenite—Bitulithic Roads and Pavements…" 58 *Municipal and County Engineering* (June 1920): 242–44; For the resulting stability, see Provost Hubbard, "The Selection and Proportioning of Sands for Sheet Asphalt Paving Mixtures," Asphalt Association Circular No. 15 (New York n.d. 1922?). For Warren Brothers national organization, see 19 district offices advertised in 10 *Highway Engineer and Contractor* (Feb. 1924): 87.

18. C.A. Talley, "Suggestions for Handling Asphalt Shipments in Tank Cars," 67 *Good Roads* (Nov. 1924): 143–45; P.S. Sharples, "Methods of Unloading Tank Cars," 47 *Municipal Engineering* (Oct. 1914): 256–59; I.W. Patterson, "Rhode Island State Highway Department Adopts a New Method of Handling Bitumens," 59 *Municipal and County Engineering* (July 1920): 6. For the rise of California asphalt, see 38 *Municipal Engineering* (June 1910): 423.

19. 38 *Municipal Engineering* (March 1910): 215; 10 n.s. *Good Roads* (3 July 1915): 58–59; 48 *Municipal Engineering* (Jan. 1915): 68.

20. "Oil and Tar Distributors," 40 *Good Roads* (May 1911): 189–92; T.M. Roache, "Asphalt Macadam Roadways," 12 *Good Roads* (March 1911): 112–13; R. Hopkins "Use of Labor-Saving Devices in Highway Construction," 58 *Municipal and County Engineering* (March 1920): 118–20; W.E. Worcester, "Asphalt Distributors and the Maintenance of Bituminous Roads," 69 *Good Roads* (Jan. 1926): 25.

21. 41 *Municipal Engineering* (Aug. 1911): 211; 42 *Municipal Engineering* (March 1912): 203.

22. See Chapter 3, above.

23. 66 *Scientific American* (8 Aug. 1908 Supplement): 92–94; for auto statistics see Clay McShane, "Urban Pathways," chapter 4 in Joel Tarr, *Technology and the Rise of the Networked City in Europe and America* (Philadelphia, 1988), 68; 63 *Engineering News*(24 Feb. 1910): 233–34.

24. Robert West Howard, *The Horse in America* (Chicago, 1965), 215.

25. 54 *Engineering Record* (10 March 1906): 515; 53 *Engineering Record* (27 Jan. 1906): 104; 56 *Engineering Record* (14 Dec. 1907): 659.

26. 59 *Engineering Record* (15 May 1909): 619; 57 *Engineering Record* (20 June 1908): 767.

27. L.W. Page, "Good Roads and How to Build Them," 106 *Scientific American* (16 March 1912): 236–38; W.G. Harper, "Road Building in New York State," 65 *Engineering News* (2 Feb. 1911): 128–29.

28. "Oiled macadam roads in California not an unchallenged success," 71 *Engineering News* (14 May 1914): 1069; editorial, "One Way to Curb Bad Roads," 70 *Engineering News* (23 Sept. 1913): 617; 73 *Engineering News* (18 Feb. 1915): 357; 73 *Engineering News* (28 Jan. 1915): 189; 68 *Engineering News* (10 Oct. 1912): 683; U.S. Dept. of Transportation, Federal Highway Administration, *America's Highways: 1776–1976* (Washington, D.C., GPO, 1976), 37; 106 *Scientific American* (16 March 1912): 234.

29. The editors of 38 *Engineering and Contracting* (25 Sept. 1912): 337 deplored the opposition of *Engineering News* and *Engineering Record* to national indebtedness for highway building; 71 *Engineering News* (29 Jan. 1914): 263–64; 71 *Engineering News* (5 March 1914): 529.

30. 68 *EngineeringNews* (12 Dec. 1912): 1113; 64 *Engineering News* (22 Dec. 1910): 685.

31. 72 *Engineering News* (26 Nov. 1914): 1058–61.

32. 70 *Engineering News* (14 Aug. 1913): 293; S.E. Fitch, Highway Supt., Chautauqua County, N.Y. "Experience with Bitumen Macadam Highways in New York," Asphalt Assn. Circular #38 (1926), 9–10.

33. A.W. Dean, "State Highways in Massachusetts," 68 *Engineering News* (15 Aug. 1912): 282–84.

34. This and the following two paragraphs are based on T.M. Ripley, "Lessons in Road Maintenance for New York State," 75 *Engineering News* (11 May 1916): 886–89. See also editorial comment at page 907.

Chapter 8
Gasoline Power and Highways, 1908–1918

1. 108 *Scientific American* (18 Jan. 1913): 61, 66; 40 *Engineering and Contracting* (16 July 1913): 57.

2. 108 *Scientific American* (28 June 1913): 574.

3. 73 *Engineering News* (28 Jan. 1915): 174. See also 75 *Engineering News* (23 March 1916): 567, and 115 *Scientific American* (16 Dec. 1916): 554.

4. Automobile Manufacturers Association, *Automobile Facts and Figures* (New York, 1938), 4; John Rae, *The American Automobile* (Chicago, 1965), 32; James L. Allhands, *Tools of the Earthmover* (Huntsville, Texas, 1951), 263–69.

5. James A. Wren, et al., *Motor Trucks of America* (Ann Arbor, Mich. 1979), 30–31; H.L. Barber, *Story of the Automobile* (Chicago, 1917), 231 ff.; Allhands, *supra* note 4, 275.

6. Wren, *supra* note 5, 34, 58, 60; Robert F. Karolevitz, *This Was Trucking* (Seattle, Wash., 1966), 43; Floyd Clymer, *Those Wonderful Old Automobiles* (New York, 1993), 165.

7. 2 *American City* (July 1910): 49; 54 *Engineering Record* (15 Dec. 1906): 673.

8. 58 *Engineering Record* (26 Sept. 1908): 338 and (26 Dec. 1908): 731–32.

9. 106 *Scientific American* (16 March 1912): 236–238.

10. 109 *Scientific American* (6 Sept. 1913): 178.

11. 58 *Engineering Record* (24 Oct. 1908): 451; 54 *Engineering Record* (1 Sept. 1906): 252.

12. 107 *The Engineer* (London, 10 April 1909): 456; 117 *The Engineer* (London, 9 July 1914): 55.

13. Rae, *supra* note 4, 51; Wren, *supra* note 5, 33.

14. For a description of solid and cushion tires, see 7 *Public Roads* (June 1926): 69–82; Allhands, *supra* note 4, 275; for problems with solid rubber tires, see 45 *Engineering and Contracting* (19 April 1916): 366; for role of Goodyear in developing pneumatics for trucks, see 16 *American City* (April 1917): 426, 433.

15. 54 *Engineering Record* (22 Sept. 1906): 309; 45 *Engineering and Contracting* (19 April 1916): 362.

16. Rae, *supra* note 4, 70, 97, 123, 129.

17. Wren, *supra* note 5, 73; *Automobile Facts and Figures*, *supra* note 4, 4.

18. 79 *Engineering News Record* (19 July 1917): 98.

19. 79 *Engineering News Record* (29 Nov. 1917): 1032–33.

20. 79 *Engineering News Record* (6 Dec. 1917): 1048–49.

21. 79 *Engineering News Record* (29 Nov. 1917): 1035; 118 *Scientific American* (5 Jan. 1918): 10–14, 40.

22. 80 *Engineering News Record* (11 April 1918): 693.

23. 79 *Engineering News Record* (22 Nov. 1917): 954–56.

24. 81 *Engineering News Record* (11 July 1918): 106; U.S. Department of Transportation, Federal Highway Administration, *America's Highways: 1776–1976* (Washington, D.C., 1876), 98.

25. Alfred Lief, *The Firestone Story* (New York, 1951), 15–25, 98–99. That not every truck manufacturer appreciated the revolution in truck tires is evident in the appearance of a "road builder" truck made by the Garfield Motor Company of Lima, Ohio, which had wide tread *steel wheels* with no rubber, 78 *Engineering News* (19 April 1917): 176.

26. Philip Scheidrowitz and T.R. Dawson, eds., *History of the Rubber Industry* (Cambridge, England, 1952), 112–13; Lief, *supra* note 25, 103.

27. Lief, *supra* note 25, 99.

28. Paul W. Litchfield, *Industrial Voyage* (New York, 1954), 141–44. For an excellent account of the Goodyear firm's role in developing tires, see Hugh Allen, *The House of Goodyear* (Akron, Ohio, 1937), 22–77.

29. 68 *Literary Digest* (8 Jan. 1921): 78; Litchfield, *supra* note 28, 145.

30. 12 *Cycle and Automobile Trade Journal* (1 Aug. 1907): 41–42.

31. 80 *Engineering News Record* (25 April 1918): 798–99 and (18 April 1918): 778.

32. 1 *Public Roads* (Feb. 1919): 25. Asphalt wearing surface on a waterbound macadam foundation continued to command respect in 1917 prior to the almost catastrophic breakdown of such roads that happened so widely in 1918; see American Highway Assn., *Good Roads Yearbook* (Baltimore, Md., 1917), 298.

33. 1 *Public Roads* (June 1918): 21; 86 *Engineering News Record* (31 March 1921): 553; 58 *Municipal and County Engineering* (April 1920): 161–63. For the role of Bureau of Public Roads testing of tire types see E.B. Smith, Bureau of Public Roads, "Present Status of Truck Tire Tests ...," 13 *Highway Engineer and Contractor* (Sept. 1925): 61–63.

34. Federal Highway Administration, U.S. Department of Transportation, *America's Highways: 1776–1976* (Washington, D.C., GPO, 1976), 98.

35. 76 *Engineering News Record* (21 April 1921): 534 and (5 May 1921): 783–84.

36. 42 *U.S. Statutes at Large* (Washington, D.C., GPO 1921), 212, 1321, Act of 9 Nov. 1921 amending 11 July 1916 highway act, and p. 660 authorizing appropriations for post roads in fiscal years 1923, 1924, and 1925; 88 *Engineering News Record* (15 June 1922): 1015 and (29 June 1922): 1097, 87 *Engineering News Record* (17 Nov. 1921): 831.

37. 86 *Engineering News Record* (10 Feb. 1921): 272.

38. *American Highways*, 113.

39. *American Highways*, 109–10, 114.

40. *American Highways*, 105. The New York State Highway Commission was so disillusioned with asphalt highways that it decided to restrict its highway contracts to concrete even though this decision led to difficulties in finding bidders on several large-scale jobs, 84 *Engineering News Record* (20 May 1920): 1036; less wealthy states continued to favor variant forms of asphalt. See E.B. Olbrick, North Carolina Highway Commission, "Development of Bituminous Base and Sand-Asphalt Pavements," 10 *Highway Engineer and Contractor* (Feb. 1924): 55–60.

Chapter 9
Cement, Concrete, and Mixers

1. 93 *Journal of the Franklin Institute* (March 1873): 204; *Encyclopedia Britannica* (Chicago, 1998), 15:323 and 10:899. A Frenchman, Francis Louis Vicat, by chemical analysis gave scientific precision to what British engineers had discovered empirically, *Encyclopedia Universalis* (Paris, France, 1989), 5:806. See also 70 *The Engineer* (London, 7 Dec. 1900): 724 and H.C. Badder, "Invention and Early Development of Portland Cement" 25 *Concrete* (Oct. 1924): 119. For a chronology of significant steps in the evolution of cement and concrete, see R.L. Humphrey, Pres., National Assn. of Cement Users, 10 *Municipal Engineering* (Feb. 1906): 89–92. Significantly, this listing of cement landmarks makes no mention of concrete highways.

2. Robert W. Leslie, *History of the Portland Cement Industry* (Chicago, 1924), 3, has a picture of a mill erected in 1824 to supply cement for the Erie Canal. *Encyclopedia Americana* (Danbury, Conn., 1995), 6:155. For the history of early cement makers in the U.S., see 54 *Engineering News* (7 Dec. 1905): 613 and Edwin C. Eckel, *Cements, Limes and Plasters* (New York, 1905); Howard Newlon, Jr., ed., *A Selection of Historic American Papers on Concrete, 1876–1926* (Detroit, 1976), especially the first essay; S.B. Newberry, "American Portland Cement," 20 *Municipal Engineering* (April 1901): 206–09.

3. 41 *Engineering News* (2 March 1899): 135; 50 *Engineering Record* (16 July 1904): 54 and 41 *Engineering Record* (26 Sept. 1903): 357; 5 *Engineering News* (18 Jan. 1906): 62–64. For distrust of U.S. cement, see J.W. Dickinson, "Progress with the Manufacturing of American Portland Cement," 14 *Municipal Engineering* (March, 1898): 128–134.

4. George W. Tillson, *Street Pavements and Paving Materials* (New York, 1912), 120; Austin T. Byrne, *A Treatise on Highway Construction* (New York, 1893), 250.

5. 74 *Engineering News* (5 Aug. 1915): 275; 73 *Engineering News* (4 Feb. 1915): 239–40; 23 *Engineering Record* (29 March 1890): 307. Eight different cement makers at this date were shipping eight different-sized barrels, giving some indication of the acute need for standard-

ization. At this date, some U.S. barrel makers were shipping knocked-down barrels to England, where wood was scarce, to ship cement back to the U.S. For the differences between Portland and natural cement, see 26 *Municipal Engineering* (April 1904): 242.

6. 38 *Engineering and Contracting* (9 Oct. 1912): 395.

7. 72 *Engineering News* (23 July 1904): 94–95; 53 *Engineering Record* (27 Jan. 1906): 91–92 and (20 Jan. 1906): 62. On the variability of laboratory tests, see R.W. Lesley, "Cement and Cement Testing Laboratories." 16 *Municipal Engineering* (Jan. 1899): 53.

8. 50 *Engineering Record* (23 July 1904): 94–95; 28 *The Engineer* (London, 31 Dec. 1869): 427; 30 *The Engineer* (London, 18 Nov. 1870): 343; 52 *Engineering Record* (16 Dec. 1905): 698. In the United States, scientific investigators of cement lagged far behind Europe. The scientific findings of Feret as early as 1870 in France were not duplicated in the United States until the 1920s, and then regarded as though they were original discoveries. See 88 *Engineering News Record* (5 Jan. 1922): 20–22. For the importance of the quality of sand, see 15 *Municipal Engineering* (Nov. 1898): 303–304.

9. Byrne, *supra* note 4, 202; Tillson *supra* note 4, 407. Some sources indicate the Bellefontaine concrete was laid in 1893, e.g., Charles E. Singer, ed., *A History of Technology* (Oxford, 1990), 4:539. Singer also credits P. Jantzen of Elbing, Germany, with first using concrete highway paving. See also the 25-year retrospect on concrete in 88 *Engineering News Record* (5 Jan. 1922): 20–22; 6 *Paving and Municipal Engineering* (April 1894): 158. For the reluctance of engineers to use cement, see 12 *Good Roads* (March 1911): 119.

10. 53 *Engineering Record* (9 June 1906): 719; 77 *Scientific American* supplement (28 March 1914): 200 for this and the two following paragraphs. A writer in 48 *Municipal Engineering* (June 1915): 373 felt that concrete reflected "sunlight and heat so powerfully as to be very uncomfortable in hot weather and very injurious to the eyesight," and suggested adding lampblack to the mixture. This quotation is from Ira O. Baker, *A Treatise on Roads and Pavements* (New York, 1903), 272.

11. 5 *American City* (Nov., 1911): 289–290.

12. 21 *The Engineer* (London, 18 May 1866): 357.

13. 24 *Engineering News* (5 July 1890): 16.

14. Byrne, *supra* note 4, 606–07; 43 *Engineering Record* (15 Aug. 1903): 189.

15. Baker, *supra* note 10, 378–79; 71 *Engineering News* (12 March 1914): 575; 18 *Municipal Engineering* (Jan. 1900): 30.

16. 94 *Scientific American* (12 May 1906): 388–89; 92 *Engineering News Record* (8 May 1924): 829–30.

17. 92 *Engineering News Record* (8 May 1924): 828–30; (3 Jan. 1924): 36–39; 39 *Engineering and Contracting* (7 May 1913): 517.

18. 43 *Engineering and Contracting* (7 April 1915): 326 and (10 Feb. 1915): 113.

19. 43 *Engineering and Contracting* (30 June 1915): 582; 73 *Engineering News* (15 April 1915): 716.

20. 73 *Engineering News* (13 May 1915): 960, (21 Jan. 1915): 144 and 75 *Engineering News* (9 March 1916): 488. T.L. Smith originally produced steel wheelbarrows of high quality and captured a large share of the market, even though his barrows cost more than most. From making barrows, he moved up to making concrete mixers shortly after 1900. 3 *Successful Methods* (June 1921).

21. 37 *Engineering and Contracting* (12 June 1912): 660.

22. 38 *Engineering and Contracting* (10 July 1912): 44–46; 40 *Engineering and Contracting* (9 July 1913): 30.

23. 55 *Engineering Record* (11 May 1907): 580; 41 *Engineering and Contracting* (27 May 1914): 599.

24. 37 *Engineering and Contracting* (14 Feb. 1912): 172.

25. 41 *Engineering and Contracting* (4 March 1914): 263; 42 *Engineering and Contracting* (15 July 1914): 70.

26. Halbert P. Gillett, *Earthwork and Its Cost* (New York, 1912), 5–6.

27. 38 *Engineering and Contracting* (13 Nov. 1912): 538–540.

Chapter 10
Concrete Highways: The Boom Years

1. 54 *Municipal Engineering* (March 1918): 104–06; American Highway Association, *Good Roads Yearbook* (Washington, D.C., 1917), 475; 44 *Municipal Engineering* (Feb. 1913): 131.

2. "End Road Building Monopoly and Save People's Money," Asphalt Association, *Circular Number Two* (New York, 1919). For a view of prewar New York State highway contracts by type of paving, see 72 *Engineering News* (24 Sept. 1914): 650 (waterbound macadam, 286 miles; such macadam with oiled topping, 20 miles; penetration method macadam, 352 miles; concrete, 217 miles; concrete with asphalt topping, 8 miles; asphalt block, 6 miles; stone block, 1 mile; other, 18 miles).

3. C.H. Conner, "State Cement Manufacturing: A Highway Administration Policy," 10 *Highway Engineer and Contractor*, (Feb. 1924): 20.

4. 86 *Engineering News Record* (10 March 1921): 410; 87 *Engineering News Record* (8 Nov. 1921): 751; 91 *Engineering News Record* (6 Sept. 1923): 407; 86 *Engineering News Record* (28 April 1921): 736 and (26 May 1921): 909.

5. 91 *Engineering News Record* (5 July 1922): 37.

6. 90 *Engineering News Record* (29 March 1923): 602; 90 *Engineering News Record* (3 May 1923): 808; 90 *Engineering News Record* (7 June 1923): 1021; For the smaller sack issue, see 90 *Engineering News Record* (29 March 1923): 565; (17 April 1923): 722, and (21 June 1923): 1069. As late as 1925, at least one supplier was still claiming that many contractors preferred cloth sacks, 27 *Cement* (October 1925): 45.

7. A.T. Goldbeck, Bureau of Public Roads, "Should Cement Be Made Better for Highways?" 13 *Highway Engineer and Contractor* (Aug. 1925): 57; The Bureau of Standards Screen Scales for Testing Sieves were graded as follows:

	Openings in inches	Wire size in inches
#10	.0787	.0272
#20	.0331	.0165
#50	.0117	.0074
#100	.0059	.0040
#200	.0029	.0021

8. 3 *Public Roads* (May 1920): 26; "Growth of a Great Industry," 10 *Highway Engineer and Contractor* (Jan. 1924): 57.

9. A.A. Levison, "Bulking of Moist Sand," 11 *Highway Engineer and Contractor* (Sept. 1924): 55–57.

10. A.T. Goldbeck, BPR, "Crushed Stone and Gravel for Concrete Highways," 13 *Highway Engineer and Contractor* (Aug. 1925): 43–45; A.T. Goldbeck, BPR, "Bulking of Moist Sands," 11 *Highway Engineer and Contractor* (Sept. 1924): 55–57.

11. 82 *Engineering News Record* (9 Jan. 1919): 117; 78 *Engineering News* (17 May 1917): 372; 14 *Highway Engineer and Contractor* (March 1926): 49.

12. F.S. Greene, New York Highway Commission, "High Cost of Maintenance of Light Macadam Highways," 83 *Engineering News Record* (21 Aug. 1919): 353–55; Guy Syford, Tacoma, Washington, to BPR, 9 Jan. 1920 and reply 15 Jan. 1920, BPR Central Files, 1912–1950, 450. 40. Concrete Roads, Box 1507, Record Group 30, National Records Center. There are many similar letters in this file.

13. 82 *Engineering News Record* (19 June 1919): 1237.

14. Asphalt Association *Circular Number Three* and *Circular Number Eight* (New York, n.d. 1920?)

15. J.E. Pennypacker, "Procedure in the Construction of Bituminous Macadam Roadways," 58 *Municipal and County Engineering* (March 1920): 101–03; Prevost Hubbard, "Results of the Bates Road Experiments During 1922 with Special Reference to Asphalt Pavements," Asphalt Association *Circular Number Twenty-Two* (New York, n.d. 1922?); "Progress of Asphalt Paving Construction is Revealed by Important Papers Presented at Detroit Conference," 68 *Good Roads* (Dec. 1925): 310–13, 320, 326; Prevost Hubbard, "Research Looking to Improve Asphalt Mixtures," 12 *Highway Engineer and Contractor* (Feb. 1925): 41–45.

16. Asphalt Association, *Asphalt Emulsions* (Lexington, Ky., n.d. 1986?), 2, quoting the federal Highway Administration's "highway statistics."

17. Clifford Richardson, "The Importance of Adequate Drainage and Foundations for Road and Street Surfaces," 56 *Municipal and County Engineering* (April 1919): 146–49; Wilt Connell, Pennsylvania Highway Department, "Economy Should Govern Selection of Highway Types," 13 *Highway Engineer and Contractor* (Aug. 1925): 55–56.

18. A.T. Goldbeck, Test Engineer, BPR, paper presented before the American Road Builders Association meeting, 58 *Municipal and County Engineering* (April 1920): 160–61.

19. For a sampling of laboratory and testing services, see advertisements in 58 *Municipal and County Engineering* (March 1920): 142–43; For a challenge to the value of laboratory testing, see C.A. Kenyon, "Bituminous Highway Construction," 38 *Municipal Engineering* (Feb. 1910): 85–88.

20. 45 *Engineering and Contracting* (1 March 1916): 208; 40 *Engineering and Contracting* (6 Aug. 1913): 153.

21. "Practical hints on the selection, operation and maintenance of paving mixers…," 88 *Engineering News Record* (23 Feb. 1922): 320–23.

22. 90 *Engineering News Record* (11 Jan. 1923): 95.

23. 89 *Engineering News Record* (9 Nov. 1922): 817 and 91 *Engineering News Record* (13 Dec. 1923): 998.

24. 94 *Engineering News Record* (23 April 1925): 709; 91 *Engineering News Record* (6 Sept. 1923): 407; 92 *Engineering News Record* (20 March 1924): 509; 90 *Engineering News Record* (11 Jan. 1923): 93.

25. A.R. Lash to Bureau of Public Roads, 10 Nov. 1920, BPR Central Files, 1912–1950, file 456, 40. Concrete Roads, Box 1506, Record Group 30, National Records Center; 91 *Engineering News Record* (19 July 1923): 120. Since mixers tended to have a useful life of about five years, about one-fifth of the approximately 15,000 in use in the U.S. in the 1920s had to be replaced each year. This underscores the importance of careful maintenance. See 88 *Engineering News Record* (5 Jan. 1922): 14, and L.P. Lessard, "The Care of Concrete Mixers," 60 *Municipal and County Engineering* (May 1921): 23–24.

26. 54 *Engineering Record* (22 Sept. 1906): 332–333; and (24 Nov. 1906): 589.

27. 42 *Engineering and Contractor* (2 Sept. 1914): 237.

28. 43 *Engineering and Contracting* (3 March 1915): 203; 42 *Engineering and Contracting* (9 Dec. 1914): 556; 50 *Municipal Engineering* (April 1916): 140–45; E.G. Carr, "Machine Finishing Concrete Roads," 56 *Municipal and County Engineering* (April 1919): 132–34.

29. 118 *Scientific American* (9 Feb. 1918): 129; 46 *Engineering and Contracting* (1 Nov. 1916): 382.

30. 91 *Engineering News Record* (6 Sept. 1923): 406; 92 *Engineering News Record* (29 May 1924): 955–56. One-lane construction to allow one-way traffic during construction may have been preferred rather than detours, but the cost to the contractor was substantially higher. One the other hand, diverting traffic to less soundly constructed secondary roads often led to the need for expensive repairs to the detours, so there were hidden costs in the use of detours; see 88 *Engineering News Record* (12 Jan. 1922): 47 and 90 *Engineering News Record* (21 June 1923): 1088.

31. 82 *Engineering News Record* (24 April 1919): 831–34 and (13 March 1919): 503, (12 June 1919): 1140, 1150.

32. 84 *Engineering News Record* (18 March 1920): 583.

33. 84 *Engineering News Record* (15 Jan. 1920): 122; 86 *Engineering News Record* (9 June 1921): 981; 87 *Engineering News Record* (11 Aug. 1921): 243; 68 *Municipal Engineering* (Feb. 1925): 65–67. A study conducted in 1925 surveying 11,000 contractors showed they averaged only 1¾% profits after state and federal taxes, and even this figure omitted interest on paid in capital. This was in contrast to the 5.5% average profit from manufacturing, 95 *Engineering News Record* (17 Sept. 1925): 456–459.

34. 84 *Engineering News Record* (5 Feb. 1920): 298.

35. 88 *Engineering News Record* (23 Feb. 1922): 304.

36. B.H. Piepmeier, Illinois Highway Division Engineer, "Economic Choices of Road Construction Plant Units and Layouts," 61 *Municipal and County Engineering* (July 1921): 21; 84 *Engineering News Record* (5 Feb. 1920): 273; and (1 Jan. 1920): 8–10; J.E. Pennybacker, ed., *Good Roads Yearbook* (New York 1917): 328 ff.; 78 *Engineering News* (26 April 1917): 207; 6 *Public Roads* (Dec. 1925): 220–232.

37. 43 *Engineering and Contracting* (10 Feb. 1915): 116.

38. 82 *Engineering News Record* (1 May 1919): 886; 84 *Engineering News Record* (17 June 1920): 1204; for the economics of paper versus cloth sacks, see 74 *Engineering News* (2 Sept. 1915): 468. By 1921, a contractor reported fabricating a mechanical sack shaker which salvaged 8 sacks worth in a day, saving far more than the $4.00 wage previously paid to a laborer to do the shaking, 87 *Engineering News Record* (19 Dec. 1921): 1075.

39. "Efficiency in Concrete Road Constitution," 6 *Good Roads* (Feb. 1926): 269–277; 79 *Engineering News* (29 Dec. 1917): 1217.

40. 43 *Engineering and Contracting* (23 June 1915): 564. Side forms for laying slab were only one type of form. Retaining walls, culverts, and bridges called for different styles of form. See 45 *Engineering News* (30 March 1916): 613.

41. 90 *Engineering News Record* (11 Jan. 1923): 95; 95 *Engineering News Record* (17 Dec. 1925): 1014; A.H. Hunter, "How to Get the Best Surface on a Concrete Road," 55 *Municipal and County Engineering* (Aug. 1917): 47; 25 *Concrete* (Sept. 1924): 103–04; C.H. Conner, "Relation of Form Setting to Riding Qualities of Concrete Pavements," 68 *Municipal and County Engineering* (March 1925): 111–116; 94 *Engineering News Record* (19 March 1925): 477–78.

42. 73 *Engineering News* (18 Feb. 1915): 354; 84 *Engineering News Record* (1 Jan. 1920): 28–31.

43. 56 *Municipal and County Engineering* (Jan. 1919): 11–13; 84 *Engineering News Record* (1 Jan. 1920): 8–9. The contractor's decision to use either industrial rail or trucks hinged not solely on cost. In wet or sandy soil, the railway was preferable, but once one lane of fully cured slab was open, it sometimes paid the contractor to use trucks on the completed slab and give up the railway to save on rental charges. See 26 *Concrete* (June 1925): 205. Early fears that hauling wet concrete for several miles would lead to separation of components and weaken resulting concrete were eased when tests conducted by the Bureau of Public Roads indicated wet mix remained workable even after a two-hour haul. See 87 *Engineering News Record* (20 Oct. 1921): 636–37; 4 *Public Roads* (Dec. 1921): 22; chief, Bureau of Public Roads to K.C. Lyon, Hyattsville, Md., 31 Aug. 1921, Record Group 30, National Records Center, Central Files 1912–1950, file 450, 40. Concrete Roads, Box 1506.

44. 6 *Public Roads* (Jan. 1926): 241.

45. 40 *Engineering News and Contracting* (18 Feb. 1914): 211–14.

46. 90 *Engineering News Record* (11 Jan. 1923): 81; 24 *Concrete* (June 1924): 241–42; 54 *Municipal Engineering* (April 1918): 134–37.

47. J.L. Harrison, Bureau of Public Roads, "Efficiency in Concrete Road Construction," 69 *Municipal and County Engineering* 9 Dec. 1925): 311–321; 6 *Good Roads* (Feb. 1926): 269–277; 45 *Engineering and Contracting* (26 April 1916): 385; 14 *Highway Engineer and Contractor* (April 1926): 60; 24 *Concrete* (June 1924): 244.

48. 24 *Cement* (June 1924): 244; 84 *Engineering News Record* (1 Jan. 1920): 33; A.H. Johnson, "Recent Developments in Concrete Highway Construction," 57 *Municipal and County Engineering* (Nov. 1919): 204–206; 88 *Engineering News Record* (15 June 1922): 996–998; 69 *Good Roads* (Jan. 1926): 18.

49. 81 *Engineering News Record* (26 Sept. 1918): 595.

50. 44 *Municipal Engineering* (June 1913): 566; 87 *Engineering News Record* (27 July 1921): 139; Chief, Bureau of Public Roads, to F.D. King, New Orleans, La., 17 June 1921, Record Group 30, National Record Center, BPR Central File, 1921–1950, file 450. 40 Concrete Roads, Box 1506; 24 *Concrete* (Jan. 1924): 10; 69 *Municipal and County Engineering* (Aug. 1925): 113–114.

51. 92 *Engineering News Record* (19 June 1924): 1050.

52. 69 *Good Roads* (Oct. 1926): 324; 93 *Engineering News Record* (28 Aug. 1924): 361; 54 *Municipal Engineering* (April 1918): 134–137; 51 *Municipal Engineering* (6 July 1916): 13–15.

53. 48 *Municipal Engineering* (June 1915): 361; 14 *Highway Engineer and Contractor* (June 1926): 64; 75 *Engineering News* (20 April 1916): 768–769; 94 *Engineering News Record* (29 Jan. 1925): 214.

54. 45 *Engineering and Contracting* (9 Feb. 1916): 129; H.C. Clemmer, "Can We Cut Down the Curing Period for Concrete Roads?" 10 *Highway Engineer and Contractor* (March 1924): 56–59; 11 *Highway Engineer and Contractor* (Aug. 1924): 39; 92 *Engineering News Record* (3 April 1924): 554.

55. See, for example, the New Hampshire specification, 28 *Concrete* (Jan. 1926): 17.

56. 28 *Concrete* (Jan. 1926): 17; For progress from the costly failures of 1913 to the successes of 1923, see W.D.P. Warren, "Developments in Concrete Paving Designs," 64 *Municipal and County Engineering* (March 1923): 89–91; For statistics on miles of concrete highway, see 69 *Good Roads* (March 1926): 114; 88 *Engineering News Record* (26 Jan. 1922):

135; Asphalt Association *Circular #51* (New York, n.d.) [1927]; For a step-by-step account of how contractors could produce slab efficiently, see "Efficiency in Concrete Road Construction," 6 *Public Roads* (Nov. 1925): 194–202.

57. "A Mile of Concrete Road," 68 *Good Roads* (Aug. 1925): 191; "A Mile of Concrete Pavement," 10 *Highway Engineer and Contractor* (Jan. 1924): 60.

Chapter 11
Retrospective on a Revolution

1. Report of Chief, Bureau of Public Roads, Thomas H. Macdonald, to Secretary of Agriculture, Annual Report, Dept. of Agriculture, 15 Oct. 1926, pp. 1, 7–8, 24.

2. If further justification is needed to sustain the contention that the highway revolution had largely been accomplished by the middle '20s and what followed was simply "more of the same," see U.S. Dept. of Transportation, Federal Highway Administration, *America's Highways: 1776–1976*, which points out that while federal funding increased from millions in the 1920s to billions in the 1970s, the same basic procedures instituted in the beginning years of federal road aid were still being followed 60 years later.

BIBLIOGRAPHY

The major sources for this volume were journals, for the most part engineering journals and those closely related to engineering. These are listed below alphabetically with my comments: *America City* proved to be especially helpful in tracing the introduction of machinery. *Asphalt Forum* and *Asphalt Circulars* are essential for this aspect of the industry. *Civil Engineering*, the journal of the American Society of Civil Engineers and *Transactions* of ASCE were also essential. *Concrete* gave useful coverage for the 1920s. For the European background of much machinery, my best source was the superb British journal *The Engineer*, published in London. *Engineering and Contracting* is an outgrowth of the earlier publication, *Good Roads*. Without question, my most important source was *Engineering News*, the outstanding journal in the field which merged with its rival, *Engineering Record*, to become *Engineering News Record*. For the period prior to the Federal Road Act of 1916, *Engineering Magazine* is useful, and *The Highway Engineer and Contractor* was useful for the 1920s. The British Petroleum Company's house organ *Horizon* offered insights on asphalt. The *Journal of the Franklin Institute* is especially valuable for the early 19th century years. In the *Journal of Urban History*, see especially the work of Clay McShane. One of the best of the journals for applied engineering or the business aspects of technology is *Municipal Engineering*, which began as *Paving and Municipal Engineering* and ended as *Municipal and County Engineering*. *Public Roads*, published by the Bureau of Public Roads and the Department of Agriculture, was uniquely valuable beginning with the first issue in 1918. *Scientific American* provided extended coverage on technological innovations in the road-building industry for the whole span of 19th- and 20th-century years treated in this study. While *Technology and Culture* contained a few excellent articles of vital interest to any consideration of highway construction, its coverage of this field in general was surprisingly scanty.

For the years embraced in this study, 1895–1925, the volumes of *Engineering News* and *Engineering News Record* have excellent indexes in each volume. There are separately published indexes for the years 1884–1891, but these are nowhere near as detailed as the indexes appearing in the individual volumes. For engineering journals in general, the Association of Engineering societies in 1892 published *Descriptive Index of Current Engineering Literature, 1884–1891* (Chicago, 1892). And Francis E. Galloupe compiled *An Index to Engineering Periodicals: 1883–1887* (New York, Engineering News Publishing Co. 1888). The *Industrial Arts Index* (New York, H.W. Wilson Co.) picks up in 1913 but there is no coverage for the years 1891–1912.

While the foregoing journals provided most of the journal articles used in this study, occasional articles of interest appeared in the following journals: *Americana, Atlantic Monthly, Cassier's Magazine, Century Magazine, Collier's, Cosmopolitan, Dial, Fortune, Forum, Harper's Weekly, Illustrated World, Literary Digest, Mississippi Valley Historical Review, North American Review, Outlook, Overland Monthly, St. Nicholas, Science, Scribner's Magazine, Technical World Magazine, World's Works,* and *World Today.*

The books contributing to this study are listed alphabetically by author to simplify retrieval, even though this separates the several categories involved. T.R. Agg, *The Construction of Roads and Pavements* (New York, 1916 et seq.), offers an especially useful glossary. Allhands, James L., *Tools of an Earthmover* (Huntsville, Texas, 1951) is obviously a labor of love by an experienced contractor. It is imperfectly documented but one must be grateful to the compiler for this comprehensive and fully illustrated volume. The American Highway Association, *Good Roads Yearbook* (Baltimore, 1912–1917) offers lists of contractors, advertisements with pictures of equipment, descriptions of various construction techniques and historical accounts. Automobile Manufacturers Association, *Automobile Facts and Figures* (New York, 1938). Baker, Ira O. *A Treatise on Roads and Pavements* (New York, Wiley & Sons, 1903 et seq.) is one of the more useful textbooks, especially for its many illustrations of equipment. Barber, Henry L. *The Story of the Automobile* (Chicago, 1917) and Bateman, John H., *Highway Engineering: A Textbook* (New York, 1920 et seq.) another in J. Wiley and Sons' useful series of textbooks which, taken collectively over many years, help one to trace the evolution of road-building machinery. Blackford, Mansel G. and Kerr, K. Austin, *B.F. Goodrich, Tradition and Transformation* (Columbus, Ohio, 1996). Blanchard, Arthur H. Ed., *American Highway Engineer's Handbook* (New York, 1919). Blanchard, Arthur H. and Drowne, Henry B., *Textbook of Highway Engineering* (New York, 1913). Burner, David, *Herbert Hoover: A Public Life* (New York, 1979). Byrne, Austin, *Treatise on Highway Construction* (New York, 1892). Many subsequent editions with fine steel engravings of machinery in text and in advertising sections. Calhoun, Daniel H. *The American Civil Engineer* (Cambridge, Mass. 1960). Chatburn, George R., *Highway and Highway Transportation* (New York, 1923). Clymer, Floyd, *Those Wonderful Old Automobiles* (New York, 1953). Connecticut Highway Commissioner's Office, *Forty Years of Highway Development in Connecticut, 1895–1935* (New Haven, 1937). Critchlow, Donald T., *Studebaker: The Life and Death of An American Corporation* (Bloomington, Indiana, 1996). Currey, Josiah Seymour, *Manufacturing and Wholesale Industries of Chicago*, volume two of this three-volume work has an extensive account of the Link Belt Company. Daumas, Maurice, *A History of Technology and Invention* (New York, 1969), the E.R. Kennedy translation. Alphaudrey, Marie Fernande, *Dictionnaire des Inventeurs Français* (Paris, 1963), a useful source for the famous French road-builder, Tresaquet, who is surprisingly neglected by French encyclopedias and biographical dictionaries. Drake, Reymond L. and Rhode, Robert T., *Classic American Steamrollers: 1871 through 1935 Photo Archive* (Hudson, Wisconsin, 2001). Dunsheath, Perry, ed. *A Century of Technology: 1851–1951* (New York, 1951) offers good coverage on origins of cement. Derry, T.K., *A Short History of Technology* (Oxford, 1960). Dundonald, Thomas Cochrane, Earl of, *Autobiography of a Seaman* (London, 1890) early exponent of asphalt. Evans, Oliver, *The Abortion of the Young Steam Engineer's Guide* (Philadelphia, 1805). Earle, J.B.F., *A Century of Road Materials: A History of the Roadstone Division of Tarmac* (Oxford, 1971), for the British experience with asphalt. Frost, Harwood, *The Art of Roadmaking* (New York, 1910) offers an extensive bibliography. Gibbs, Sir Alexander, *The Story of Telford: The Rise of Civil Engineering* (London, 1938). Gillette, Halbert Powers, *Handbook of Cost Data for Contractors and Engineers* (New York, 1910 et seq.; title varies); *Earthwork and Its Cost* (New York, 1903 et seq.). These volumes are a treasure trove of detailed information on the practical problems confronting contractors. Goodland, Stephen B., *Getting There: The Epic Struggle Between Road and Rail in the American Century* (New York, 1996). Grimble, Jan, *The Sea Wolf: The Life of Admiral Cochran* (Edinburgh, 2000) more on asphalt. Hall, Clayton H., *Baltimore: Its History and Its People* (New York, 1912) early use of macadam in the U.S. Hetzel, Frederick V. and Albright, Russell K., *Belt Conveyors and Belt Elevators* (New York, 1944, 3rd edition). Hilles, William Clark, "The Good Road Movement in the United States, 1880–1916," Duke University History Department M.A. thesis, 1958, typescript. Hollins, William, *Remarks on the Intercourse of Baltimore with the Western Country With the View of the Communication Proposed Between the Atlantic and the Western States* (Baltimore, 1818). Holt, W. Stull, *The Bureau of Public Roads: Its History, Activities and Organization* (Baltimore, 1923).

Howard, Robert West, *The Horse in America* (New York, 1965). Howe, Henry, *Memoirs of the Most Eminent American Mechanics* (New York, 1842), includes Telford but not McAdam and devotes six pages to road-making. Hulbert, Archer B. et al., *The Future of Road-making in America* (Cleveland, 1905). This is volume XV in the series *Historic Highways of America*, and *The Old National Road* (Columbus, Ohio, 1901). Iles, George, *Leading American Inventors* (New York, 1912). Johnson, Brian, *Steam Traction Engines, Wagons, and Rollers* (London, 1979) colored plate illustrations including portable steam engines,. Johnson, Paul C. *Farm Power in the Making of America* (Des Moines, 1975). Jordan, Philip D. *The National Road* (New York, 1978). Karolevitz, Robert F. *This Was Trucking: A Pictorial History of the First Quarter Century of Commercial Motor Vehicles* (Seattle 1966). Kirby, R., Withington, S., Darling, A., and Kilgour, F., *Engineering in History* (New York, 1956). Kirby, Richard Shelton and Laurson, Philip Gustav, *Early Years of Modern Civil Engineering* (New Haven, 1932). Law, Henry, *Rudiments of the Art of Constructing Roads* (London, 1850) excellent account of details of macadam construction with illustrations of the hand tools employed. Lay, M.G., *Ways of the World* (New Brunswick, N.J., 1992) a British view of road making. Leslie, Robert W., *History of the Portland Cement Industry* (Chicago, 1924). Lewis, Nelson Peter, *The Planning of the Modern City* (New York, 1923). Lief, Alfred, *The Firestone Story* (New York, 1951). Link Belt Co., *Modern Methods Applied to Elevating and Conveying Materials and the Transmission of Power* (Chicago, 1902). Litchfield, Paul W. *Industrial Voyage* (Garder City, New York, 1954), insights on the Goodyear 12-year effort for a successful pneumatic truck tire. Mason, Paul P. "The League of American Wheelmen and the Good-Roads Movement, 1880–1905," a dissertation, University of Michigan, 1957, available via UM dissertation service. McAdam, John Loudon, *Remarks on the Present System of Road-Making* (Baltimore, MD 1821, 4th edition and first in U.S.). One of the most important sources for this study, a classic. McBeth, Brian S., *Gunboats, Corruption and Claims: Foreign Intervention in Venezuela, 1899–1908*, a major source for the Barber Asphalt Company's asphalt. McDonald, Terrence, *The Parameters of Urban Fiscal Policy* (Berkeley, California, 1980). McShane, Clay, *Down the Asphalt Path: The Automobile and the American City* (New York, 1994) extensive source notes. Mascetti, Raymond W., "A Pioneer in Connecticut Road Construction: A Biographical Sketch of Joseph Mascetti," unpublished typescript, available in Torrington, Conn. Historical Society, 1994. Melosi, Martin, *The Sanitary City: Urban Infrastructure from Colonial Times to the Present* (Baltimore, MD, 2000) extensive bibliography. Maynell, Lawrence, *Thomas Telford* (London, 1957). Mitchell, Mary H., *History of New*

Haven County, Connecticut (Boston, 1930) for Eli Whitney Blake's stone crusher. Newton, Howard Jr., *A Selection of Historic American Papers on Concrete, 1876–1926* (Detroit, Mich. 1976). Nordin, Dennis, *Rich Harvest: History of the Grange, 1887–1900* (Columbia, Missouri, 1997). Oglesby, Clarkson H., *Highway Engineering* (New York, 1934, 1st ed.). Peckham, S.F. *Solid Bitumens* (New York, 1909). Olson, Sherry H., *Baltimore: The Building of an American City* (Baltimore, 1980). Owens, Hamilton, *Baltimore on the Chesapeake* (Garden City, New York, 1941). Peck, Dickson, *National Standards in a Modern Economy* (New York, 1956). Pollak, Emil and Martyl, eds, *Selections from the Chronicle: The Fascinating World of Early Tools and Trades* (Needham, NJ, 1991). The *Chronicle* is the newsletter of the Early American Industries Association, useful for origins of the steam-powered endless link belt in the ice industry. Pope, Albert Augustus, *The Movement for Better Roads* (Boston, 1892), and *Road Making as a Branch of Instruction in Colleges* (Boston, 1892). Pannell, John Percival Masterman, *An Illustrated History of Civil Engineering* (London, 1964). Rae, John, *The Road and the Car in American Life* (Cambridge, 1971), *The American Automobile Industry* (Chicago, 1965), and *American Automobile Manufacturer: The First Forty Years* (Philadelphia, 1959). Raitz, Karl, ed., *The National Road* (Baltimore, 1996). Rayner, Derek, *Road Rollers* (Haverfordwest, Pembrokeshire, 2001). British and some foreign rollers illustrated. Reynolds, Tom, *The History of the Asphalt Institute* (Lexington, KY, 1994). Richardson, Clifford, *The Modern Asphalt Pavement* (New York, 1905) a uniquely useful source. Rhode, Robert T., *The Harvest Story: Recollections of Old Time Threshermen* (West Lafayette, IN, 2001) for traction engines. Roe, Joseph W., *Connecticut Inventors* (New Haven, 1934) for Eli Whitney Blake and stone crusher. Schidrowitz, P. and Dawson, T.R. eds., *History of the Rubber Industry* (Cambridge, England, 1952). Schneider, Morris Francis, *The National Road* (Columbus, Ohio, 1975). Seely, Bruce, *Building the American Highway System: Engineers as Policy Makers* (Philadelphia, 1987). The outstanding monograph on the subject. A top-down study primarily concerned with policy formation, financing, etc. rather than the tactical details of construction. Shaler, Nathaniel Southgate, *The Autobiography of Nathaniel Southgate Shaler* (Boston, 1909), and *American Highways* (New York, 1896). Singer, Charles, Holmyard E.J., and Hall, A.R., eds., *A History of Technology* (Oxford, 1954–1990) especially volumes 4 or 5 for "Roads to 1900." Spencer, Herbert, "History of the Asphalt Institute" (College Park, MD, typescript, 1969–1970). Stine, Jeffery K., *Nelson P. Lewis and the City Efficient* (Chicago, 1981). Syrett, Harold C., *The City of Brooklyn, 1865–1898: A Political History* (New York, 1944). Tarr, Joel A. *Technology and the Rise of the Networked City in Europe and America* (Philadelphia, 1988). Thurston, Robert H., *A History of the Growth of the Steam Engine* (Ithaca, NY, 1939). Tillson, George W., *Street Pavements and Paving Materials* (New York, 1912). Tate, Warren, *Cochrane: The Life of Admiral the Earl of Dundonald* (London, 1965). White, John H., *American Locomotives: An Engineering History* (Baltimore, 1968), and *A Short History of American Locomotive Builders in the Steam Era* (Washington, D.C., 1982). Wik, Raymond M., *Steam Power on the American Farm* (Philadelphia, 1958), especially useful for the origins of the portable steam engine. Wixom, C.W., *ARBA Pictorial History of Road Building* (Washington, D.C., 1975), an American Road Builders Assn. publication with many excellent photographs of construction equipment. Williamson, Harold F. and Myers, Kenneth H., II, *Designed for Digging: The First 75 Years of the Bucyrus-Eric Company* (Evanston, IL, 1955). Wren, James A. et al., *Motor Trucks of America* (Ann Arbor, MI, 1979), Yow, John, *Are We There Yet?* (Atlanta, 2002), American Road Builders and Transportation Association publication heavily illustrated.

State and Federal publications contain a wealth of material on highway construction. Particularly useful are the annual reports of the Secretary of Agriculture containing the reports of subordinate units: the Office of Road Inquiry (ORI) 1893–1899; the Office of Public Road Inquiry (OPRI) 1899–1905; Office of Public Roads (OPR) 1905–1915; Office of Public Roads and Rural Engineering (OPRRE) 1915–1918; Bureau of Public Roads (BPR) 1918–1956. The *Statutes at Large*, especially volume 39 containing the 1916 highway legislation, are critical. So too are the debates in the *Congressional Record* leading up to the 1916 legislation. The Department of Commerce *Statistical Abstract of the United States*. Successive tables report total road miles, but not until 1916 do multiple tables offer fuller details. The U.S. Department of Transportation Federal Highway Administration publication, *America's Highways, 1776–1976* (GPO, Washington, 1977) offers a comprehensive view with voluminous notes. The Massachusetts Highway Commission *Annual Reports* for the years 1913 to 1919 were especially helpful, as was the Connecticut Highway Commission's *Biennial Report* for 1901–1902.

INDEX